Narrative Inquiry

Narrative Inquiry

A Dynamic Approach

Colette Daiute

The Graduate Center,
City University of New York

Los Angeles | London | New Delhi
Singapore | Washington DC

Los Angeles | London | New Delhi
Singapore | Washington DC

FOR INFORMATION:

SAGE Publications, Inc.
2455 Teller Road
Thousand Oaks, California 91320
E-mail: order@sagepub.com

SAGE Publications Ltd.
1 Oliver's Yard
55 City Road
London EC1Y 1SP
United Kingdom

SAGE Publications India Pvt. Ltd.
B 1/I 1 Mohan Cooperative Industrial Area
Mathura Road, New Delhi 110 044
India

SAGE Publications Asia-Pacific Pte. Ltd.
3 Church Street
#10-04 Samsung Hub
Singapore 049483

Acquisitions Editor: Helen Salmon
Assistant Editor: Katie Guarino
Editorial Assistant: Kaitlin Coghill
Production Editor: Libby Larson
Copy Editor: Judy Selhorst
Typesetter: C&M Digitals (P) Ltd.
Proofreader: Theresa Kay
Indexer: Sylvia Coates
Cover Designer: Michael Dubowe
Marketing Manager: Nicole Elliott
Permissions Editor: Karen Ehrmann

Copyright © 2014 by SAGE Publications, Inc.

Printed in the United States of America

Library of Congress Cataloging-in-Publication Data

Daiute, Colette.

Narrative inquiry : a dynamic approach / Collete Daiute, The Graduate Center, City University of New York.

pages cm
Includes bibliographical references and index.

ISBN 978-1-4522-7448-5 (pbk. : alk. paper)
ISBN 978-1-4833-1304-7 (web pdf)

1. Narrative inquiry (Research method) I. Title.

H61.295.D35 2013
001.4′33—dc23   2013024069

This book is printed on acid-free paper.

13 14 15 16 17 10 9 8 7 6 5 4 3 2 1

Brief Contents

Detailed Contents

Tables and Figures

Preface

This book focuses on narrating as an activity in life and in research. As a longtime student of language and languages, I have found narrative to be a fascinating, albeit subtle, means of enacting human relations, reflection, and development. As a professor of psychology and education working with students across the human sciences, I have found that building inquiry on narrating in daily life has helped both beginning and experienced researchers appreciate narrative and extend that appreciation to their research. It is such active qualities of narrative use in daily life and the close appreciation of narrative in research that are the inspiration for the approach in this book.

This approach to inquiry highlights the dynamic nature of narrating in several ways: Narrating is a natural human activity, a research activity, and a process for using research to create new knowledge, practices, and policies. The principles of narrative inquiry build on a theory of interaction and use, with implications for narrative research design and narrative analysis. This approach complements most other forms of narrative inquiry, in particular adding to other approaches close listening and reading for expressive meaning beyond themes and content analysis. Narrating in life and in research connect in this theory of use, with narratives as brilliant means of human relations, always set in some context, including power relations. Interpersonal, institutional, and intra-personal interactions flow in narratives, such as when a teen narrates to connect with a peer, an adult social worker to connect with a client, a refugee from war to connect with a new society where expectations are unclear, or a willing participant in a research interview about stereotyping to connect with the issues of interest. How those dynamics occur systematically—albeit often tacitly in daily life—offers insights for narrative inquiry.

As a researcher, I have used the methods presented here with colleagues, students, and participants, young and mature, in my research projects. These dynamic narrative analyses have helped us deepen our understandings not only of narrative meanings but also of the value of narrating to develop meaning in process, suggesting new ideas and questions about the phenomena we study. In addition to offering systematic theory-based methods for narrative analysis, this approach employs narrative theory and process to analyze other discourse forms, like letters and expository expressions.

After teaching qualitative research methods for many years, I have increasingly built on interdisciplinary scholarship to focus on the expressive detail of narrative for a method accessible to beginning and experienced researchers. My hope is to communicate with a range of researchers by explaining how the qualities that speakers and writers use each day are applicable to research. To invite readers of this book to experience what I have found to be interesting and productive narrative inquiry, I offer practical theoretical principles, numerous illustrative examples, and processes of narrative research design and narrative analysis, including ideas for involving participants in narrative practices beyond the research. I have developed these activities and explanations in courses on qualitative research, narrative inquiry, and discourse theory and analysis with undergraduate students, graduate students, and experienced researchers attending professional development seminars. My previous books and research articles present results of these approaches, and I work in this instructional text to advance the approach as well as to describe what has worked well for me and for my students in the past. In the spirit of dynamic narrating—a relational expressive process of use and diversity—I also welcome interacting with you, the reader, about what works for you and what can be improved in future editions.

Acknowledgments

This book is dedicated to my students—students of research, human development, education, and social sciences. I cannot name all with whom I have worked since 1980 at Teachers College Columbia University, from 1983 to 1994 at the Harvard Graduate School of Education, and since 1994 at the Graduate Center, City University of New York, but I hope all my students see this book and accept my acknowledgment. Before completing my doctorate, I also taught literacy skills to students across age groups, and, although that work was not in a research program, it helped me understand the complexity and beauty of narrative in ways that led to my eventual research focus. I thank all those previous students and especially those whose research involved processes presented in this book. I refer to some of the work with and by past and current students in the chapters of this book and the references. Thank you all. I also look forward to applying and extending these research methods with new students.

I am grateful to SAGE Publications, in particular my editor, Helen Salmon, for shepherding this project through acquisition, reviews, production, and beyond, with her generous and thoughtful understanding of the purpose, spirit, and specifics of this project; to Vicki Knight for rekindling interest in my idea for a book after several years of percolation; to Kaitlin Coghill, Judy Selhorst, and Libby Larson for their enthusiastic and careful attention to detail. I also extend my sincere thanks to the reviewers whose rigorous readings and prior experience helped me express my ideas more clearly: Thalia M. Mulvihill, Ball State University; Trena M. Paulus, University of Tennessee; Katherine Chaddock, University of South Carolina; Mary Louise Gomez, University of Wisconsin–Madison; Ann K. Brooks, Texas State University; Jana Sladkova, University of Massachusetts, Lowell; Linda R. Weber, State University of New York, Institute of Technology; Karina Korostelina, George Mason University; Lisbeth A. Berbary, University of Waterloo; Richard Buttny, Syracuse University; C. Amelia Davis, Georgia Southern University, and Jane M. Agee, the University at Albany, State University of New York. Your close reading was impressive and most helpful.

To colleagues with whom I have collaborated on narrative research and other studies, I am grateful for your embracing some of these methods before they had broader currency and for critical and creative discussions about our research. Special acknowledgments to Patricia Botero Gomez, Zena Eisenberg, Vera Vasconcellos, Tinde Kovacs-Cerovic, Luka Lucić, Chana Etengoff, Phil Kreniske, Vienna Messina, Maja Ninkovic, Jana Sladkova, Ralitsa Todorova, Cynthia Lightfoot, and Maja Turniski for our recent narrative research and writing together.

Finally, this is the first book I've written without being able to discuss it with my dad. The encouragement of my mom, Doris; my son, Jack; and members of my extended family has been especially supportive at this busy time.

Introduction

The power of narrative is not so much that it is *about* life but that it interacts *in* life. Narrative is an ancient product of human culture, enhanced today with technologies, personal mobilities, and intercultural connections. In this complex world, narrating has become a tool people use to engage with diverse others and with the mutual development of society and the self. This book explains and illustrates that narrating is a social process occurring in everyday life and, thus, in research interactions. It offers an approach to narrative inquiry that builds on the practices of daily life, where we use storytelling to *do* things—to connect with other people, to deal with social structures defining our lives, to make sense out of what is going on around us, to craft our own way of fitting in with those situations, and sometimes to change them. In this process, narrating interweaves diverse perspectives of people with varied influence, experience, knowledge, and goals. Prior narrative research tends to emphasize either individual personal voice or ideological discourse, even though evidence abounds that the personal and the political interact in everyday narrating. Narrative inquiry has also, in the past, focused in particular on the individual, but this book draws on recent research accounting for individual *and* societal relations in meaning, learning, development, and social change. Building on such findings, narrative inquiry presented here is sensitive to contexts characterized by social media, diverse personal experiences, inequalities, migration, conflict, and standpoints. Contemporary research can and must address such complexities.

This book is for researchers and scholars (both beginning and experienced) who seek ideas and examples for gathering, eliciting, and analyzing narrative and other discourses to address their research questions. It also reaches out to readers interested in systematic field-based methods that blur the boundaries between qualitative and quantitative methods. This approach extends to designs with numerous participants, maintaining the richness of narrative including and beyond individual case studies. This integrative approach offers research strategies applied to a range of projects addressing questions across cultural settings with diverse challenges and opportunities.

Chapter 1 explains the appeal of narrative inquiry, the rationale for this dynamic narrating approach, and four guiding principles (use, relationship, diversity, materiality). Chapter 2 puts narrative theory to work by focusing on how to design research that allows for dynamic narrating. Chapters 3 through 6 extend the theory-based approach with practical narrative inquiry strategies, including values analysis, plot analysis, script analysis, significance analysis, character mapping, and time analysis. These strategies are illustrated with examples from prior funded and published research and guidelines readers can apply to their own projects. Chapter 7 discusses how researchers make observations from those narrative analyses and present findings of dynamic narrative inquiry, also relating them to other approaches. All the chapters demonstrate that any concerns about researchers having to learn certain skills, like how to identify plots, should be diminished by the knowledge that everyone naturally uses plots (and other narrative devices) in everyday discourse. Translating such natural language strategies to research analysis strategies is, therefore, logical and beneficial.

I have developed and refined this dynamic narrating approach while teaching at the Graduate Center of City University of New York, before that at Harvard University, and over the past decade in professional development seminars at universities and conferences across the United States as well as in Europe, South America, South Asia, and Africa. My students, colleagues, and I have applied these methods in research projects in educational contexts, community centers, human rights agencies, and workplace settings, addressing issues like migration, learning, cultural diversity, violent conflict, displacement, and resource inequalities. Our work demonstrates that this approach is well suited to research in situations of practice, diversity, and development in changing times and places.

A number of the tables from this book are available for readers to download and complete at **www.sagepub.com/daiute.**

About the Author

Colette Daiute is Professor of Psychology at the Graduate Center, City University of New York. She is on the faculty of the Ph.D. program in Human Development and teaches courses on theory, research, and methods in the social sciences, attended by students across a wide range of disciplines. Dr. Daiute does research in diverse settings, including community centers, educational institutions, human rights organizations, television and computer technology environments, and informal community gatherings. Her most recent research has focused on child and youth development in extremely challenging and rapidly changing environments. Organizations funding this research most recently include the Spencer Foundation, the United States Institute of Peace, and the National Council of Teachers of English. Her prior book publications include *Human Development and Political Violence* (Cambridge University Press, 2010); *International Perspectives on Youth Conflict and Development,* edited with Zeynep Beykont, Craig Higson-Smith, and Larry Nucci (Oxford University Press, 2006); and *Narrative Analysis: Studying the Development of Individuals in Society,* edited with Cynthia Lightfoot (SAGE Publications, 2004). Her recent journal articles include "Human Development in Global Systems," *Global Studies Journal* (2012); "'Trouble' in, around, and between Narratives," *Narrative Inquiry* (2011); "Situated Cultural Development among Youth Separated by War," *International Journal of Intercultural Relations,* with Luka Lucic' (2010); and "The Rights of Children, the Rights of Nations: Developmental Theory and the Politics of Children's Rights," *Journal of Social Issues* (2008). Dr. Daiute has conducted professional development workshops on narrative inquiry, youth-and-society development, and research design for practice and policy implications. Colette Daiute has been a keynote speaker at conferences internationally, as well as in the United States. She has proudly guided students' theses and dissertations in settings as varied as mental health institutions, nongovernmental organizations, preschool through college education, human resources departments, physical health organizations, social service agencies, technology use, and creative arts arenas, focusing on issues including immigration, postwar community rebuilding, displacement, teaching, learning, television, and computer media development. In addition to teaching courses at the City University of New York, Dr. Daiute is a coordinator of the ongoing "Narrating Change" seminar of the Center for the Humanities at the Graduate Center, CUNY.

1

The Appeal of Narrative in Research

I saw the bird flattened on the ground outside my door. One of the kindergarten children walked toward me slowly, crying. That's when I knew it was time to act.

The very brief narrative above occurs amid myriad spheres of social relations. These relations are not all apparent, but understanding narrative meaning requires understanding narrating as an interactive process. As researchers we enhance our methods *if* we know how to read narratives as complex social processes. This opening **narrative** expresses a sequence of two past events.[1] The narrative involves action ("walked," "act") and consciousness ("saw," "crying," "knew"). From the little bit that is there, one can imagine possible settings: "Kindergarten" suggests a school context; characters include the implicit narrator "I," apparently in a position of responsibility and power ("it was time to act"). This bit of narrative also sits amid possible plots—some kind of conflict on a school playground—with characters, the "child," the "I" character, and the "bird" (depending on how the story develops). This brief narrative seems to convey life quite naturally with a story of an encounter involving a person, nature, and an institution—a child, a bird, and a teacher, school principal, or other adult—within a broader series of imaginable events. The ending "it was time to act" implies that the bird's demise involved something more than disease or old age, compelling the "I" character to intervene. Details like the dead bird, the crying child, and the urgency to act hint at some sort of trouble, piquing the reader's desire to know what happened. That 30 words invoke so much meaning demands a dynamic narrative approach.

Narratives are accounts of daily life, stories that spring from the imagination, vignettes of daily life, news reports of events of public interest, histories, gossip, and other oral and written accounts in past, present, and future time. Narratives tend to include characters—human or otherwise—presented in spatial and temporal contexts to share some meaningful experience or idea. More than a set of features, **narrating** is the interaction of expressions and contexts in ways that render relationships among characters and events prominent. Even when details of the context are unknown to a reader or listener, a narrative like the one above points beyond its brevity and pulls in the careful reader/listener's curiosity and ideas about the surrounding situation. As a "product of social life and human social activity" (Wertsch & Tulviste, 1992, p. 551), narrating is **culture** in action.

The power of narrative is not so much that it is *about* life but that it interacts *in* life. Narrative is an ancient product of human culture and an activity that keeps producing cultural innovations. With current technologies, human mobility, and the resulting intercultural connections, narrating has become a tool people use to engage with diverse others, to develop personally, and to contribute to the development of society. Narrating is a uniquely human form of expression and intelligence, and it occurs in both verbal and nonverbal forms. Thousands of years ago, people shared experience in pictorial scenes still preserved in caves, later in the form of oral epics by travelers who shared events across distant places. Since the invention of writing, generations across cultures have narrated religious, historical, legal, literary, popular, social, and other traditions. Studies of narrative across civilizations show that **meaning** resides in expressive form—in its style, linguistic flourishes, organizational format, and visual features—as well as literally in the words referring to persons, places, things, and actions. Over time, cultures establish ways for speakers and writers to recount events and to show why the events are important.

Facebook, for example, is a massive contemporary epic narrative. People use Facebook and other social media to do much of their connecting in conformity with social-relational practices established over time while also crafting self-presentations to assert some individuality. Much of the meaning in social networking occurs in *how* the narrator puts words and images together and thereby connects personal experience to a vast network of actual and imagined audiences. Most remarkable is that human babies learn the nuances of language and narrative long before they get Facebook accounts, and in doing so they acquire skills created by humankind slowly over thousands of years. Every interaction, including the ways that friends, family, and others share pictures and anecdotes, becomes part of the material people draw on for their personal narratives, not only to share experiences but also to become persons recognized as good or bad, heroes or villains. While the words "My child is so clever and cute!" do not appear, this recent Facebook posting about Sophie demonstrates how clever and cute she is: "Sophie began to read yesterday!!!! Not yet 3, she held up the book confidently, began with 'onceuponatime,' turned each page deliberately, and soon, maybe, she'll hold the book right side up!" The narrative of Sophie's early encounter with a book uses the details of the story, the posting itself, and the parent's attempt to appear just short of bragging by admitting that the child was, after all, holding the book upside down. **Narrative inquiry** should be sensitive to such interweaving of implied and stated meanings. Dynamic narrating is a theory and practice researchers can use to learn from meaning-making processes people use every day.

INTRODUCTION TO DYNAMIC NARRATING

This introduction to the social and cultural nature of narrating sets the scene for dynamic narrative inquiry. **Dynamic narrating** is a social process occurring in life and, thus, should be the basis of **research**. This book explains and guides such an approach to narrative research in the social sciences, building on practices of daily life, where people use storytelling to do things—to connect with other people, to deal with social structures defining their lives, to make sense of what is going on around them, to craft a way of fitting in with various contexts, and sometimes to change them. In this process, narrating integrates perspectives of diverse individuals and groups with varied influence, experience, knowledge, and goals related to an issue of research interest. If you are, for example, studying the effects of recent immigration policies in the United States, you could interview people entering the country for different reasons, such as people seeking work, refugees from war zones, young people joining family members, immigrants already in the country, or public officials, including social service professionals, employers, and educators working with immigrants. In addition to interviewing some of these actors in the immigration process, you could examine official documents or media stories to gain insights about immigration policies, perceptions, and impacts. That research design would provide material for analysis of shared and divergent meanings about immigration. In this book, I define **narrative meaning** in terms of such interplay among actors—people whose perspectives merge and diverge in social and political processes—and I apply this definition for systematic research sensitive to language use.

The guiding idea of **dynamic narrative inquiry** is that narrating **mediates** experience, knowledge, learning, and social change. When acknowledging this active, functional nature of narrative, a researcher focuses on what narratives do as much as on what they say. Consistent with this view, narrative researchers focus on narrative expression as it interacts with situation and purpose. This book explains and illustrates that process by presenting various dynamic features of narrative working together much like colors in a kaleidoscope when a researcher applies them in research. In the remainder of this chapter, I further define the dynamic nature of narrative, explain why researchers are interested in narrative, and present four principles to guide narrative inquiry.

Narrating Is a Natural and Artful Human Activity

Scholars of narrative understand that, beyond being a discursive form, narrating is a basic, necessary, and fascinating human activity. Because dynamic narrative inquiry draws on narrating in daily life, a discussion about its qualities is foundational. Narrative seems to copy life events. Something about the sleeping-waking cycles of life translates well into the "Once upon a time" and "and so that's how it came to be"—beginning, middle, and end—structure of narrated experience. What is particularly powerful about narrating is the fertility of this apparently mundane cultural practice for recounting events, "**landscapes of action**" (Bruner, 1986), in ways that animate why those events matter, "**landscapes of consciousness**" (Bruner, 1986).

Words in context. People use the ordering of events in narrative form to guide perception, expression, and interpretation of those events. For example, from a young age, children learn to recognize the cues of rising suspense in a story, perhaps even sitting alert until they notice story elements suggesting that everything will turn out okay. The repeated "Someone's been sitting in my chair . . . eating my porridge . . . sleeping in my bed . . ." in the British fairy tale "Goldilocks and the Three Bears," for example, creates an anticipation about the interloper to the bears' home and possible consequences for that protagonist when discovered (Cundall, 1851). After hearing the story of a family of bears returning to their woodland home that is not quite how they left it, even very young children familiar with the story want to shout out to the unsuspecting bears that someone has been sitting in their chairs, eating their breakfast, and ultimately falling asleep in one of their beds. From early on, the young child listening to a reading of the story becomes emotionally involved with the rising action of the plot. The interwoven phases of meaning in the bears-and-girl story plot—a little girl intruding on the family home, the attendant turn of events, the listener's feeling of suspense, and more—can be mined for deep understanding in research. Young children's interactions with characters, places, and events that they never experienced or that never occurred attest to the basic nature of narrative. Understanding a story is as much about context as about words, because, for example, someone relating to a story would have heard it (or stories like it) before, would observe the reactions of others in the context, would have some sense of how to behave during a reading, and would use any illustrations to augment details. All this involves paying attention to how the story is told.

Meaning in how *the story is told*. Stories communicate with a variety of features that narrators use not only to share specific messages but also to hint at why they are telling *this* story in *this* way at *this* time. The various features of narrative create recognizable expressions indicating that "this is a story" with interactive devices individuals use to achieve their goals. Beyond any literal meanings learned over time among members of a community (and written in a dictionary) are the implicit meanings, the words between the words that members of the culture understand as expectations, possibilities, and taboos (Labov & Waletzky, 1967/1997, discussed in detail in Chapter 5). For example, the brief narrative "There was a war here and everyone feels bad about it" conveys literal and implicit meanings in Bosnia, where a young person wrote it as part of a postwar youth history project in a community center (Daiute, 2010). The passive construction, "There was a war here," for example, implies that the war was imposed on the Bosnians when their capital city was under siege for several years, and "everyone feels bad about it" applies to the local people, the commonly accepted major victims of the 1990s wars in the Balkans. In contrast is the superficially similar narrative written by a youth in Serbia (for the same project): ". . . the news is that we are again under an embargo. They all got scared and mad and started . . . fights about our responsibility in all this mess. . . ." Although these narratives are both about war and express painful emotions, one enacts the passivity of a declared victim, whereas the other takes an active stance and addresses the issue of responsibility. In addition to the passive and active forms of the sentences, collecting narratives of local living histories to read alongside these two brief but rich stories reveals responsibility in the one case ("fights about our responsibility in all this mess . . .") and lack of control in the other ("There was a war here"). Such nuances of narrative expression are ripe for application in narrative inquiry, across cultures and languages in terms of local practices.

Cultural variation of a basic tool. The specific forms for interweaving narrative action and consciousness differ across cultures. Children in all cultures grow up learning about the accepted practices in their environments, at first in oral story form and then in literature, religious rites, social media, and other genres (Heath, 1983). Along the way, given the opportunity to tell and to write stories for responsive audiences, people become good at narrating *within* cultural norms, not only to entertain others but also as a means of connecting, **sense making**, and thriving. In local settings, children are initiated into the mores and practices of their cultures via narrative. Those cultural differences have to do with the structure of the language—such as how a fairy tale or folktale in Spanish or Swahili builds suspense or manages to convey a moral without spoiling the pleasure of the story. The qualities applied for narrative inquiry in this book are based in English and languages of other western cultures, but readers may consider and alter the qualities applied herein as appropriate to their preferred languages. The point is that most cultures use available linguistic devices for interactive narrating (Bruner, 1986).

The Development of Narrative in Life

Narrative is one of the major cultural processes guiding children's **development** from early in life. From birth and across contexts, people use narrative to interact in the world. Using narrative as a means for participating in the world integrates human biology, such as the ability to speak, and cultural inventions, such as the capacity to create literature (Donald, 1993). Researchers have explained that children develop the ability to narrate as others tell stories around them (Miller, Hoogstra, Mintz, Fung, & Williams, 1993; Nelson, 1998). One explanation relevant to the current inquiry is that children become familiar with cultural routines in the context of daily activities like having meals, bathing, and celebrating family milestones (Nelson, 1998). As they mature, young people focus increasingly on broader social contexts, like school, where different expectations, like those for proper classroom behavior, organize activity and meaning (Cazden, 2001). Children narrating experience in mainstream American schools, for example, are expected to share facts, while the home cultures of many American children value stories that entertain, share role models, or serve other developmental functions than reporting facts (Cazden, 2001; Heath, 1983).

Storytelling socializes young people via cultural values shared during routine events that parents, teachers, employers, and others repeat and reinforce. In turn, children and adolescents exert effort to socialize those around them, by infusing personal details and desires into scripts (routine ways of explaining routine events) and transforming them into nuanced stories (Daiute & Nelson, 1997). It is, for example, through storytelling that families let their children know the kinds of persons they are and will become (Miller et al., 1993). Once they have mastered the basics of the narrative genre by around age 11 (Berman & Slobin, 1994), young people take increasing control over social-relational processes linking persons and contexts—that is, they gain control over the impact of their stories on others. Because storytelling is, moreover, a means of presenting oneself to others and to one's own reflection, children, like adults, use it to perform identities and reflect on them (Bamberg, 2004a; Daiute, 2004; Reyes, 2011). Physical events—a salient word, glance, movement, or physical arrangement—are embodied in these interactions among author/speaker, audiences, and self-subject (Bakhtin, 1986). In this way, storytelling embeds institutional values, power relations, circumstances of the physical environment, and individual motivations (Fairclough, 2010; Harré & van Langenhove, 1999) in ritual narrations or scripts (Nelson, 1998).

Different social **scripts** may co-occur; they may be integrated, like plots and subplots, and they may clash, resulting in a story that seems incoherent. Social scripts have also been referred to as dominant ideologies (Foucault, 2001), ways of knowing (Gilligan, 1993), cultural scripts (Nelson, 2007), master narratives (Solis, 2004), and collective memories (Wertsch, 2002). These social scripts organize perception and action (discussed further in Chapter 4). Storytelling shapes public life, and individuals transform public life in their own personal stories. It is through storytelling that societies indicate who belongs and who does not. It is, moreover, through storytelling that leaders justify war and peace, as their political arguments are based on certain sequences of causes and effects, motivations, and involvements of individuals and groups. National stories are often adopted by individuals, a process that sometimes suppresses the voices of those left out of any official story (Amsterdam & Bruner, 2000; Scott, 1992). Prior research shows that children and youth adjust their personal stories to the preferred narratives in their societies, toward organizing personal accounts in terms of victimization in one situation and responsibility in another (Daiute, 2010; Daiute, Buteau, & Rawlins, 2001). Young people also use narrating to challenge stereotypes (Daiute, 2010). Narrating then becomes a means for advancing society.

Drawing on this knowledge about the social and cultural nature of narrating, researchers can broaden beyond assumptions that narrative is primarily relevant to research interested in individual experiences, perspectives, and life histories. Instead, it is the range of narratives that participants in research, like people in everyday life, use to interact with those in their surround, including researchers. The multiplicity of narratives that each individual uses to connect with and change a social milieu is what researchers should explore.

A brief review of reasons for the increasing interest in narrative inquiry will set the foundation for the approach in this book.

WHAT IS THE APPEAL OF NARRATING IN RESEARCH?

Building toward the dynamic narrating approach requires a brief review of the major arguments for narrative in contemporary research. Researchers embarking on narrative inquiry should become familiar with different ways of appreciating narrative for research purposes as well as in life. "Narrative research has many forms, uses a variety of analytic practices, and is rooted in different social and humanities disciplines" (Cresswell, 2013, p. 70). Arguments for narrative research draw on scholarship as varied as literary theory, human development theory, psychodynamic theory, cultural anthropology, sociolinguistics, and sociology, among other disciplines. Different disciplinary perspectives lead to some different emphases, such as a focus on process and change by developmental, psychodynamic, and health psychologists, a focus on identity and identity conflicts by social psychologists, a focus on meaning by philosophers, a focus on culture by anthropologists, a focus on aesthetics by literary scholars, and a focus on language in context, including social and power relations, by sociolinguists and discourse theorists.

The major differences that play out in narrative inquiry design and analysis pertain to whether and how experience and meaning are defined as authentic reports, constructions, or patterns of use. Although these three ways of thinking about narrative in research can work together, narrative researchers should understand the implications of resulting differences for the design, analysis, and interpretation of their projects. The purposes of this review are to orient readers to the appeal of narrative inquiry and to build on prior approaches with an increased focus on narrating as a relational activity.

The appeal of narrative, most agree, is that it expresses personal experience. Narrative inquiry typically focuses on experience and the meaning of experience from the perspective of people living it in reality or in imagination rather than to identify objective truths. Differences in how scholars define narrative determine their beliefs about the location and operation of personal experience—such as whether it is primarily *in* the individual or distributed *across* symbolic and physical spaces where individuals interact to create and transform meaning. Illustrating the range of reasons for doing a narrative approach, the following narrative by a college student serves as an anchor. After presenting the narrative and its origin, I interpret it briefly in terms of the report, construction, and use rationales for narrative inquiry.

> The conflict happened in the middle of the day when I went with my friend for a drink. I am [a] non smoker but one guy was very rude and he was keeping his cigarette in front of my nose. I kindly asked him to move his cigarette to the side, he did not pay attention to me but instead purposely was blowing the smoke towards me. I was upset . . . and I told him he was a primitive Neanderthals . . . I felt very upset.

This narrative by a youth in a study of the effects of political violence and transition anchors this discussion of three major rationales for narrative inquiry. Twenty-one-year-old Z was born in 1987, a few years before the beginning of the wars that broke apart the country of Yugoslavia. When Z's city of Sarajevo was under siege for three years, she was a child. Her prime school years were disrupted by cancellations due to bombing, street sniping, lack of electrical power, food, and other resources. A community-based project involving Z's generation in the writing of a social history elicited narratives of daily life a decade after the war (Daiute, 2010). During the time of the workshops, many youth like Z participated in activities at community centers, often devoted to helping with neighborhood rebuilding efforts, youth skills, and social life. The need for out-of-school activities highlighted young people's welcome of opportunities to narrate from diverse perspectives, not only the perspectives dictated to them. Z and her peers in Bosnia, Croatia, Serbia, and the United States responded to an invitation to write about conflicts of daily life. Z wrote the narrative above about a conflict with a peer.

It may be surprising that, given her childhood growing up in war, Z's story seems mundane. Nevertheless, the fact that people do not always narrate the experiences researchers may seek is relevant to appreciating narrative as tool for interacting in complex ways with the extant circumstances. In fact, few of the 137 participants in the same study as Z directly addressed "the war." Instead, they used their narratives to consider the present time, including but not only consequences of war, in very different ways. To illustrate the appeal of narrating for researchers considering narrative inquiry, I discuss Z's narrative and a few other examples in terms of each rationale for narrative inquiry below.

Narrative Report

A common rationale for using narrative in research projects is to gather information about personal experiences, memories, feelings, and knowledge. This rationale, which I refer to as the narrative **report**, is based, albeit often implicitly, on several assumptions. These assumptions include that people have access to past events in memory, that they recount those events as the events occurred or were experienced, and that narrative accounts provide insights about the person, his or her group, and the individual's deeply held understandings of the subject of interest.

In spite of the range of disciplines and theories informing narrative inquiry, many researchers emphasize certain features, including the individual's experience, authentic expression of that experience, identity, and identity processes (Clandinin & Connelly, 2000; Cresswell, 2013). Narrative research designed to elicit personal reports mentions "authenticity" and "spontaneity," available in individual perspectives often referred to as "voices" (Cresswell, 2013; Gilligan, 1993). Emphasizing the individual narrative report also tends to emphasize coherence, to smooth over tensions that render the individual voice confused and confusing. When trying to understand how people make sense of life and the problems scholars study, researchers often identify narrative as important for the particular, idiosyncratic, deeply held experiences of being in this world, as compared to the more general indications noted on surveys or responses in controlled experiments.

Another common goal of narrative reporting is to empower the voices and perspectives of those who have been silenced or excluded from some public hearings of personal experience (Harding, 1988). On this view, narrative research serves to enter previously excluded voices into a broader public forum. Such research introduces novel and sometimes critical interpretations of life by people in diverse situations whose experiences are not considered mainstream or ideal (Harding, 1988). With those voices increasingly in the foreground rather than the background of public life, researchers can take them increasingly seriously by focusing on the nuances, diversities, and powerful uses of narrating within as well as across social groups. Narrative expression can be or can feel personally life affirming. Power comes from the social nature of narrating, the interactive nature of personal stories and collective voices narrating a situation, place, or insight.

Research emphasizing narrative reports tends to include interviews, repeated interviews, or life stories to glean a person's or a group's authentic basic truths (McAdams, 2005). Narrative inquiry focuses on stories and/or on the storied nature of discourse (such as chronological order) by analyzing themes, structures (such as turning points), or interactions (Denzin & Lincoln, 2011; Riessman, 2007). As noted by a leading scholar of narrative inquiry, "A good narrative analysis prompts the researcher to look beyond the surface of the text" (Riessman, 2007, p. 13). There are numerous ways to look beyond the surface of the text. There are also numerous hints to profound meaning in narrative expression.

One way narrative researchers go beyond the surface is by identifying "themes"—defined in this way after a comparative analysis of qualitative research scholarship: "Themes are abstract (and often fuzzy) constructs that link not only expressions found in texts but also expressions found in images, sounds, and objects . . . as the conceptual linking of expressions. . . . Themes come both from the data (an inductive approach) and from the investigator's prior theoretical understanding of the phenomenon under study (an a priori approach)" (Ryan & Bernard, 2003, pp. 87–88). What counts as "theme," "content," and "expression" differs in interesting ways across approaches to narrative inquiry. Nevertheless, what is common in valuing narrative as a report of personal subjectivities (memories and feelings about experiences) is that the content or theme is authentic and embodied in a specific person. For that reason, perhaps, themes require reading beyond the surface of the text. In the absence of the connection of themes to narrative expression and a way of connecting surface expression to deep structure, themes remain in the mind of the researcher and difficult to identify.

Researchers, of course, work from theoretical perspectives, which means that those relying on theories like personality development (Lieblich, Tuval-Mashiach, & Zilber, 1998; Spence, 1984) might identify meaning in narrative in terms of psychological conflicts with others and one's own history (Erikson, 1994; Lieblich et al., 1998), or feminist theories focusing on oppressions and consequences of oppression (Chase & Rogers, 2001; Harding, 1988). Grounded theory is another approach used to create themes that emerge as self-conscious interactions of the researcher's perspective with narratives and other discursive data (Charmaz, 2006; Corbin & Strauss, 2007).

Emphasizing Z's narrative for its individual authenticity would involve noticing topics—peer conflict, changing social mores, such as the fact that smoking in public places is no longer always accepted, and, most important, Z's feeling upset about the smoker's rude behavior. A researcher seeking a meaningful theme might wonder if some intergroup tensions were playing out between Z and the smoker, if Z had a history of conflicts with men, or if her harsh judgment was a relational habit. Such questions could be addressed with additional narratives or interviews, a life history, observations of Z with her peers, perhaps directly addressing Z's orientations to peers, male peers, that person, or something about him.

Research that values narrative inquiry for individuality and coherence indicates a preference for case studies to remain personal, abstracting away from within-person diversities and common uses of narrative across individuals. Reading Z's character and relation to this narrative would be a priority in a case study. With the emphasis on creating a narrative profile, a case study would seek meaning in terms of principles of character, motivations buried in the narrative, a need to avoid certain painful events, and strategies for doing so, such as what restorying might produce (Hermans & Hermans-Jansen, 2001). In terms of ongoing methods for analyzing this and other narratives by Z, research emphasizing individual authenticity—the report approach to narrative inquiry—may caution the researcher to avoid influencing the interaction as much as possible. The reason for this is that the report is intended to be the authentic voice of the individual.

From the perspective of grounded theory (Charmaz, 2006; Corbin & Strauss, 2007), a beginning analysis would focus on topics (like smoking), characters, conflicts, and reactions, to create categories of social relations. Such an inward look is valuable and an aspect of narrating. Nevertheless, because human development is a dynamic sociocultural process, reducing discourse to the individual or to an identity group could minimize the interaction of an individual in constant interaction with diverse others and the individual in diverse situations, thereby provoking within-person diversity and complexity. Research designs can also allow for such diversities as well as any essential truths.

While grounded theory excavates individual meaning, a constructive perspective assumes a broader gaze on narrating in context, as a process of increased awareness about self or relevant issues. The state of the art of narrative inquiry provides insights for increasingly precise analyses of narrators' interactions with others. Another major reason researchers cite for doing narrative inquiry is that narrative is a creative process.

Narrative Construction

Some scholars focus on narrating as a developmental process—whereby persons become themselves through the stories they tell (Polkinghorne, 1991). This constructive nature of narrating is appealing because it involves people in creating meaning and a sense of who they are.

Researchers do systematic studies to examine how narrating interacts with the development of identity, thereby acknowledging the process nature of narrating in research. Narrative psychologists have, for example, explored literary features such as "chapters" (McAdams, 2005), "turning points" (McLean & Pratt, 2006), coherence (Linde, 1993; Smorti, Pananti, & Rizzo, 2010), and continuity (Clandinin & Connelly, 2000), in particular to learn about narrators' identity development and health.

This rationale for narrative research emphasizing **construction** builds in part on psychodynamic theory that personality is the story one tells (McAdams, 2005; Ochs & Capps, 2002; Polkinghorne, 1991). This constructive view is also appealing for studying and promoting well-being or socialization to social norms (Chase & Rogers, 2001; Ochs & Capps, 2002). Storytelling treatments are based on the idea that creating a new story to explain traumatic events or to make sense of those events can provide healthier guidelines for perception and action. Researchers have, for example, found that narrating a disruptive event like an earthquake and its aftermath led to increased calm among the college student participants (Smorti, Del Buffa, & Matteini, 2007). Interacting with narrative can impose sense on chaos and familiarity on strangeness. Researchers focusing on identity and well-being construction also tend to emphasize coherence and conformity in their designs and analyses with narrative (Baerger & McAdams, 1999). While coherence may be important at times to mental health and social conformity, it can actually undermine the study of identity development when it glosses over the inevitable conflicts and within-person diversities. For this reason, researchers need to expand beyond an emphasis on narrative report to include broader social dimensions and their vicissitudes.

The appeal of narrating for its constructive function extends beyond the narrative text and individual to various kinds of interactions. Some researchers emphasizing the constructive function of narrative for identity development highlight the interactive nature of narrating. This strand of research on identity development mines tensions in the process, in part because it defines narrating in conversations or **small stories** (Bamberg, 2004a; Korobov, 2009; Ochs & Capps, 2002). Small story research, for example, examines the formation of male ideals exchanged during conversations among preadolescent boys talking about girls (Bamberg, 2004b) and studies college students discussing their romantic relationships (Korobov, 2009). The research design simulates settings for peer group conversation as closely as possible, such as asking friends to "chat among themselves" during a delay in starting the presumptive research activity (Korobov, 2009). In this approach, researchers examine turn-taking patterns and other strategies, like irony, as means of conveying acceptable conversation about such matters and, thus, about related ideals. These designs emphasize narrating for identity development in conversations, which the researchers analyze for enacted qualities like agency/passivity and constancy/change (Bamberg, 2008).

The construction rationale acknowledges, even invites, tension and contradiction, often enlivened by defining narratives as always interacting in the environment, as occurs in actual conversation. The construction rationale thus argues that ". . . the domain for analyzing counter positions is the social realm of interaction in which narratives are implemented rather than the stories per se" (Bamberg, 2004a). When examining narratives in the context of everyday activities, it becomes clear that people use narrating not only to report or to construct personal experiences but also to interact with diverse environments—people, objects, and situations—including research settings.

Approaches emphasizing narrative construction would appreciate Z's narrative in ways that are explicitly social—that is, as among persons rather than primarily for what the social situation invokes within her and the history that has created her personality. Reading Z's narrative in terms of its value as a constructive process would turn outward more than inward, as with a report reading. As a construction process, Z's narrative would yield some additional insights about how she felt about the people, place, and history related to her narrative of the rude smoker. An emphasis on zooming out to the interaction of the smoking incident, asking about it, observing other events in the same place, or reproducing peer conflicts might address questions about how Z was performing not only the stable identity she had crafted up to the age of 21 but also how she was continuing to develop that identity. What occurred before, after, and during the narration would be relevant to the researcher emphasizing narrative construction. The researcher's consideration about seeking or eliciting additional narratives to inform the analysis and interpretation might include presenting Z with the narrative and asking her about those surrounding events and her current interpretation.

Alternatively, the researcher might observe or construct conversational events with individuals or groups of similar profiles relevant to the research questions framed, perhaps as "What bugs you in public places or society these days?" Use of the colloquial "bugs you" would indicate interpersonal issues rather than big issues, as those microaggressions of everyday life tend to be material for ongoing self-construction. Brief anecdotes or longer sagas can be helpful in figuring out the meaning of an event and its relation to a researcher's questions, for the narrator as well as for the audience. In other words, the point and relevance of a memorable event often become clear in the telling, in the social interaction among researchers and their subjects, as among friends or other interlocutors. Analyses would identify self-presentation and self-reflection moves, like self-aggrandizing (Oliveira, 1999) or playing with irony (Korobov, 2009), within the text and in a recorded interactional context. Analyses presented in Chapters 5 and 6 of this book are especially relevant to such a reading.

Narrative research has indicated that in addition to being an activity for reporting personal experience and constructing identity, narrating is an activity for engaging with the world. An emphasis on activity, relationships, and diversity is important in this global era, characterized by increasing plurality of experiences, intercultural contact, conflict, and resource inequality. Research must, thus, be sensitive to these complexities as they interact in expression. Toward that end, the use theory of narrative provides an explanation and analytic approach for understanding narrating as an activity of critical and creative sense making about the environment as well as about the self.

Narrative Use

Valuing narrative for its use quality extends prior emphases by highlighting the fact that narrating is a sense-making process—a process for figuring out what's going on in the world and how one fits. According to this theory, narrating is an activity for creating identity as well as for sharing experience, but more than that, it is an activity for figuring out what is going on in the environment and how one fits—in brief, for problem solving about experience (Nelson, 1998, 2007). Another source for this view is the philosopher Wittgenstein (1953), who defined meaning as use: "Now, what do the words of this language *signify*?—What is supposed to show what they signify, if not the kind of use they have?" (p. 6).

When zooming out from the individual in this way, identity fades as a focal issue of research while the interaction of social and personal activities and perspectives comes into focus. Within this broader process of narrating to interact in the world, one crafts and tests out self-presentations both for how others respond and how one feels in the wake of interaction (Spence, 1984; Turkle, 1997). Inevitably, given the diverse contexts where people participate across the life span, these experiments at being—aided in part by storytelling—continue. A 70-year-old participating in her first meeting of the local senior citizen group might, for example, feel as attentive as a high school freshman to all the implicit rules of what people talk about and what they don't, which personal experiences they share, which they don't share, and how they make friends. Narrating creates a symbolic reality as a person remembers it or would like it to be, so researchers must extend the idea that narrative is a construction process to allow for how people use narrating to interpret their experiences.

A dynamic narrating approach assumes that in research, as in life, people address one another guided by the situation, expectations, and rapport, rather than only in terms of an individual's knowledge about an issue. A dynamic narrating perspective assumes there are myriad influences on what people say or write and that these influences are expressed in the research narratives, whether the researcher accounts for them or not. Very often interviewees do not explicitly mention the issues of interest to the researcher. For example, participants in a study on gender roles in workplace practices may avoid mentioning gender or discrimination because they know that differences of opinion about such issues cause conflicts at work, or they may mention an issue because the researcher has asked about it several times. A researcher interested in gender discrimination and also sensitive to the dynamics of narrating could ask a participant to narrate from the perspectives of females *and* males or for audiences of males and females. The participant would then be performing ideas about gender in relation to diverse situations rather than only talking about gender. The researcher could analyze for dynamic cues to meaning rather than only explicit mentions of "gender," "discrimination," or synonyms. Another language-sensitive option consistent with dynamic narrating would be to present several narratives expressing gender discrimination and interpretations for the participant to judge in terms of whether she or he relates to the story in a positive way, a negative way, not at all, or would like to adjust the telling.

Eliciting personal stories in research is an advance in social science, but this must occur with awareness of the fact that narratives are language, language is social, language use constructs meaning, and that meaning is fraught with relational realities and dilemmas. Also destabilizing the idea that narrating would be in any singular way authentic is a fact that many beginning researchers notice: Participants often check with the researcher for "Is that what you want?" Acknowledging and adjusting to the creative nature of narrating is the way to address this. This is not a problem but an indication that researchers must design studies with the awareness that research discourses are social and directed. In these ways, narratives are interactions rather than reports or personal constructions.

Emphasizing the use quality of narrating involves defining meaning in interaction with explicit or implied others, in relation to social structures, power relations, and one's own needs and goals. Participants in research, as in life, use multiple narrating experiences, engaging diverse narrator stances with diverse audiences and purposes (connecting, inquiring, advising) to express their complex range of knowledge, experiences, and intentions. Narrating is, thus, oriented externally, first acquired by interacting with experts—like parents and older children—in the culture, then becoming a tool available for use. This approach adds to prior inquiry by employing basic knowledge of how language works.

A poignant example of how meaning includes social context comes from a news report about speeches at the Republican and Democratic conventions to nominate the 2012 U.S. presidential candidates. This quote from the news report explains that what each political party emphasized in its speeches was precisely the opposite of the party platform and its historical position: "The two back-to-back conventions are highlighting an interesting role reversal between the political parties. The Republicans, who in the past eagerly waged a culture war, tried to emphasize economic issues, while the Democrats, stuck with a bad economy, were no longer running away from social issues that once petrified their strategists" (Baker, 2012). This reporter alerts readers to the fact that the meaning of each speech must be understood in the context of history (that one party typically emphasized the economy and the other emphasized social issues), current facts (the party of the incumbent president was being blamed for a bad economy, and the other party for being hostile to the economic needs of poor and middle-class Americans), and public opinion at the time about each party's weaknesses. What all this means for researchers wanting to understand how their subjects think and feel about topics of interest is that a large part of narrative meaning is not stated at all or may contradict what is stated.

Reading Z's narrative with an emphasis on use involves establishing the context with which she was interacting, actually and virtually, to account for the presentation she wanted to make with the story for others. Because Z wrote the narrative in the context of a community center with progressive values, the issue of past behavior was much in the air. Even the use of the term "Neanderthal" had come to refer to those who were unable to move beyond the war and many suspected to be holding on to the past mentalities, like hatred of people of ethnic groups different from their own. A researcher who observes narrative situations, makes notes, and gathers narratives or other documents by the focal participants and their interlocutors can consider such interactions, as is explained in Chapter 2 of this book. Qualities of narratives are also relevant for precisely identifying performed meanings, as explained in all subsequent chapters of this book. Rather than doing extended interviews or a life history, as would be consistent with the report rationale for narrative inquiry, a researcher focused on learning about narrative use would involve participants in personally meaningful activities involving narrative and other discourses (letter writing, mission statements, and so on) directed to different audiences with whom the participant would want to interact in different ways. For example, in this narrative where she is merged with the "I" character, Z is critical of a person exhibiting behaviors the narrative expresses as bad. In that way, Z uses the narrative to perform her distance from past behavior, indicated not only by the portrayal of the smoker's rude behavior but also by summarizing him as a "Neanderthal"—a prehuman species living thousands of years ago. As explained in Chapters 2 and 3, emphasizing the use value of narrating involved Z in sharing accounts that were not only autobiographical but also focused on others and imaginary scenes. The purpose of such diverse narrating is to shift judgment away from the individual as an explicit focus, which tends to restrict expression toward a perceived ideal. In narratives about adults in the community and in fictional stories, for example, Z comes across in a different way, still distancing from the past but expanding her range of narrative vision, at least to express another's possible perspective:

> . . . there is one old man that is really primitive. Whenever he enters the trolley he rudely tells someone to get up so that he can sit, as if that is someone's duty and not just a show of good manners. This is why the old man got into conflicts many times with others, and he always gets a "shorter end of the stick." The conflict is never resolved.

In yet a third narrative, Z crafts a completely different approach. Rather than distancing, she enacts connections with others, cooperation rather than harsh judgment, and a comparatively positive demeanor:

> The news that the building could not be built came because the property was illegally purchased, and government does not approve building on that place. People were crushed, angry, and upset. At the end, by strike, they won and the building will be built.

In a letter to a public official, Z extends further with the plea "give the opportunity to youth and they will show you what they can do."

Having four opportunities to express experience, knowledge, and imagination in relation to issues of interest, Z comes across as complex. Acknowledging that narrating is a clever human invention for performing meaning, researchers pay close attention to narrative expression, thereby eliciting complexity rather than making individual authenticity or coherence the priority. The story at the beginning of this chapter, for example, sounds like it could be about how a bird died, but focusing on the telling suggests it could instead be about the narrator. Details like the repeated "I" and the action leading up to the high point of the narrator's recognition "it was time to act," among other elements of this emerging story, implicate the narrator as protagonist. Because narrating is embedded in life—with all its social pressures, such as public opinion, in just the way that researchers would like to discover—the main message often unfolds with how the story unfolds in context.

Narrative use focuses closely on expression, and, for this reason, after mastering some analytic strategies, researchers can work in precise ways. Understanding narrative uses requires providing multiple opportunities for people to narrate from different perspectives (self, other) and for different audiences (audiences of peers or adult authorities like teachers or politicians). Emphasizing narrative use is not incompatible with appreciating the individual report or self-construction, but the appeal of narrating for how people use it to mediate interactions in the world adds a strand of meaning that is often missed with other approaches.

Building on this brief review of the appeal of narrative inquiry, the next section presents four principles to guide dynamic narrative inquiry, as explained and illustrated in subsequent chapters. This narrative approach offers insights to complement prior and other approaches, but it can also offer new kinds of information.

PRINCIPLES OF DYNAMIC NARRATING IN RESEARCH

Dynamic narrative theory provides a foundation for principles to guide research design and analysis. Rather than being a window into people's minds and hearts, storytelling is a cultural tool (like other discourse genres and symbol systems) for managing (mediating) self-society relationships (Vygotsky, 1978, p. 55). As a **cultural tool**, narrating is, thus, a psychosocial mediator or "conductor of human influence on the object of activity . . . externally oriented . . . aimed at mastering and triumphing over nature . . . and . . . as a means of internal activity aimed at mastering one's self" (Vygotsky, 1978, p. 55).

This theoretical insight is brought to life with the dynamic narrating principles defined in this chapter, explaining that narrating is a process of use—to do things in the world in relation to diverse other people and the physical and symbolic environments. The principles of use, relation, materiality, and diversity guide the work of narrative inquiry design, analysis, and integration in the chapters to come. A brief statement of each principle provides a foundation for researchers using this book, researchers paying attention to sociocultural meaning in the style and context of narrative discourse. Subsequent chapters work with these principles for research design and analysis.

The Use Principle

The **use principle** highlights the fact that discourse is activity. Narrating functions as a tool to mediate individual and societal interactions, so researchers can design activities where participants have the opportunity to use narrating flexibly to interact with and reflect on the issues of interest. Research consistent with this principle would sample multiple narratives from diverse positions to learn about meaning by comparing diverse uses. Because people use narrating to contest historical and cultural narratives and not only to conform to them, research designs should allow for and even encourage narrating from critical stances as well as to conform to accepted expressions. Put most simply, a research design can elicit narrative use by studying it in activities that are meaningful to people, where people can reflect from different perspectives around the phenomenon of interest and for different purposes. Eliciting narratives in meaningful situations will elicit meaning in use, and varying important purposes and interactions in those meaningful situations will bring diverse dimensions of meaning to life. If, for example, a researcher is interested in how people deal with conflict in relationships, he or she can invite participants to narrate from their relationship partners' perspectives as well as from their own. Respecting the use principle also means examining how people employ narrative elements to express themselves socially, as well as studying what they say literally. A researcher studying public opinion about political candidates could, for example, consider how candidates' speeches over time relate to different news reports about the candidates and voters' narratives on similar issues.

The Relation Principle

The **relation principle** is that narrators interact with present and implied others, objects, and ideas in environments, so we should design research with narrating in terms of different narrator-audience-issue relations. Narrating is a relationally complex process, because for each telling and listening arrangement, the narrator must consider which details to select, how to arrange them to highlight the most interesting points to maintain the listeners' attention, how to present him- or herself in the telling, how to avoid certain taboos, and how to suggest a better life with the story. Recounting the same event at another time, in another place, or in another social arrangement would provoke some change in the meaning, because narratives embed audience, time, and place, implicitly as well as explicitly. For this reason, research designs should observe, elicit, and analyze the narratives participants share in relation to diverse circumstances. Whether participants mention issues like race, gender, or political persuasion is likely to be determined by the present and presumed listeners and readers of the narrative. What may loom large as an expectation or a taboo in an interview about voting preferences and ethnicity with a person of the same ethnic group is likely to differ from what looms large in an interview on the same issue with someone from another ethnic group. Likewise, what emerges in a narrative framed as one's own experiences with a certain difficult situation is likely to differ from what emerges in a narrative about another person's plight. Ignoring such relational complexity—variation of narrator stance and meaning—and any contradictions in favor of coherence could seriously limit the results of a study.

Narrating is dynamic because it is a social-relational activity. According to discourse theory, knowledge and identity are created in the context of culturally meaningful activities in verbal and nonverbal practices, as each linguistic utterance is a response in "the chain of communication" where "no utterance is the first to break the silence of the universe" (Bakhtin, 1986, p. 69). Interaction occurs "when the listener perceives and understands the meaning (language meaning) of speech, [and] he simultaneously takes an active, responsive attitude toward it. He either agrees or disagrees with it (completely or partially)" (Bakhtin, 1986, p. 68). The interactive process of person-in-world has been identified in the narrative quality of *"addressivity"* (Bakhtin, 1986).

Addressivity is a quality of each meaningful utterance, a word, brief narrative, or novel, responding to others in the present, prior, or future moments of history. Whether in the room or in the imagination, those others have contributed in some way to the motivation for an utterance—a definition, explanation, or justification—and a basis for response or resistance. The insight for narrative inquiry is that writers and thinkers, like speakers, direct language to audiences distant or imagined, such as others who may judge them, as well as to actual audiences in the immediate context. Because people select what to say, what not to say, and how to say it in relation to their views about expectations of these audiences, they become part of each text. This concept of addressivity brings context—those to whom a narrative is directed—into the meaning of a narrative text.

Consistent with that view, narrators work with features, like plot, to read, re-create, and respond to expectations and sanctions where they live. The narrator of the story at the beginning of this chapter was, for example, using a basic plot to interact with assumptions about playgrounds and adults' responsibilities to protect children. The first sentence sets up a problem or trouble that launches the story ("I saw the bird flattened on the ground . . ."), a consequence and complicating action ("One of the . . . children walked toward me . . . crying"), and what appears in this unfinished story to be a high point or turning point ("That's when I knew it was time to act"). The reader or listener who understands this bit of story draws on clues about the context (school context indicated by "kindergarten"), characters ("children," "bird," "I"), and cultural mores ("it was time to act"), thereby interacting with that context and the narrator who created that story world. Aided by plot structure in this way, narrative is not only a memory of reality but also a means to an end, such as to present oneself as a good person, a serious person, or some other kind of person. The process of narrating interweaves such goals in accounts of specific events to show researchers the diverse realities subjects perceive.

Ironically, much research tries to limit the relational dimension, in part because it creates dissonance and in part because the emphasis is typically on conformity and truth. Survey research, for example, minimizes participants' language production. And, as discussed above, research with narrative often emphasizes coherence. Those may be important goals over the life course, but to achieve a coherent sense of self, individuals go through the process of dealing with conflict, tension, and contradiction. Those dynamics are embedded in the narrative process, albeit often unexpressed in favor of a good story or the right story—so research designs must allow the expression of multiple stories relevant to the inquiry. The relation principle contributes to dynamic narrative inquiry by providing guidelines for designing and analyzing for complex narrating. The concrete elements of narrative also contribute to meaning.

The Materiality Principle

The **materiality principle** accounts for the fact that narrating is firmly rooted in actual life, so narrative inquiry is also embedded in life. The physical features, like exclamations (!) or repetitions, and the structural features, like prosaic openings (e.g., "Once upon a time"), contribute to meaning, so we pay attention to those features in narrative analysis. As illustrated in Chapter 5, for example, exclamations (among other detailed narrative features) indicate what is especially important to the narrator. Also, as presented in

Chapter 4, elements of plots, like openings, indicate the narrator's stance on narrated events. "Once upon a time," for example, indicates that the narrator wants us to judge her story as a comment on life from a distance rather than exactly as *her* life. When designing research, we should, therefore, consider the concreteness of meaning in discursive acts and elements, such as whether the genre is autobiography or fiction and the specific features that go along with each, such as whether the referent of the "I" character is the author or an imagined other. Important messages may or may not be stated (often the most contentious ones are *not* explicit). Like the Democrats and Republicans mentioned earlier in this chapter, narrators use the features of their discourse cleverly to express or to hide meanings in appeals to their audiences at specific times and in specific places.

Meaning doesn't float vaguely in the act of narrating to then disappear from the airwaves or into participants' memories, writings, or transcripts of their speech. Meaning is, instead, material because narratives are symbolic systems inextricably linked to persons, contexts, cultures, and circumstances of their histories and expressive moments. When I share an experience of my day, those in earshot, viewers of an e-mail subject line, blog, or online conversation, understand (or can venture a good guess about) why I am sharing the story, how to respond, and what not to say. The meanings come from the patterns of symbols rather than only the literal words. The words "This was the day I had been waiting for!" have meaning, but the arrangement of "This was the day" followed by "I had been waiting for" points demonstrably to the day as an anticipated event rather than just another day. Those arrangements, like the sounds and referents of the words, embody meaning.

Narratives appear to mirror events in everyday life, but even more than that, meaning is material because it integrates biological qualities, like vocalization and hearing, with culture, like agreements about when we share stories and which stories are worth telling. This blend of material and cultural life is expressed with the concept of the cultural tool—a symbolic process developed in human relations for interacting purposefully in the world. The quintessential cultural tool is language, which people use to interact with one other, their environments, and the myriad symbolic realities created in cultural histories (Vygotsky, 1978).

Narrating is also material because it provides specific elements pointing to meaning outside the narrative as well as within it. A simple illustration is a parent's pointing to a dangerous object, alerting the other parent and the baby to steer clear of the object. The parent's use of a finger and any wounds from past perils with this object are physical, while the means for creating shared attention among the family group are cultural. Pointing an index finger progresses symbolically to the use of pronouns that point in written language to persons, places, objects, or ideas in the physical or conceptual world outside the text. Pointing to an approaching snake, for example, refers to the snake object, expresses an urgent call to attention, and, over time, expresses an understanding that a similar object could present danger. With the aid of devices like pointing and the routines where these devices take on meaning, narrating creates a scenario that leads to future action. This is important when analyzing narratives in research to acknowledge that what people say is often intentional rather than only factual. Verbal pointing techniques—referred to as **indexicals**—connect expressions to contexts because they point somewhere in the world (Reyes, 2011). That research participants use narrative to indicate what they intend to say should be included as research data.

Another example of the materiality of meaning that has implications for research comes from a study with multimodal forms of narrating. In a project to compose a library book about fourth and fifth graders' lives, children digitized photographs they had taken of interesting places in their neighborhoods, used digital drawing tools, and used a standard word-processing program. Analyses of the completed book and the composing process showed that children who had difficulty writing used the physical features of a multimodal computer system to extend their abilities to complete social studies assignments (Daiute & Morse, 1993). For example, one boy whose major difficulty was maintaining attention on writing tasks used computer commands to shift—hyperactively—among visual, oral, and written elements of the class database of material about the students' home neighborhoods. In contrast, a very verbally skilled girl who was also very slow to realize she had ideas to share played with multiple visual tools, including a scanned image of a Hershey bar wrapper and a drawing tool to alter that image. This play with visual and digital tools, in turn, sparked the girl's memory of her departed grandfather, whom she described in a touching narrative about their relationship symbolized by sharing favorite candies. How these young people employed diverse computer tools was integrated into the meaning of their final compositions. The boy who hyperactively selected among different composing modes created a complete text with interwoven aural and visual imagery. The girl used an image as a motivating springboard for a parallel verbal narrative. In summary, highlighted in this example of multimodal composing are the young people's abilities to use various media to enhance personal skills and preferred ways of working to create meaning. These examples suggest meanings that the researchers might have missed had they ignored the physical composing process. Likewise, the features of narrative (like plot and exclamations) are highly relevant, albeit underused, as clues to understanding meaning in narrative research.

The Diversity Principle

The **diversity principle** refers to differences within and across individuals and groups in narrators' stances—purposes, feelings, and thoughts—in relation to their audiences at the time of telling. This kind of diversity is like a network of connections rather than primarily inside the narrator or about narrator identity. Researchers often design their studies based on diversities between groups distinguished by categories like gender, ethnicity, and citizenship. Such factors play a role in narrator experiences, but they do not completely define individual or group experiences or their tellings, as is explained with the diversity principle. Categories like gender and ethnicity, which are presumed to be within individuals, are complicated when narrators have the opportunity to imagine various situations from the perspectives of diverse others, including adversaries in a conflict, unfamiliar groups or those of another age group as well as from their own perspectives. A common narrative—or script (see Chapter 4)—might emerge from an analysis of narratives by participants who had an opportunity to tell several versions of a story. Given the complexity of contemporary life and human relations, assuming unitary experience based on predetermined factors may not, however, offer the kinds of personal nuance researchers often want from narrative inquiry. Narrating diversity does not mean giving up one's point of view or giving in to another point of view; rather, it involves acknowledging one's complexity and sensitivity to others and environments.

In summary, narrating is an activity of oral, written, and visual communication. Discursive activities, like speaking, writing, choreographed movement, and signage, not only express symbolic thinking but also form it and develop it (Parker, 2005). Narrators use myriad elements, including characters, settings, plots with events that set stories in motion (also referred to as "trouble"; Bruner, 2002; Daiute, 2011), high points or climaxes (Labov & Waletzky, 1967/1997), resolutions, and morals as building blocks for sharing experience, feelings, and intentions. This communicative nature of narrating—*how* people express themselves—is central to *what* people are saying in research projects. That there is so much in a narrative text means that researchers can read context in the text, in large part, with a theory of use. Dynamic narrating also extends beyond prior approaches that emphasize the individuality of each person's voice, focusing instead on the networking quality that humans use to connect with their social and physical environments. Defining narrating and applying the dynamic process to research design and analysis continue across the chapters of this book. For now, a narrating experience is a step toward understanding the process.

RESEARCHER NARRATING

As someone who has used narrative to interact in your own life, you can do the following activities as steps toward doing narrative inquiry. These activities might remind you that you tell, write, or imagine narratives on a daily basis. They might bring the definitions of narrative above to life for you, or they might add weight to the preceding explanations of the appeal of narrative inquiry. Your own narratives, written or dictated as I suggest below, might also serve as examples to use for practice with various narrative analysis strategies presented in later chapters of this book. (If you dictate your narratives, you can transcribe them for closer study with activities in later chapters of this book.)

- Write about a good childhood experience. What happened? Who was involved? (You can use pseudonyms—that is, invented names.) How did everyone think and feel about the event? How did it all turn out?
- Write about an event you observed and consider humorous (or write about a difficult childhood experience). What happened? Who was involved? (You can use pseudonyms.) How did everyone think and feel about the event? How did it all turn out?
- After writing these narratives, consider the following: What makes them narratives? What are the features? How do these narratives rely on knowledge of the context, audience, narrator, and other factors? What questions do these writings raise for you about narrative and the narrating process?
- Imagine yourself as someone who might listen to or read one of your narratives. Then, redo it imagining that potential audience.

Doing the narrating you are interested in for your research is also a way to consider whether and how your research plan is likely to yield the kind of material you will need and would like to analyze. Many researchers also use narrating in their work by making notes about the research process and experiences, sometimes even when they are not eliciting narrative discourse.

PLAN FOR PRESENTING DYNAMIC NARRATIVE THEORY AND PROCESS

The theory and process of dynamic narrative inquiry unfold in relation to research activities in this book. Chapter 2 presents an approach to dynamic narrative inquiry design, and Chapters 3 through 6 focus on different narrative analysis strategies consistent with this theory. Chapter 2 is an ideal next step for gaining a sense of factors to consider when designing a narrative research project. After that, you can read and do the activities in Chapters 3 through 6 in any order. I present **strategies** including values analysis (Chapter 3), plot analysis (Chapter 4), significance analysis (Chapter 5), character mapping (Chapter 6), and time analysis (Chapter 6) in an order that explores narrative meaning first in a broader social interactive sense (with values), then in terms of narrative structure (with plot), followed by narrative features anchored in, but not limited to, specific kinds of expressions (significance, character, time). Chapter 7 focuses on ways to transform analyses into findings.

For a more detailed overview of the book, see Table 1.1 (on pages 28–29), which presents the process strategies of subsequent chapters in terms of the principles of dynamic narrating discussed in this chapter. The table offers a summary of the major principles of dynamic narrating, defines them briefly, and points to subsequent chapters presenting practical inquiry strategies that apply each principle, with examples and materials.

Each chapter includes a brief overview, an introduction to the foundational concept(s) for the methodological strategy with an example, an explanation of the method and its potential contribution, an interactive example, examples of the strategies in previous published research, a detailed description of the process for applying the strategy in new research, a chapter summary, and a brief transition to the next chapter. Following this progression of concepts and activities will provide you with a good understanding of dynamic narrative inquiry by the end of the book.

CONCLUSION AND NEXT

Researchers have expressed several different rationales for narrative inquiry, including wanting to gain insights about personal experiences and understandings of issues related to their research, wanting to learn about the construction of knowledge and identity, and wanting to assess similarities and differences in ways of knowing across individuals and groups. That narratives are tools

Table 1.1 Plan for Focus on Dynamic Narrating Design and Analysis Strategies

Dynamic narrating principle	Defined	Focal chapters applying each principle in detail (see chapters for methods, examples, implications)
Use principle	People *use* narrative to make sense of what's going on in their environments and how they fit, so researchers should build on this natural use of narrating for design and analysis in narrative inquiry.	All design and analysis strategies across Chapters 2 through 6 apply this principle. Chapter 7 discusses strategies for determining how analyses across the chapters combine to address research questions in terms of how participants used narratives to make sense of the issues of researcher interest.
Relation principle	Narrators select and organize their expressions interactively in relation to others likely to communicate with and/or to judge them. These may be interpersonal relations, intergroup relations, and/or relations with society more broadly.	**Chapter 2:** The *activity-meaning system design* is useful for guiding the sampling and collection of narratives by stakeholders with different perspectives on the research questions and issues of interest. **Chapter 3:** *Values analysis* examines how narratives by the different stakeholders interact with the research issues of interest and one another. **Chapter 6:** *Character mapping analysis* identifies interactions of characters (and objects) in narratives as they relate to issues in the context and the research issues.
Diversity principle	Because narrating is an interaction with others, it is not a neutral process. Narrating is, instead, defined by the perspectives of people (groups, institutions, and so on) in positions of different influence (power), cultural familiarity (e.g., ethnicity, gender), practices, resources, and so on. Such diverse perspectives with which narrators interact must be considered in narrative research design/analysis.	**Chapter 2:** The *activity-meaning system design* suggests purposefully including stakeholders positioned in different ways around the issues of interest (e.g., influence, knowledge, goals) around the research questions and issue of interest. **Chapter 3:** *Values analysis* involves examining how the stakeholder narratives relate with their uptake (*performing*), rejection (*contesting*), and transformation (*centering*) of values identified in the first part of the analysis. **Chapter 5:** *Significance analysis* identifies narrator individuality by the use of unique patterns of nuance in narratives (*evaluative devices*) as those relate to others' narratives and the context. **Chapter 6:** Patterns of narrative *time analysis* offer additional unique information about narrators' individual and collective subjective orientations to the issues of interest.

Dynamic narrating principle	Defined	Focal chapters applying each principle in detail (see chapters for methods, examples, implications)
Materiality principle	Narrating is a physical process, rooted in the settings, scenarios, expressive features, and social relations of daily life, enacted verbally (also visually and in movement) and with inflections for effect beyond literal meaning (e.g., dialogue, intensifiers, metaphors, repetitions). The symbolic qualities of narrating link so closely to perception, action, and language use common in daily life that they create meaning that integrates symbolic and material expression.	**Chapter 4:** *Plot analysis* (e.g., setting, conflict, resolution strategies) indicates the narrator's perceptual and interpretive framing of specific narrated events, thereby shaping the meaning. **Chapter 5:** *Significance analysis* identifies the physically expressive features of narratives (e.g., repetitions, emphases, and verbal and nonverbal markers) for their shaping of meaning. **Chapter 6:** *Time analysis* follows the chronological organization in a narrative to address the fact that narratives have a finite period of expression defined by narrative structure (plot with beginning, middle, end). Time markings engage sense and symbolic responses rather than only mirroring real time.

people use is a relatively novel idea for conducting narrative research design and analysis. This idea builds on prior explanations for narrative inquiry and expands the inquiry process for new insights and precision.

Dynamic narrating is, in summary, a concept emphasizing the interactive, communicative, purposeful nature of narrating, leading to strands of meaning researchers can identify to enhance findings about human problems, understandings, and behaviors. Dynamic narrating highlights the interactive quality of narrative for making sense of life events, people, and objects and for developing life in the symbolic realm. As a shared cultural tool (developed and used in culturally relevant ways), narrating is a relational process, occurring within a system of diverse situations and diverse perspectives from an individual's point of view while always implicating others. This process of sense making occurs with the use of language forms, like narrative, and serves to organize (mediate) people's interactions in the world. Narrating is purposeful; for example, we use it to present ourselves in ways that connect or disconnect with the social and political milieu or to suggest different views of how things could be. Narrating is also a means for imagining possible worlds (Bruner, 1986). These creative and imitative dimensions together enact narrative meaning.

Drawing on such knowledge about narrating in daily life for research design and analysis is long overdue. This dynamic narrating approach extends knowledge about mundane narrating to the design of research acknowledging that people *use* narratives (they don't pour meanings into them) to relate to social, physical, and symbolic environments (people don't narrate only for interviewers or themselves), to employ features of the genre to create meaning (people don't just speak through narratives to meaning in some other place; meaning evolves with the narrative such that narrator and audience are changed in the process), and to engage a tension between culturally accepted stories and alternatives leading to social change. Because this approach to narrative inquiry draws on the history of human communication, researchers employing it can move beyond the qualitative versus quantitative methods divide. We blur that distinction by acknowledging the combination of the naturalistic and systematic qualities of storytelling. This is not only a mixed-methods approach including qualitative and quantitative analyses but also an integrated approach drawing on the naturalness and diversity of the cultural practice of narrating.

Chapter 2 presents an approach to designing narrative inquiry consistent with the principles of dynamic narrating discussed in this chapter.

Notes

Narratives by Z on pages 9 and 18 are from *Human Development and Political Violence* by Colette Daiute. Copyright © 2010 Colette Daiute. Reprinted with the permission of Cambridge University Press.

1. Terms appearing in boldface type are defined in the glossary.

2

Designing Dynamic Narrative Research

People use narrating all the time in daily life, sometimes communicating to friends about last evening's adventures or plans for tomorrow, sometimes to personal journals with sagas about problems, sometimes in more public realms like news reports, class summaries, or other accounts of "what happened." Researchers can learn from such interactions, sampling narratives during spontaneous interactions in life or in research settings. Researchers can also build on such natural narrative processes—practices, features, and functions of everyday narrating—to design data collection and analysis. Aware of the principles of dynamic narrating (as discussed in Chapter 1)—that people *use* narrating to interact purposefully (albeit not always explicitly) *with others, their environments, and themselves* in *diverse ways*—researchers can plan studies that involve narrating as a rich relational process.

This chapter begins with an example of a novice researcher observing narrating in life and builds on the observation to create a research design—the process of interest in this chapter. The chapter defines the concept activity-meaning system as a framework, the features of research designs consistent with that concept, examples of activity-meaning system designs in previous research, and a summary of the dynamic narrative inquiry research design process.

BEGINNING NARRATIVE INQUIRY

A conversation among young people on a college visit developed into a research question and draft research design. Nathan, a volunteer in a college recruitment program, overheard visiting students talking about what it might be like to go to college there. After guiding the group of prospective students around the college, Nathan thought about one of their conversations. Then, when writing for a class assignment, Nathan made notes about the interaction. He wrote his notes as a narrative with another narrative embedded in it. Nathan's narrative read:

> One of the recruits, a girl I'll call Allison, said "Imagine you're here next year, and you're all settled and it's the first Saturday night, and, like, you want to party." Another student from her high school, Jackson, said "Ok, yea, I'm game. Let's party." Matt another kid from their town said, "Remember the time when it was Maria's 17th birthday and her parents gave her money for five friends to go to the club? That was awesome!" Maria got specific "Okay, so here's the invite list. Maria in, Jackson in, Matt in,—Allison in—it *is* her birthday, after all!" (all laughed.) So, one more? Bradley, Allison's brother, Bradley? Okay?" "Naaa," said Allison, "he's too young to get into a college party. Okay, my cousin, Lina? She was loud but fun at my other cousin's birthday." "Sure" added Jackson, but Maria countered with "How 'bout Jennie? Not too young, not too loud, not too much in the family, not . . ." "But, she's illegal!" griped Matt. "Like not in age! But, like 'illegal'?" "What?" said Maria, seemingly stunned. "So what!!!" chorused the others.

Nathan was intrigued with the interaction among the potential students, wondering, "How do these adolescents think about who's in and who's out? What do they know about different kinds of 'illegal'—illegal to drink, illegal immigrant?" Nathan had been impressed that the group was "all colors of the rainbow," as he wrote elsewhere in his notes, but then this "illegal" thing came up. How do these almost-college students come to understand friendship in their families, peer circles, local politics, the media, or other places? This conversation and the questions it provoked in a researcher interested in social relations became a catalyst for a study with networks of narratives around the issues of intergroup relations and the spreading of such ideas in narratives among friends, families, and nations. The spontaneous narrative Nathan heard and then embedded in his own narrative notes led to a design for inquiry into how adolescents develop their ideas about social inclusion and exclusion. Because narratives do not occur in isolation, researchers do well to consider social contexts.

NARRATING IN CONTEXT

Narrating is an activity people use to mediate—manage—interactions that matter to them. Narrators recount experiences and tell stories to solve problems, to make friends, to pursue opportunities, to live good lives. This sense-making function of narrating involves using narrative as a tool to figure out what is going on in the environment, how one fits, and how situations might be better. For these reasons, narrating is a process that occurs within a complex network of social structural, interpersonal, and environmental relations. As the basis for research design, the next section expands the definition of narrative, in particular as interacting in social systems.

Narratives and Narrative Interactivity

If you listen (or read) as people tell (or write) about events, in their lives, in others' lives, or in imagined lives, you are hearing (or reading) narratives. In narrative inquiry, oral and written narratives are the obvious focal point of research. As defined in Chapter 1, narratives are accounts of events in chronological sequence (Labov & Waletzky, 1967/1997). According to that definition, the brief oral account "I saw the bird flattened on the ground outside my door. One of the kindergarten children walked toward me slowly, crying. That's when I knew it was time to act" is a narrative, as is the longer one by Z, both presented in Chapter 1. At the same time, extended oral life histories and very long novels are narratives. Journalistic reports of public events, newsworthy interpersonal interactions, and accounts of observations in fieldwork are narratives, too.

Narratives that simulate events in the world are, in summary, the most obvious narratives. Narratives simulate events in past, present, future, or, more typically, mixed time, as they describe characters, actions, dialogue, and other lifelike qualities in settings. Narratives differ from abstract informational discourse, like answers to direct questions about one's knowledge (e.g., "I know there is a problem with intergroup relations in the United States"), and reflections, like those in essays about reasons for changes in immigration policies; however, narrators also interact with such non-narrative discourses, as explained below. More than a specific set of features, narratives interact with contexts.

Much of everyday discourse is narrative, so narratives are often interwoven. In addition, as explained in Chapter 1, much of culture is created in narratives, which means that narratives by many different sources—different persons, roles, institutions, and so on—intermingle in a process of **narrative interactivity**. Nathan's notes, for example, include interwoven narratives. The narrative is a beginning researcher's account of an episode in an event beginning with dialogue, "One of the recruits, a girl I'll call Allison, said . . . ," to a climax, "'So what!!!' chorused the others." Within that narrative is a future story by the students on the tour, beginning with "Imagine you're here next year . . . ," and within that there is the narrative about Maria's 17th birthday party. Nathan's narrative is, moreover, woven within the context of his taking a class that required him to make notes about potentially interesting research topics related to ethnicity in the United States. These narratives within a narrative are relevant to inquiry because a researcher can identify narratives as well as craft them, select appropriate segments to study, and include them in a data set for narrative inquiry.

As human civilization has become increasingly complex, in part because of the symbolic tools in our midst, like writing, voice recording, video, and the Internet, to name a few technological advances, so have scholars' understandings of narrative. Scholars now, for example, consider narrative as more than representations of events in chronological order. **Small stories** are conversations in everyday discourse, described this way "both for literal (these tend to be brief stories) and metaphorical reasons (i.e., in the spirit of a late modern focus on the micro, fleeting aspects of lived experience)" (Bamberg & Georgakopoulou, 2008, p. 379). The conversation among Nathan's recruits, for example, became a small story. Although defining what constitutes a small story is still ongoing in narrative research, what distinguishes small stories from other conversations is the unfolding of events into a narrative account, by conversationalists shifting positions as authors and characters. Small story researchers consider the small story process as often leading to self-discovery.

Narrative has also come to refer to a worldview, a certain way of presenting events, the normality and morality of those events, characters, and related factors (Foucault, 2001). For example, a report of the end of a war can be seen as a victory for one side and a loss for the other. (This concept of narrative is discussed in more detail in Chapter 4 related to script analysis.) Such a broad societal explanation, also referred to as master narrative or dominant discourse (Foucault, 2001), is often considered a narrative. Because narratives in life are rarely separated completely from other forms of discourse, like abstract informational responses to direct questions or expressions of opinion, it is useful for researchers to recognize the interactivity of narrating with a range of contexts and discourses. The next section considers **narrative systems** and their implications for narrative inquiry.

With expanding definitions of narrative as an account of an event, a conversation in which a story unfolds, and a way of understanding the world, narrative is understood to be a social process. The context of narrative is, thus, an ecology—a **system** of settings, institutions, physical environments, formal and informal social relations, and events. When hearing narratives in daily life or imagining a narrative relevant to a research project, a researcher would, thus, consider a broad set of relevant relationships. For example, notes by Nathan at the beginning of this chapter draw on the practice of guiding prospective college students around a school, the informal interaction among friends, and research practices (note taking, reflecting on an informal interaction), all within the setting of an institution of higher education. As a college tour guide, Nathan represents the college, an institution with specific values, requirements, and other qualities that determine at least to some extent how he narrates a day in the life of a student to these recruits. The students' families are also somehow involved in the narrative of the college tour, in informal ways (perhaps observing their youth go off on the college tour or texting them about how it was going) and formal ways (having helped in the application process, such as to narrow the list of potential colleges for feasibility, cost, or other factors). Defining narrative as a social process—as in dynamic narrative inquiry—means that the person narrating in the midst of this system of relations is influenced by and influencing others in discourse. The central text for Nathan's emerging research design is his narrative of a conversation, and around that, in his research design, are other narratives and relevant documents, such as the assignment for his class.

People whose different interests, experiences, and positions in life relevant to the research question navigate this meaning-making system. The researcher who learns about relationships relevant to a project increases validity by becoming aware of the network of meanings rather than only individual expressions. Anthropologists offer wisdom about this process for ethnographic research, which includes gathering narratives they overhear or that emerge in their interviews, along with the common practice of having spent time in the culture, in situations related to the research topic, and with people involved in those practices (O'Reilly, 2012). When the research goal is to identify shared cultural mores, the focus of gathering narratives from diverse **perspectives** is primarily to triangulate them—that is, to find the common beliefs across diverse perspectives. When the goal is to examine change or development, differences across perspectives are also important because they indicate catalytic conflicts and, ideally, debates within and among narratives. Studying narrating in social contexts is enhanced with appropriate research designs.

THE NEED FOR DESIGN IN NARRATIVE INQUIRY

The observations that narrative inquiry is important because narrating is a common practice in everyday life *and* that narrative research requires design may seem somewhat contradictory. Nevertheless, applying narrative in life to narrative inquiry is long overdue. As discussed in Chapter 1, narrating is a basic life process for interacting in and developing in the world. Even though narrators are not always aware of the rules they are using, they conform to a basic structure of how to tell a story. Narrators select and organize details to serve different purposes—such as to connect with others, to entertain, to persuade, to attend to environments, to identify problems coming their way, and to narrate solutions when possible. That narrators—young and old—use narratives for those ends (often implicitly) means that researchers can use them too.

With the increasing call for narrative inquiry, it is imperative that researchers extend beyond including narratives only as anecdotes, as often occurs. Individual anecdotes may express an issue or truth, but there is much more to learn from multiple stories considered in relation to one another. Researchers can conduct formal inquiry with narratives and **narrative analysis** without losing the qualitative value of sharing experience. They can conduct systematic narrative inquiry while respecting the natural features of discourse. In order to do that, a researcher imagines a realistic system where individual narratives might interact and designs a study with that system in mind. Even when the audiences of a narrative are nowhere in sight or sound, a context-sensitive researcher begins to imagine, "What just happened to spark that story? Who is the audience? How is the story serving the storyteller?" **Research design** involves thinking about the processes of gathering and eliciting narratives—which occur everywhere—for research purposes. Recognizing spontaneous narratives in everyday life, as Nathan did, can be the beginning of narrative inquiry.

Recognizing, Gathering, and Eliciting Narratives for Research

Researchers interested in narrative inquiry may notice narratives they overhear in public life, read on the Internet, or find in archives like newspapers or histories, as long as they follow ethical practices. (A brief discussion of ethical considerations and procedures appears later in this chapter.) A researcher interested in the dating practices of college students could, for example, gather narratives overheard in the cafeteria or read in blogs. Narratives reported in prior research are also available for reflection and examination, citing the original research reference. Gathering narratives in public life has an appeal consistent with rationales for narrative inquiry to access authentic voices and experience, but there are several risks and cautions when selecting isolated narratives out of context. Consistent with defining narrating as a social-relational process, researchers should try to learn as much as possible about the narrator's context and interlocutors—that is, the social relations and purposes, such as who is involved, what is their role in society, and what is their position vis-à-vis the narrator (including their power over the narrator). This process can be guided with dynamic narrating principles, especially when the researcher wants to identify tensions or contradictions around an issue as well as coherence or cultural norms.

As mentioned in Chapter 1, narratives are not only reports of what happened or what one remembers; they are also dynamic means for relating to others and for problem solving. What prompts a person to share an experience may bring to light a fact, concern, or curiosity that influences the unfolding of the narrative. Sketching the network of relationships and issues that may matter for a research project is helpful, not so much because the researcher should (or can) know everything that might influence participants in a narrative study. Instead, when researchers imagine the possible range of interacting factors facing potential participants—such as expectations and taboos—the research design can be all the more sensitive to what participants might share, or not, in relation to the questions of interest.

From Curiosity to Research Questions

With the narrative he heard and then transcribed from experience, Nathan posed questions and subsequently created a design by asking how other people in different positions in the college scene and beyond were making sense of undocumented citizen status at the beginning of the 21st century—a time of relatively massive global migration and technologically enhanced interconnection and fear about that movement. The questions Nathan posed after overhearing a conversation that touched on illegality could, furthermore, lead to research designs that might improve the mission and practice of educating young adults from diverse backgrounds at Nathan's college. To build on Nathan's notes, a researcher could inquire into college practices for assigning roommates, policies regarding participation in clubs based on ethnicity and other interests, and so on. Prior research about how children and youth think about social exclusion and inclusion would, for example, offer insights about what to ask and how to design a study (Killen, 2007; Ruck, Park, Killen, & Crystal, 2011). With knowledge from prior research, a researcher like Nathan considers how a specific conversation created a relevant context for these issues. Similar situations, like narrating about someone else's party or another kind of event, would provide scenarios for research about how adolescents and young adults in different circumstances deliberate the issues.

A researcher gathering narratives in public life can maintain a context-sensitive approach by addressing the following questions: Where/when was this narrative expressed? Who was the narrator conversing with (performing for, arguing with)—in present, past, or imagined situations? Who might the narrator have had in mind? What might have been the purpose of this narrative—the broader use of the narrative that guided the selection of details or organization of characters and events as narrated? What do I, as the researcher, wish I had access to for a fuller account of the system of narratives involved? The researcher won't be able to answer all these questions, but by asking them he or she could gain insights into what else to include to shed light on the narratives and issues of interest in the study.

Building on the principles of dynamic narrating (described in Chapter 1), the next section presents the concepts activity-meaning system and activity-meaning system design, with examples from prior research, and guidelines for planning activity-meaning system designs in new projects.

ACTIVITY-MEANING SYSTEM DESIGNS

Activity-meaning system is a useful concept for organizing dynamic narrative inquiry. An activity-meaning system depicts an environment of everyday life—a cross-context slice of life—wherein relationships across different points of view by different actors in the system interact in some way. Table 2.1 lists and defines the dimensions of research designs in meaningful activity systems: (a) having a research focus or question where narrating plays a role in expressing and developing meaning, (b) identifying or creating space-time contexts where narrators interact in familiar and extended ways with others and environments, (c) recognizing the key **participants** in diverse relevant social and intra-personal relations (**actors/stakeholders**), and (d) gathering and eliciting narrating activities by stakeholders for subsequent narrative analyses addressing the relation, materiality, diversity, and use functions of narrating.

Like a snapshot's relation to reality, an activity-meaning system is not an obviously bounded unit. Just as a snapshot includes relevant elements of a scene, some in the foreground, others in the background, from the photographer's point of view, an activity-meaning system includes participants who interact directly and indirectly in the creation of meaning around an issue. Numerous possible voices came into play, for example, as Nathan considered his research design.

Table 2.1	Overview of Activity-Meaning System Research Design Dimensions

Dimensions of activity and meaning systems	Relevance to narrative inquiry design
Research focus and question with narrating as a cultural tool to use for making sense of the environment and how the narrator fits	Pay attention to the real-life contexts where people share, make sense of, and transform their experience and knowledge.
Space-time activity that is culturally relevant	Identify key elements of the place, time, purpose—the cultural relevance—to maintain and highlight in the design. Sample relevant activities familiar to participants, extend those activities with consistent systematic narrating activities for analysis, and/or create similar activities.
Interacting **stakeholders** with different perspectives on the issue of interest (Stakeholders are people whose perspectives—interests, experience, knowledge—play out in relevant activities and interact across the activity-meaning system.)	Identify key stakeholders—those for whom the meaningful activities matter and may differ in important ways.
Specific **narrating activities** (Narratives sampled and/or elicited should allow for dynamic narrating, diverse expressions of experiences and knowledge by focal participants for diverse relevant purposes and diverse audiences and contexts.)	Gather or elicit specific narrative activities and narrative texts that are likely to put those dimensions of the activity-meaning system into play and relief for subsequent analysis. Check the design to imagine how the relational, diversity, materiality, and use principles may play out to reveal participating sense making in the design and subsequent analysis.
Narrative analyses	See Chapters 3–6.

In relation to Nathan's emerging research about how college students come to label others "illegal," possible influences on a group of college students would have to do with their family experiences, family immigration histories, family lore about immigration, personal experiences with peers, local community interactions around immigration, and the participants' knowledge and developing ideologies about immigration. With those stakeholders, any specific research narratives would interact across space, beyond the college setting where, for example, Nathan met a group of high school students and began his research, to the prospective students' hometowns, the United States or beyond. With such spatial relevance to the individual and collective student narratives in Nathan's emerging research project, is a concept of time that would perhaps reach back to the experiences of the students' grandparents, perhaps Nathan's relatives, and forward to the students' eventual attendance at Nathan's college. A researcher, like Nathan, wanting to understand the development of youth understandings and opinions about contemporary immigration might consider the time dimension of the mid- to late 20th century via experiences of grandparents and great-grandparents and a space dimension of the local area, the broader United States, and immigrants' countries of origin. It is not that narratives from all these time and space dimensions must be included, but considering them can strengthen the ultimate selections for the narrative research design.

I drew on **cultural-historical activity theory** to develop the concept of "activity-meaning system" for research design (Daiute, 2008). Scholars have recently built on the **sociohistorical theories** of Vygotsky and others (originally formulated at the beginning of the 20th century and extended today) to explain how individuals' minds, personalities, and identities are social rather than self-contained and naturally unfolding. "Activity theory is an integrated approach to the human sciences that . . . takes the object-oriented, artifact-mediated collective activity system as the unit of analysis, thus bridging the gulf between the individual subject and the societal structure" (Engeström, Miettinen, & Punamäki, 1999, back cover). These systems involve "multiple interacting activity systems focused on a partially shared object" (Engeström, 2009, p. 307), "aimed at the formation of the motivational-needs sphere" (Polivanova, 2006, p. 81) and sensitive to "the world of human relations" (Polivanova, 2006, p. 81). Of course, researchers considering collective activity systems have numerous relationships and factors to consider, which renders the research design and analysis processes complex. Nevertheless, describing the broader context and range of interactions that may impinge on a narrative process or on an individual narrative enriches an inquiry beyond research assuming that narrative is confined to an individual biography (Engeström, 2009). This means that researchers studying individuals—their lives, their understandings of their lives, their specific challenges or phenomena of interest—must consider narratives in interaction. When researchers sample and examine narratives for indications of how they embody and connect relationships, research designs can be sensitive to the fact that narratives are interactions within social systems.

A metaphor may also be helpful for defining activity-meaning system. An activity-meaning system is like a cluster of spider webs, with each narrative in the midst of connected webs. Each strand in a web is connected through a spider and the spider's activity. Imagine each silky strand as a communication channel to somewhere else in the web, to another spider or to another web connected at a corner. The web includes dimensions of space (the substance where the spider sits and the space where the web hangs) and dimensions of time (the web was not there yesterday, may not be tomorrow, and changes with the spider's movements and entry of the sought-after food that is the primary purpose of the web). Each spider has interests in its territory—hoping that any small insects or bits of food caught in the web will be in its territory rather than in another spider's adjoining weblet. Not all is competition, however, because if a large bug gets caught, there may be plenty to share among neighboring spiders. If those spiders could tell their stories, they would certainly be situated in their webby time and space, somehow communicating in rhythmic tension of competition and cooperation with other spiders in the neighborhood. From the perspective of a spider's story, should there be one, the meaning of the web is more than about catching bugs to eat; it's about where the web hangs, other spiders, challenges, opportunities, and other arachnid details. The metaphor ends here, as spiders are not narratives and do not have the capacities of narrators, but the structure of their multiple webs offers an image that is useful for researchers considering the relational nature of narrating in an activity-meaning system design.

Relational Dynamics in Activity-Meaning System Designs

The recognition that each narrative (like any utterance) interacts with prior ones historically and in the present is offered across the disciplines of literary theory (Bakhtin, 1986), sociolinguistics (Labov & Waletzky, 1967/1997), developmental psychology (Vygotsky, 1978), philosophy (Austin, 1962), discourse theory (Fairclough, 2010; Wortham, 2001), and narrative theory (Daiute, 2011; Nelson, 1998). Currently, these ideas are extending into discussions of research methods.

A scholar studying the novel made what remains today an innovative explanation of narrating as an interactive, conversational process, across historical time and spaces, as well as within present face-to-face interactions:

Persuasive discourse—as opposed to one that is externally authoritarian—is, as it is affirmed through assimilation, tightly interwoven with "one's own word." In the everyday rounds of our consciousness, the internally persuasive word is half ours and half someone else's. . . . It is not so much interpreted by us as it is further, that is, freely, developed, applied to new material. . . . (Bakhtin, 1935/1981, p. 345)

This and other theoretical statements influence theory and, to some extent, methods in narrative inquiry today. Nevertheless, extensions to detailed narrative design and analysis are a relatively original step of dynamic narrative inquiry. Literary theorists have explained that since all knowledge and experience are created socially, even longer apparently singly authored texts, like novels, political treatises, policy statements, organizational mission statements, and educational curricula, function as "utterances" in "complex chains of communication" (Bakhtin, 1986, p. 69). In this way, narratives are turns in a broader societal conversation—such as among groups with different perspectives on an issue and even by an individual at different times or in different situations.

Activity-meaning systems make visible and audible the network of relationships and interactions in which each narrative occurs. Researchers highlight narrative use when they ask interviewees to narrate for different relevant purposes, from different perspectives (such as in the first person and in the third person), for different audiences and different contexts. Inviting narrator-audience relations with different genres and across positive and negative experiences are design strategies that have offered evocative information beyond what is expressed from single points of view. Creating an activity-meaning system design can begin with a sketch that establishes the possible more and less involved interlocutors in a narrative inquiry.

DRAFTING ACTIVITY-MEANING SYSTEM DESIGNS

The process of creating an **activity-meaning system design** begins in various ways, such as with narratives in the wild—spontaneous narratives in everyday life—and/or with a plan to elicit narratives. Working with the dimensions listed in Table 2.1 and expanded in Table 2.2, consider an activity-meaning system for research related to college students' understandings of immigration policies.

As shown in Table 2.2, Nathan drafted **research questions**: How do young people become involved in understanding "illegal" when undocumented people may not mention this fact? What's going on in the near and far environments around this issue that teens might have interacted with? How does this relate to social exclusion and inclusion? Applying an activity-meaning system design to Nathan's emerging inquiry, you can imagine interactions around young people's

Table 2.2	Dimensions for an Activity-Meaning System Design for Research Generated by Nathan's Narrative of Students' Mention of "Illegal!" and an Alternative

Using this table: Use this table for practice working with activity-meaning system designs. Read the notes indicating Nathan's design choices (in the middle column), then note (in the right-hand column) possible alternatives for each dimension if you were designing a similar study. Based on Nathan's notes about the young people at the college tour, what research question(s) would you pose; what period of time and range of place, stakeholders, and stakeholder narratives would you consider sampling in your alternative design?

Dimension of activity and meaning	*Activity-meaning system design around Nathan's narrative with prospective college students mentioning "illegal"*	*Alternative dimensions that could be generated from Nathan's notes*
Research issue of interest and research question(s)	How do youth become involved in understanding "illegal" and legal citizen status? What's going on in the near and far environments around this issue that participants might have interacted with? How do these interactions relate to youths' feelings about social exclusion and inclusion?	
Space-time dimensions relevant to the interacting individual, group, and societal narratives around the research focus and/or question(s)	*Space:* visit to a college; college student volunteer and prospective attendees; imagined context of the party being discussed; imagined context of family conversation. *Time:* college visit; period of proposal and demise of Dream Act; two generations experiencing immigration in different situations.	
Stakeholders interacting from different perspectives on the issue of interest	Adolescents, future college students; experiences of parents, grandparents, older cousins; U.S. public realm, Dream Act policies; media coverage.	
Specific narrating activities (tasks)	Gather or elicit specific narrative activities and texts that put those dimensions of the activity-meaning system into play for subsequent analysis.	
Reasonable expectation to allow for dynamic narrating	Check the design to imagine how the relational, diversity, materiality, and use principles may play out to reveal participating sense making in the design and subsequent analysis.	

feelings of inclusion and exclusion in U.S. society. The space dimension includes the places where Nathan heard the small story—the college recruitment program, other spaces where the youth might have interacted with peers or family mentioning these issues, and public discourse in the United States, where issues of immigration have become increasingly contentious in debates about policy and everyday life. The time dimension spans out from the college visit to the period of policy making related to the Dream Act (formally the Development, Relief, and Education for Alien Minors Act) and the lifetimes of three influencing generations—those of the college students, their parents, and their grandparents. The stakeholder dimension then becomes clear. Table 2.2 mentions some stakeholders—those whose narratives are likely to be part of the system of interactions—including other college students (perhaps groups that Nathan would be showing around his college), family members of those students in the original group, probably two generations growing up during very different times in U.S. immigration history, and documents related to current policy, such as Congress' repeated failed attempts to pass the act.

The dimension of specific narrating activities is a place for noting the narratives and other expressions a researcher would like to consider and needs to gather or elicit as the pivotal meaning-making activities within this system of relations. As the term *system* suggests, the diverse narrator perspectives are not neutral but connected by relations of power—with some having more status and influence in a society and thus over different narrators, some having more resources for spreading their stories, some having better storytelling skills, and some garnering more sympathy for their plights.

You can practice creating an activity-meaning system by considering design decisions that differ from the ones presented in Table 2.2 for the draft of Nathan's study.

The qualities of narratives themselves also have a role in narrating activities and, thus, must be considered in the research design. Narratives of personal experience highlighting the first-person, "I" character emphasize different perspectives and other story elements from narratives of imagined experience—fictional narratives. As character focus shifts, narrative processes shift as well—for example, from self-revealing autobiographical performances to observations of others. The first-person narrator is directly exposed to judgment, praise, or other personal effects. In contrast, the narrator foregrounding others is less onstage, and the omniscient narrator is in an even more distant relation to others, both stances allowing exposure of certain ideas or personal details that may be prudent to express in the absence of judgment. For example, Matt in the college visit story called Jennie "illegal," so he probably knows enough about the meaning of the word to understand at least that it is negative, and he would probably not use it were he to tell a story about the party from Jennie's point of view. Nathan's college recruits may not know about the Dream Act, proposed to ease the path to citizenship for young adults whose parents brought them to the United States or extended their stay without formal documents, but their older relatives or cousins may have mentioned the act. Such different narratives involve shifting relations among author, audience, and context.

Because narratives are not isolated expressions, maintaining the interconnected nature of meaning in social relations in real time and space is important in narrative inquiry design.

Sampling Relevant Time and Space Dimensions

Stakeholders in narrative meaning may also interact across time and space. Following Bakhtin's (1935/1981, 1986) insights, researchers identify that people narrate within historical contexts as well as in the current time of narrating. Authors also refer to different time frames in their narratives.

Narrating is often focused on the past—in part because a function of narrative is to share and to interpret recent or remote life events. Even though narrative recounts memories of past events, literary scholars, narrative psychologists, and others interested in how narrative works remind us that authors express in a present time and place—with immediate concerns and desires—as they decide what to say about the past, what to leave out, and what to project into a future time (Ricoeur, 1990). Authors are, thus, also set in time frames themselves. Nathan's study design, for example, involved sampling experiences and beliefs from the past, such as those of grandparents, who may have influenced the narratives of present-day youth sorting out issues of legal citizenship. In addition to the youth stakeholders, grandparents or others might be influencing present-day narratives. The present circumstances of narrative expression are anchors for researcher decisions about the appropriate dimensions to sample. Narrative speakers' and authors' present situations in place, like time, are the podium for orchestrating how events unfold across near and far spatial contexts, as will be discussed in relation to prior studies presented below. Because narrators play with time and space implicitly in daily life, researchers do well to recognize that fact when they are designing their research.

To draw on real-life narrating, I usually design my projects within meaningful activities that relevant participants would normally do in familiar contexts. Examples include telling stories about needs in community projects, discussing obstacles in educational practices, dramatizing relations in play sessions, projecting decision-making processes in legal contexts, narrating an ideal outcome in a political campaign, and recounting one's journey in an immigration support group. Along with the organizers of those settings, such as community leaders, educators, public officials, and young people, research designers must include narrating (and other activities) in ways that are consistent with the goals in the setting. This means that some of the social and structural relations relevant to expressions are defined in the setting, as are the material qualities and diversities. Some community organizations devoted to displaced children and families, for example, emphasize painting or essay writing, which my research complements with narratives, while other settings emphasize performance, which my research complements with letter writing or interviewing. Research designers benefit from embedding narrating activities in settings of practice, because those typically enact the interplay of real-life goals, pressures, and inspirations across a range of temporal and spatial contexts.

When a neutral context is more appropriate than the actual context of practice, such as when the research involves interviewing veterans transitioning from the military to college, narrating provides a way to invoke each setting (Messina, 2013). Veterans are no longer in the field, and interviewing in a college classroom or dining hall may violate participants' anonymity. Nevertheless, those contexts can be invoked with invitations to share experiences from both contexts (Messina, 2013). For example, asking participants to tell about a time when they realized that college was similar to military life and a time when they realized that college was different from military life engages different kinds of memories, experiences, and reflections. Meaningful contexts where veterans narrate also occur in blogs, used by people who must communicate this way because of distances or who prefer to meet others virtually rather than face-to-face. Whether entering ongoing sports activities, schools, clubs, Twitter feeds, or blogs, researchers seeking the dynamic nature of narrating create activity-meaning system designs.

Identifying Stakeholders in a Narrative Inquiry Design

When designing narrative inquiry, researchers consider diverse stakeholders who are likely to interact with the author or speaker narrative meaning. Identifying stakeholders involves the researcher in knowing or imagining key individuals and groups with whom the focal participant might be interacting with a narrative. The researchers, peers, and others, present or imagined, are audiences. Other less direct but no less important interlocutors might be the participant's cultural group, with whom he or she wants to maintain solidarity in narrative content or manner. A researcher cannot include every possible relevant stakeholder, but identifying some likely to have similar perspectives and some likely to have different perspectives on the issue is the most important criterion. Also important is identifying situations when the participant might be likely to share an event differently for different purposes, with different focal characters, and for different audiences.

Criteria that researchers should consider when identifying the range of stakeholders around an issue include (a) sampling different perspectives on the issue, (b) allowing focal participants to narrate from different perspectives (accounts for different personal purposes, the participants' understanding of different perspectives on the issue, and so on), and (c) inviting participants to narrate for different audiences (whose presence [actually or virtually] might be relevant to the speaker/author in some way, such as to invoke power influences, affiliation influences, and the like). The number of expressions by the focal stakeholder and others has to do with the nature of the research questions. For example, research questions seeking change over time would require gathering narratives before, after, and perhaps in the midst of an intervention; research questions inquiring about participants' understandings related to different activities and purposes would involve eliciting a narrative for each relevant purpose; and/or research questions sensitive to narrating for different audiences and the attendant social relations would invite a narrative for each relevant audience.

The activity-meaning system design can be more or less complex, depending on the research question, the phase of research (such as whether it is a pilot study or a comprehensive study), and researcher resources (such as the amount of time available to carry out the study and financial resources for gathering different kinds of data). While many researchers prefer to collect their own narratives, publicly available databases of narratives can also be quite relevant and appropriate. These include but are by no means limited to the Occupy Sandy Storyline database (http://www.sandystoryline.com), the Child Language Data Exchange System (CHILDES; see MacWhinney, 2000), and numerous blogs.

Author, narrator, character, audience actors/stakeholders. The person speaking or writing a narrative is, of course, a stakeholder—someone who cares about the issues of research focus, someone who experiences consequences of the issues in some way and narrates to address those facts. Although the person narrating is often presumed to be merged with the narrative content, characters, and orientation, following literary theory it becomes clear that the author crafts a narrator stance and characters. As stated by a narrative theorist and researcher, "This differentiation between the self as character in the story and the self as speaker (animator and/or author) is extremely important because we all too often tend to collapse them too quickly in our analyses" (Bamberg, 2004a). Building on literary analysis of three strands of consciousness—author, narrator, and character—researchers can focus on these strands to analyze meaning. Considering the distinctions among author, character, and narrator can affect the research design.

The person expressing the narrative is the **author**—whether speaking or writing. The author is the major stakeholder not because the experiences are necessarily personal or authentic but because the narrative is the means the author uses to act in a context. The cultural tool of narrator provides an alter ego of sorts for an author to use as the narrative voice (point of view or guide).

The narrator is the stance (perspective, point of view, voice, or guide) the author has created for the specific story. Because narrative is a cultural invention for acting in the world, it is helpful to consider the author and the narrator as distinct. In Nathan's narrative above, the narrator is crafted from the researcher perspective. In that narrative, Nathan selects details as a careful observer—noticing action, recounting dialogue, and building to some sort of point—rather than in terms of his own actions, interactions, or feelings about the event. Even when interjecting "One of the recruits, a girl I'll call Allison . . . ," Nathan's (the author's) use of "I" is through the researcher role, inventing a pseudonym, as is typical in research to ensure subject anonymity. This distinction between narrator and author is relevant to understanding that narrated experience is shared in culturally crafted ways rather than primarily as highly personal outpourings. Other genres for that purpose are the focus of psychotherapy or stream-of-consciousness expression (Hermans & Hermans-Jansen, 2001; Spence, 1984), which would rarely occur in research.

Narrative characters may or may not be intended as merged with the author or narrator. Even when the protagonist of a narrative is expressed in the first person, "I," this "I" may be the author, the narrator, or a character created to be a participant in the narrative events. Chapter 6 focuses in detail on characters in narratives, in particular for narrative analysis.

The actual or presumed **audiences**, listeners or readers, of narratives are also stakeholders. One reason that audiences are stakeholders is that the author's conception of audience expectations, possible judgments, and ability to understand and empathize with the narrative are embedded in the narrative meaning. As discussed above, such audience factors constitute the narrative context, and audiences may also be implicated in the narrative meaning in other ways. The researcher, for example, has plenty at stake as an audience research designer, and inevitable participant.

Sampling Stakeholder Expressions

Just as a researcher must select the most relevant stakeholders for considering the focal participants' narratives, the researcher must decide which and how many expressions are reasonable given the resources available for carrying out the study. Most relevant for purposes of research design is the theoretical requirement of gathering narratives in ways that acknowledge and, ideally, maintain context. This means obtaining information about the context to have some sense of the narrators' interactive relations (including sociopolitical hierarchies, roles, other related diversities), purposes, and material-symbolic connections. Planned elicitation of narratives in activities meaningful and familiar to the participants can provide those key contextual factors. Stakeholder expressions in narrative inquiry may be as diverse as documents, mission statements, news reports, curricula, blogs, conversations, and personal narratives. As discussed below, expressions related to societal stakeholders in an inquiry about immigration could include policy statements by public officials or news reports of events related to an immigration conflict. Different narratives by a participant around the issue of immigration would also invite personal breadth. The researcher might, for example, learn more from asking people on different sides of an issue to share a narrative than from interviewing an individual many times.

To allow for relational diversity (discussed in Chapter 1), narrating activities should be varied, such as telling about an event from three different characters' perspectives, also extending beyond what people might normally do. Expanding narrating in such a way helps researchers understand the participants' range of experiences around the question of interest and helps participants gain new insights about their experience. Relationships and other features of the actual setting are, moreover, informative for narrative analysis, while interviewing people outside their familiar contexts may leave a researcher guessing about which aspects of that interview setting played a role. The benefit to participants also expands when researchers follow up for reflective discussions (see Chapter 7).

An important design feature for narrating in activity-meaning systems is addressivity—the relational interaction among narrator, audiences, situations, and issues enacted in narratives (Bakhtin, 1986). The idea is that writers and thinkers, like speakers, direct language to audiences who are sometimes implicit, such as others who may judge them, as well as to actual audiences in the immediate context. Because narrators select what to say, what not to say, and how to say it in relation to what they understand about actual and potential listeners or readers of their narratives, audiences become part of each narrative.

Recent psycholinguistic analyses implore us to consider narrative use, relation, materiality, and diversity in terms of author stance (such as narrating from the first-person "I" perspective or the third-person "he, she, or it" perspective), goals, audience, and other details of the narrating context. People use these features, intentionally or spontaneously, as tools for perceiving situations, organizing meaning, and gaining insights from the narrative experience itself. A soldier returning from war might, for example, tell about a famous battle in different ways when speaking with her husband, her children, and her classmates at college.

Practical implications of addressivity for narrative inquiry design are numerous. For example, asking participants to narrate positive and negative experiences in relation to research issues of interest also elicits very different information (Daiute, Eisenberg, & Vasconcellos, 2012; Jović, 2012). Most people have had positive and negative experiences, but, more important, asking about both invites a person to consider more and less ideal situations. Narrators tend to put their best selves out there in their stories (Oliveira, 1999), so asking a participant to narrate good and bad experiences, in relation to danger, for example, sets the research scene for the narrator's sharing more and less clear and conforming meanings. When sharing experiences that are defined as "good," "best," or positive in some other way, people tend to select exemplary material conforming to cultural ideas of what that means, as well as to present themselves in a positive light. While participants in interview studies may not want to admit feeling frightened in situations that threaten their well-being on a daily basis and that might present them as cowardly, researchers asking explicitly for stories about "difficult experiences" or "the worst experiences" provide a relatively protected context for interviewees to share personal experience and knowledge. When telling a "bad," "worst," or otherwise negative experience in some other way, an author uses the acknowledgment that the situation was not ideal, thereby providing an entrée for a story expressing (although not requiring) difficulties or challenges or a negative aspect of self or local milieu.

Table 2.3 presents relations involved in addressivity, including author stance, narrative focus, context, and audience(s). In fiction, the author is "omniscient," presenting the story from outside the action through a narrator, which may or may not be explicit, while in autobiography the narrator is also a character in the story. Employing the dimensions of first-person, third-person, and omniscient narrating listed in the table, you can create three narrating activities relevant to your research interest. You could try writing about an event yourself

Table 2.3   Narrative Relational Stances and Prompts in a Prior Study and for Your Study

Using this table: For a study you are planning or considering, think of different narrative activities that would invite your focal participant(s) to narrate in different relational stances to audiences, by shifting the focal character across first person (author's story) to third person (author share's another's story) to fictional, or omniscient (author is outside the story as narrator).

	Narrating activity 1	*Narrating activity 2*	*Narrating activity 3*
Addressivity	*Feature*		
Author/speaker stance	First person	Third person	Omniscient
Author-audience relations	Direct, author exposed	Indirect, author can observe	Open, potentially equal power
Character interactions	Defined, constrained	Available for selective play	Narrator free to play
Narrative prompt example	*Write about a time when you or someone you know had a conflict with someone the same age. What happened? How did all involved think and feel about it? How did it all turn out?*	*Write about a time when people different from you had a conflict. What happened? How did all involved think and feel about it? How did it all turn out?*	*Imagine a town near yours (but not necessarily a real town) where people gathered to protest something they thought was unfair. What was the problem? What happened? How did everyone think and feel about it? How did it all turn out?*
Narrative prompts for a study you are doing, planning, or considering doing	*Tell or write about a time when you . . .*	*Tell or write about a time when someone different from you . . .*	*Imagine a place or time when . . .*

from these three perspectives to gain insight into how varying author perspectives elicits different knowledge and experience, and/or you could consider such a framework for eliciting narratives for your research.

The following examples of activity-meaning system designs in previous published research should also be helpful to researchers designing new studies with narrating activities within activity-meaning system designs.

EXAMPLES OF ACTIVITY-MEANING SYSTEM DESIGNS

The brief descriptions below of several activity-meaning system designs in prior research illustrate the principles, elements, and design structure for dynamic narrative research. Activity-meaning systems account for spheres of influence in narrating by groups and individuals, interactions across stakeholders, across relevant time and space, and purposeful activities for within as well as across participant complexity—diversity and flexibility. Table 2.4 lists the details of these research designs in terms of activity-meaning system design dimensions.

An Activity-Meaning System Design to Study Human Rights Policy

An analysis of the effectiveness of children's rights policy offers an example of an activity-meaning system design that sampled a range of preexisting data. Key dimensions, as listed in Table 2.4—events, places, and actors involved in the geopolitical project of children's rights negotiations—are included in the system. The 1989 United Nations Convention on the Rights of the Child (CRC), like other international treaties, involves a system of interactions, including policy making, qualifying, monitoring, and reporting. I did a study to determine whether and how the treaty process was operating to ensure children's rights 20 years after the CRC was ratified. The design for this study involved identifying the major actors in the system, defined as the key stakeholders, including the U.N. Committee on the Rights of the Child. This committee participated in the development of the CRC and is devoted to monitoring, reporting, and continuing to advance the rights of children among the states party signatories and nongovernmental organizations (NGOs) in the various countries that perform another check on the states parties, in particular involving children themselves in the process. I selected stakeholders to enact the relevant roles and activities in the system and to allow tensions across the system to emerge.

Table 2.4   Dimensions of Dynamic Narrating Activity-Meaning System Research Designs for Four Prior Studies

Narrative research focus	Children's rights	Effects of war	Social development in innovative curriculum	Relations in societies and religious families with gay sons
Research question (primary question)	How are children's rights negotiated?	How do children/youth growing up during and after war make sense of conflict?	How do children make sense of intergroup relations in relation to a prevention program?	How do religious families negotiate the gay disclosure of a son?
Time-space dimension	1989–2005, international and Colombia	1945–2007, across former Yugoslavia	1980s–1990s, first-through third-grade years, 9 classrooms, 2 urban schools	Ancient religious texts; 2011 post–gay disclosure
Stakeholders interacting	1. Committee on the Rights of the Child 2. Colombia (state party to the CRC) 3. NGO report 4. Children quoted	1. Yugoslavia 2. Bosnia 3. Croatia 4. Serbia 5. United States 6. NGOs across former Yugoslavia 7. 137 youth across former Yugoslavia	1. U.S. and urban concerns about violence 2. Urban schools and classrooms using violence prevention curricula 3. 9 participating teachers 4. 150 third and fifth graders of diverse ethnic backgrounds	1. Gay men 2. Key family members 3. Clinicians working with gays 4. Religious canons
Stakeholder expressions	1. CRC treaty text 2. Memos between Committee on the Rights of the Child and Colombia 3. NGO narrative report 4. Children narrating their experiences	1. E.U. documents for country accession, conflict resolution, inclusion 2. Narratives of conflicts first person, third person, fiction 3. Letters to public officials	1. Statements about urban youth violence 2. Literacy-based violence prevention curriculum 3. 9 teachers' newcomer narratives 4. 400 narratives, first person and fiction	1. Interviews with gay men 2. Interviews with family allies 3. Interviews with clinicians 4. Excerpts regarding sexuality in Old and New Testaments

Because each document in the CRC activity-meaning system occurs within a series of meetings, it is a response to previous interactions and directed toward future ones. Documents express narrative relations in several ways, as they enact values, policies, and diverse ideological perspectives. Those interactions alongside other stakeholder documents (which is often how the powerful interact in a system) provide actor position statements for analysis. The documents in the CRC system, for example, are also dialogic because they are directed explicitly and implicitly to specific and general audiences of participants in the children's rights process. Designed as a dialogic system, the stakeholders' interactions occur via various documents, because participants could not all appear in person.

With the CRC system design established, I conducted an analysis to identify activities enacted in the CRC documents from each key stakeholder position, including qualifying, monitoring, reporting, and implementing, and added an analysis of reports on behalf of children whose rights had also been violated with narratives by more powerful actors. As shown in a report of the study, the CRC activity-meaning system is expressed in the CRC treaty and related documents, including the CRC (preamble and 54 articles); "Declarations and Reservations"; the U.N. General Assembly Security Council Item No. 63 on the Promotion and Protection of the Rights of the Child; 61st Session, the CRC Committee Consideration of Reports Submitted by States Parties under Article 44 of the Convention; Concluding Observation: Colombia, 42nd Session; and a state party report, "Third Periodic Report of Colombia, and the Alternative Report to the Report of the Government of Colombia on the Situation of the Rights of the Child." These documents represent major actors involved in stating, ensuring, and monitoring children's rights and follow a sequence of reporting and monitoring for Colombia, a state party figuring prominently in the process.

As shown in the second column of Table 2.4, these stakeholders in the human rights process are expressed in several representative documents (including the CRC Treaty, a report by the Committee on the Rights of the Child, minutes of a U.N. Security Council meeting, reports by a state party, and a report by a civil society group in that country), included to consider activities by different stakeholders in the CRC activity-meaning system. Drawing on practices such as requirements for follow-up to receipt of a document from the CRC Committee also captures this notion of discourse activity system. Periodic reports by states that have ratified the CRC, for example, are responses to a treaty requirement. Agenda items by the CRC Committee are, in turn, responses to periodic reports, which may be accepted or discussed for violations at meetings of the committee. Through such ongoing interactions, participants in the CRC system negotiate the meaning of children's rights. Analyses of those interactions revealed a process whereby the rights of nations trumped children's rights, perhaps indicating the fact that children are not only protected by legal structures but also continue to belong to those structures.

Preliminary analysis revealed differences for specific states parties in terms of any violations noted by the CRC Committee, thereby requiring additional reporting from those states parties, special activity by a group tasked to research and write an alternative report, and the inclusion of children's narratives. For that reason, I selected the actor and space of Colombia from the period when it signed the CRC up to the time of my research as a case study in the broader CRC system.

The design and subsequent values analysis (see Chapter 3) revealed a tension between children's rights and nations' rights. For example, while a value like not recruiting children to participate in armed conflict was performed across stakeholders, the U.N. monitoring report offered narratives indicating that Colombia, for example, had contested this value by its extensive recruitment of young boys in rural areas, although often through other agents, like paramilitary groups. In its report to answer that accusation, Colombia officially restated its performance of the value of not recruiting children, while the alternative report by a group of NGOs cited children who narrated specific events in which soldiers had recruited them and initiated them into violent practices that, de facto, bound them to be ongoing members of violent groups. The design of this study revealed specific sources of tension in the children's rights process. In particular, the analysis revealed that narrating processes by international and national actors, in some cases, trumped children's rights.

An Activity-Meaning System
Design to Study Impacts of Growing Up in War

An example of a research design embedded in ongoing activities of practice comes from a study in community centers across several postwar countries of the former Yugoslavia. Conceptualizing the unit of analysis across such systems was an important step toward complexity and diversity in design of developmental studies of social, political, and economic change. Narrating is especially useful for gaining an understanding of lived experiences of those changes, but, as noted previously, narratives refract a range of diverse positions.

Research questions began inquiring into issues like the following: How do people positioned differently across a political (violence) system interact in and make sense of that system and their positions in it? What threat/opportunity complexes emerge to motivate their goals and meanings? How do these results expose the power relations and figure of the child/youth in that system? How do these processes define development in this context? What activities can be highlighted to support developmental thriving? In addition to the broader design of the political-violence system, engagement with diverse genre activities can bring these relations to life for the benefit of the participants and researchers alike.

In a situation of political violence, an activity system involves making sense of the causes, manifestations, and consequences of a crisis affecting the social and physical environmental system and individuals within it. Beginning with the premise that children interact with the environments where they grow up, a research design must account for people, events, and meanings that are persuasive in the contemporary situation. This means focusing on what matters to young people growing up in different positions across time (born before, during, or after a war), geopolitical location (different postwar countries), and goals (analyzing problems in society, expressing one's personal experience, and engaging in other purposeful activities).

The former Yugoslavia is a developmental system because the youth generation was born in the country of Yugoslavia, experienced wars that broke it apart, and afterward grew up across numerous countries, some oriented toward Western Europe, others eastward toward Mecca, and still others positioned between alliances to Russia and the European Union. Unlike other political separations in the region, such as that of the Czech and Slovak Republics, the breakup of Yugoslavia was violent, which exacerbated problems and possibilities for the transitional generation orienting toward adulthood. Tensions within this system organized people's everyday lives. Rather than assuming that the generation growing up during the wars responded in only negative ways, the research explored *how* participants interacted with these tensions. By extending beyond individual sites, groups, and countries, the design made it possible for the research team to identify the tensions not only in terms of individuals' perspectives but also in terms of salient goals and opportunities in each context. Working with youth organizations across the system, the researchers asked young people what was on their minds rather than assuming that they were damaged, dangerous, or holding on to collective memories of the past.

The third column of Table 2.4 depicts dimensions of the political-violence system of the former Yugoslavia likely to have affected young people growing up in this system. The time frame possibly affecting a generation directly was quite broad, beginning with the creation of a communist state of Yugoslavia, which influenced the education, childhoods, and adult lives of the parents of the 1990s generation. Space changed dramatically during the 1990s wars, when participants were growing up, as many were displaced or lived in areas where large numbers of displaced persons arrived. As the inhabitants of the various spaces changed, the meaning of spaces changed, including the formation of new countries, as listed in Table 2.4.

The political system of the former Yugoslavia is neither naturally occurring nor necessarily functioning as a political unit, because migration and displacement continue across the region. Tensions defining distinctions across the system, however, include that the 1990s wars occurred but the origins, causes, stakes, and consequences differ depending on where one is currently standing. Disagreements about what happened, who was right, who suffered most, and so forth have played out in local and national public spaces: in the International Criminal Tribunal for the former Yugoslavia (ICTY), in neighborhoods, in the media, in places of worship, and in private conversations among family and friends. In addition, societies and individuals across the former Yugoslavia have different material and psychosocial positions within their local contexts. The activity-meaning system design provided a framework of spatial, temporal, international, and intergroup relations for reading and interpreting diverse narratives by young people across the contexts. From each of these possible influences, the young narrators interacted most poignantly with their local/national environments. That is, their narratives spoke to and from the diverse political economic circumstances where they were growing up more than to the fact of war itself (Daiute, 2010).

After immersing myself in the practices of community centers and the broader context, I designed a research workshop inviting young people to narrate events from their own perspectives (a pull for the first-person "I" character), from the perspectives of adults in their environments (third-person "he, she, it, they" characters), and in parallel fictional stories. Those narratives were set within the broader context of creating histories from young people's perspectives, with eventual publication in a community newsletter or pamphlet to be cataloged in the local library or archives. Helping out in the community and creating products like murals and newsletters was already familiar to the participants, and the narrating activities built systematically on that familiarity to allow narrators to play with different author stances—that is, with different presentations of themselves as protagonists within stories, as observers of other primary characters, and as omniscient authors outside the stories. Such variation of narrator stance has proved to be important, revealing different events, details, issues, and orientations across each narrative stance. Thus, depending on whether a narrator is telling a first-person account, such as of conflicts in everyday life, telling about others' conflicts, or creating an imaginary story set in a community conflict, he or she expresses different information and reflections on that information. In the postwar setting as in other dramatically changing places, such narrating from different perspectives was crucial to expression because there was such pressure to narrate in a certain way (such as proving people were beyond the atrocities of the war). Because of the importance of designing research to include multiple expressive opportunities, I asked participants to also do a letter-writing activity to share knowledge in addition to narrative knowledge (Daiute, 2010).

Attempting to explain how children and youth respond to violence and its aftermath, one can observe the interdependence of personal and societal goals guiding perception in everyday events and interpretations of society as manifested in conversations about public stories, diverse narratives, letters, and youth inquiries. This process was illustrated with participants' uses of cultural tools to mediate conflict, in particular the affordances of literary narratives, to negotiate tensions between what can and cannot be expressed. For example, given the national goals of Croatia to conform to standards of the European Union, motivations for social inclusion were especially intense, yielding a prohibition on war talk and ethnic talk. Young people indicated the need, moreover, to address contemporary problems and obstacles to their progress as independent adults. Such dynamics are developed within specific plot structures, emotional valences, and functions of storytelling (Daiute, 2010).

Evidence from this study in the former Yugoslavia, for example, showed how a series of narratives, letters, and evaluations of society engaged young people to think critically about the specific circumstances of their postwar locale while also instilling a sense of their potential to contribute, especially when they were active in community organizations. Specific narratives elicited and analyzed in the context of this study design are presented in Chapters 4 and 7.

An Activity-Meaning System Design in an Educational Innovation

The narrative understandings of teachers and children involved in a curriculum to promote interethnic group relations and strategies for resolving conflicts were examined in an activity-meaning system design. The creation and implementation of such a curriculum in urban schools indicates concerns about group relations in the broader society (Elliott, Hamburg, & Williams, 1998). The values and goals of the curriculum introduced a specific sensibility, with children's literature depicting different cultural groups, their ways of living, and their problems, especially around exclusion and discrimination. Third and fifth graders seemed especially appropriate to consider such issues as these children had begun to read and write, had increasing friendships outside home that might expose them to social conflicts, and could begin to take some self-determination in how to address those conflicts. Given these and other factors, the time dimension of the activity-meaning system was not only the period of implementing such a curriculum but also the one to three school years when this strand of activities might take hold. In addition to the students, stakeholders in this process were, of course, teachers who worked with the curriculum materials and interpreted them from their own cultural perspectives, which is why we sought participation from teachers of diverse ethnic backgrounds. Working with teachers of diverse backgrounds and varying narrating activities in particular to account for children's exposure to judgment over time proved particularly informative, not only about the narrating process but also about the usefulness of an activity-meaning system design. As mentioned above, varying narrator stance in relation to audience, issues, and specific narrative genres (such as autobiography or fiction) enacts interactions among actors in an activity-meaning system.

In the U.S. classrooms, as children learned curriculum strategies for resolving social conflicts, they adjusted their narratives about personal experiences of conflict to conform to those strategies, while they included more strategies that the curriculum defined as less than ideal in their fictional narratives. Since first-person narratives with the authors as protagonists exposed the authors to judgment in the context of recent classroom discussions, the researchers interpreted the children's portrayals of narrative conflicts and resolution strategies as reflecting their understandable desire to present themselves in an acceptable way. At the same time, the young authors included values counter to the curriculum in fictional stories where they narrated from outside the action and thus were less subject to direct judgment than when they were protagonists. These results, thus, show that children can use narratives rather than only speak singular coherent truths through narratives. The activity-meaning system design that embedded diverse kinds of narrating activities across third- and fifth-grade classes with teachers who interpreted the literary selections and curriculum from their own perspectives made it possible for the researchers to identify these interesting results.

What that meant in the curriculum study was that the context of the classroom was varied as audiences, with more public and private audiences across autobiographical and fictional narrating activities. In activity-meaning system research designs, we assume that the stakeholders all have some participation in the process of the focal narratives. In the curriculum study, children's narratives of personal experiences of conflict were not judged as their authentic voices or authentic voices of their ethnic group but in relation to the classroom culture created by their teacher, indicated in the way she led class discussions about literary selections and lessons on conflict. This approach of narrating in relation to dimensions of an activity-meaning system maintains a focus on each aspect as a kind of dependent variable (although not in the traditional sense). Dimensions of the activity-meaning systems are thus not independent background factors but embedded within all narratives. With sufficient foundation in **practical theoretical concepts** and identification of key comparisons to offer insights for the research questions, researchers can discuss interactions in the network of relations based on systematic analyses. In the curriculum study, for example, each participant produced a range of narratives varied for addressivity that the researchers analyzed systematically to consider children's interactions with features of the curriculum, the various teachers' implementations of the curriculum, the children's ages, their grades in school, the children's and teachers' ethnic backgrounds, and other qualities.

An Activity-Meaning System Design to Study Conflicts About Changing Sexual Practices

A study of individual, family, and societal development in relation to conflicts between family religious beliefs and the sexual orientation of a gay family member employed an activity-meaning system to account for the diverse interests involved in narrating family membership (Etengoff, 2013). The primary research questions were "How is the process of sexual orientation and sexual orientation disclosure negotiated within a religious, familial, and societal system?" and "What cultural symbols do the gay son, ally in the family, and clinician use to negotiate family relationships in the context of relevant conflicts?" To create a research design that would make audible narratives about family relationships in the context of conflicts between a family member's alliance with increasing acceptance of homosexuality in the United States and religious traditions banning the practice, in particular Orthodox Judaism and conservative Christian religions, the researcher asked stakeholders—including the gay son, a close family member chosen by the son, and clinicians—to narrate their experiences about the son's homosexual disclosure and family relations. Etengoff identified conflicts and conflict resolution strategies in narratives across these stakeholders and in religious texts mentioning marriage and appropriate sexuality. Consistent with dynamic narrating, these stakeholders mutually influenced one another in terms of how they narrated the family system—such as the nature of conflicts causing lack of harmony. Inherent in narrating relations within the strictly religious family with a gay son is the issue of homosexuality, so identifying conflicts and resolutions in those narratives offers information about the impact of changing societal structures in people's everyday lives. With 23 gay men, 15 of their key family members, and 12 clinicians, this study identified conflicts related to dealing with homophobia in the community and uses of strategies like normalizing gay sexuality to mediate such conflicts.

Narrating relationships in a religious family at the intersection of changing societal mores proved to be a complex process with some surprisingly different kinds of conflicts and strategies for mediating these conflicts. The study's results indicated that across the activity-meaning system, mutual awareness among stakeholders of what was going on in one another's lives made a difference in whether and how families addressed sexual disclosure–related conflicts, and whether humanization strategies emerged as a common way to recognize the religious diversity of the gay community (Etengoff, 2013). Investigating the issue of religious stigmas against gays with this design offered new information about the mutual formulation of perspectives and, thus, the development of sexuality in the broader context of social relations. Previous research offered important information about sexual orientation, for the most part in terms of individual identity (Etengoff, 2013) or among partners (Tolman, 2005). With a broader activity-meaning system design, Etengoff included the social-relational realm relevant to sexual orientation, as is especially poignant in the changing mores and policies at this time in history.

The next section outlines the narrative inquiry design process with the activity-meaning system framework. Having read about several studies with activity-meaning system designs, you can review dimensions of this framework listed in tables in this chapter and descriptions of researchers' applications of the dimensions in prior studies, in addition to suggestions below, as you consider this framework to guide your research.

THE DYNAMIC NARRATIVE INQUIRY DESIGN PROCESS

When designing an activity-meaning system, you might find some of the following questions related to dimensions of such designs helpful: What is your primary research question? What are several related questions? What are likely to be the temporal and spatial contexts that would influence narratives you are eliciting to address the research questions? What are some of the contexts where the issues of interest are likely to be enacted in everyday practices? What is the web of explicit and implicit communication that might have influenced the focal narratives in your study? Which actors/stakeholders would have produced expressions that might interact with your focal participants' narratives around your issues of interest? What relevant issues are likely to be expressed prominently in the practice contexts where you are doing your research? What relevant issues are likely to be silenced (discouraged or taboo) in the practice contexts where you are doing your research? What are some strategies you could employ to encourage your narrators to assume different stances with the issues of interest in relation to diverse audiences? How might your narrative prompts or selections allow narrators to address power relations and contest them? How can you vary narrative genres (autobiography/fiction), audiences (such as by varying narrator exposure as first-person to third-person observer and fiction), purposes, and narrating contexts to allow for relational flexibility? You may need to work through subsequent chapters on narrative analysis strategies to appreciate activity-meaning systems designs.

The following steps guide the design of an activity-meaning system for research with dynamic narrating:

1. Identify a research focus and read previous related research to learn about what is already known and still unclear.

2. Familiarize yourself with the relevant participants, settings, narratives, and related expressions. Ways of doing this include, but are not limited to, the following:

   2a. Like Nathan, make notes from your own experiences and observations.

   2b. Identify narratives available on the Internet as you consider appropriate narratives and narrating activities for your study.

   2c. Visit settings and do informal observation.

   2d. From those settings, create or gather narratives, interactions with narratives.

   Ethics are an important factor in gathering narratives. A full review of the standards of ethical involvement with human subjects is beyond the scope of this book, but information on this topic is widely available; one place you might start is the website of the Collaborative

Institutional Training Initiative (https://www.citiprogram.org). When gathering spontaneous narratives in public life, you should gain permission in a formal way from anyone you interact with directly and identify (naming personally or as a member of an identified group), anyone you take visual images of, and anyone considered vulnerable (children, prisoners, disabled people).

2e. Identify a few sample narratives, conversations, or other materials that seem similar to what you would hope to have as data for your research.

3. After studying your notes from your reading of previous research, observations, and so on (steps 1–2 above), draft some research questions. Research questions are the anchors of research, but you can revise and edit these anchors as needed depending on how the project unfolds. As summarized above, research questions in narrative inquiry tend to be about experience(s), knowledge, meaning-making processes, other types of processes (group processes, conflicts, and so on), associations and comparisons across individuals and groups; comparisons of individual performances across time, location, or activity. This list does not exhaust all options for research questions, but it can be helpful for researchers writing their research questions.

4. Having become familiar with and oriented toward the research focus (as in steps 1–3)—that is, having progressed from curiosity to drafting research questions—you are ready to draft an activity-meaning system design. Steps in activity-meaning system designing include the following:

4a. Review elements of activity-meaning system designs discussed in this chapter and presented in Tables 2.1 through 2.4.

4b. Using the appropriate spaces in Table 2.5 (for this and the steps below), write down your research goals, draft questions, or refined questions.

4c. Identify the time-space dimensions of narrative interactions— explicit or implicit (actual or historic). Time-space dimensions might be (a) at one time, in one setting (such as differences in narratives by individuals in hospital, community center, classroom, or other settings); (b) distributed across a specific time period (such as before and after an intervention); (c) distributed across a spatial range (such as countries, hospitals, community centers, or other settings in different locations). State these in your design roughly or specifically.

Table 2.5 Draft Activity-Meaning System Design for Your Research

Using this table: This table is useful for sketching a preliminary activity-meaning system design for your research or a possible study. First, state the research focus and a major question the study is addressing or might address. Then, consider the relevant stakeholder(s) across the dimensions appearing in the table column heads (any global, regional, and/or transnational stakeholders; institutions; groups; and/or individuals).

Research focus and question:

Dimension of activity and meaning	*Global-societal sphere of activity*	*Relevant institutional actors/ stakeholders*	*Other institutional actors/ stakeholders*	*More local interactions among individual actors/ stakeholders*	*Individual actors/ stakeholders*
Relevant stakeholders					
(Possible) Stakeholder expressions					
(Possible) Stakeholder interactions: More or less direct/indirect? Across time and/or place? Other?					
(Possible) Analyses—to be filled in after completing Chapters 3–6					

4d. Identify the stakeholders in this narrative interaction—that is, the individuals, groups, and/or institutions who have participated in the process (directly or indirectly) and have some stake in it (interest, motivation, relevant experience, knowledge).

4e. Identify stakeholder expressions—narratives or related documents— that may be direct or indirect interactions in the development of meaning you are studying.

4f. Make notes about possible outcomes you would like to gain from this inquiry.

4g. If you have hypotheses about what you might find out, note those as well.

4h. Keep principles of dynamic narrative inquiry in mind, considering the following: What is going on here—in this environment, situation, at this time? With whom is the author/speaker sharing this narrative? Why might the author/speaker be narrating in this way? How is the narrative being used to connect with others, perform a certain image, get something done, and so on? What should I include in the design to gain insights about this process? Such narrating processes relate to the place, people, time, resources, and issues going in the environment and that are, after all, a common reason people use storytelling.

4i. Read and study Chapters 3 through 6 for ideas about narrative analyses you might apply to address your research questions and designs. After doing that work, return to Table 2.5 and insert the analytic strategies you will apply or have applied.

4j. After completing those analyses, study Chapter 7 for ideas about how to make observations and identify findings to address your research questions (considering both confirming and possible disconfirming analyses).

A summary of the activity-meaning system research design process appears as a checklist in the appendix.

Creating an activity-meaning system design may require several iterative phases, such as drafting a list of possible stakeholders in addition to your focal participants, writing interview or narrative prompt protocols, and completing some of these yourself to find out what it's like to do the narrating and other interactions in your study. Reading one or more of the subsequent chapters may also bring the potential contribution of an activity-meaning system design to light for you. Therefore, keeping the term *sketch* or *draft* in mind as the process you have followed above is a good idea, so you can begin a complex realistic design for a narrative study while realizing that most researchers would reconsider the design several times, perhaps even after collecting some data and doing some analysis, as suggested in the subsequent chapters.

CONCLUSION AND NEXT

An activity-meaning system design samples narratives across actors whose interactions and mutual influences—whether explicit or implicit—play a role in the creation of meaning. Identifying stakeholders in these activity-meaning systems cannot be comprehensive or absolutely ideal, nevertheless the design can sample key expressions from key participants to bring narrative interactions characteristic of life into research settings and discourse. Sampling in this way takes much of the guesswork out of narrative analysis. The author or speaker interacting with realistic audiences other than the researcher will narrate as in life. Silences in one stakeholder position will, for example, be expressed in relation to another carefully chosen interlocutor. Raising relevant voices in, around, and between any single narrative provides social-relational data for narrative analysis, whereas studies sampling individuals out of context offer fewer touch points for analysis. Creating an activity-meaning system design, the researcher will have a sample of narratives consistent with the principle that human interaction via discourse like narrating is an active, purposeful, relational process. As researchers gather or imagine networks of interacting narratives, the mystery of qualitative narrative inquiry begins to subside, because this design system provides the material and strategies for proceeding with analysis.

In brief, when recognizing that research settings are cultural settings like social settings in everyday life, researchers design data collection in context-sensitive ways, in this case narratives and related expressions from diverse perspectives to identify meaning as worked out within the challenges and opportunities of life. In addition to providing life-based activities in an organized way that builds on the features of dynamic narrating, research designs are valuable for creating interventions and policies, as well as for evaluation of interventions.

The next four chapters focus on strategies for analyzing narratives and other documents sampled in an activity-meaning system design (or other design you have used). Having considered research design, you can proceed with the following narrative analysis chapters in any order, although I present them in a way that works for me. Chapter 3 defines and illustrates values analysis to examine the interaction of meanings across stakeholders in activity-meaning systems. Chapter 4 focuses on narrative structure (plot and script analysis), Chapter 5 on significance analysis, and Chapter 6 on character mapping and time analysis.

Note

The summary on pages 55–58 is from *Human Development and Political Violence* by Colette Daiute. Copyright © 2010 Colette Daiute. Reprinted with the permission of Cambridge University Press.

3

Values Analysis

Narrative is more than a means of communicating about personal experience. Narrating is also a means of social relations and social change, in part with the interaction of diverse values that organize meaning. Any single narrative may be organized in a way that conforms to a social norm, such as a peer group's value of equality in romantic relationships, including that females as well as males should initiate dates. Based on peer group values, for example, someone sharing an experience of a recent date might or might not mention having initiated the get-together. Narrating is also, however, more than a means of reproducing social values of the powers that be—whether those powers are peers or a government. For example, if a person's peer group shares different values about romantic relationships from those of the person's family, he or she might not include the detail about initiating a date when recounting dating stories with family members yet would include that detail when recounting stories with friends. Because people use narrating to figure out what is going on around them and what is stirring within them, values from diverse life contexts come into play when sharing experience in research. No matter how carefully controlled a narrative research design, values organize narratives, so the careful researcher must consider narrative values.

Because values are important in organizing narratives, narrative inquiry benefits from a process for analyzing values. Toward that end, the focus of this chapter is **values analysis**—a way to identify narrative meaning in terms of values expressed in and interacting with narratives. After defining narrative values, this chapter discusses values analysis, presents examples of values analysis in prior research, and outlines a values analysis process.

DEFINING NARRATIVE VALUES

Values are "culturally-specific goals, ways of knowing, experiencing, and acting in response to environmental, cultural, economic, political, and social circumstances—a definition based in socio-cultural theory" (Daiute, Stern, & Lelutiu-Weinberger, 2003, p. 85). Values are principles that people live by. Values may be enduring moral codes, situational norms, or, more likely, flexible and changing over time, situation, and other factors. Unlike rules, values are believed, at least to some extent. Nevertheless, values are enacted flexibly in daily life. Because narrating is a dynamic process, any single narrator can adopt different values he or she has learned in diverse cultural contexts of daily life.

In increasing contexts across the globe, people are not living in places where their birth cultures dominate, thereby requiring that they learn multiple cultural values (Sassen, 2008). Any young person growing up in a city, for example, learns a culture in the family, which may conform to ethnic and religious norms, a culture in school that conforms to national norms, and cultures related to participation in activities of interest or generational orientation. In this way, people's values expand, and as narrators they can select among or intermingle values in relation to their diverse groups. Expressed in actual activities, like narrating, values guide narrators, their selection of details, such as characters, connections among causes and effects of events, and the point of a story.

Another aspect of defining narrative values is to acknowledge that values are enacted rather than discussed, illustrated rather than announced. That is, narrators do not typically state values as such but are, instead, guided by them when planning or expressing narratives. Narratives report facts and imaginings, but values guide their selection and arrangement. Although usually implicit, values are extremely important aspects of narrative meaning.

An example that advances this discussion of narrative values comes from debates about gun control in the United States. Values emphasizing the constitutional right to bear arms organize the narrative "The mass shooting was done by a person, not the guns. The shooter planned for weeks, appeared to others to be in a state of rage the day before the rampage, and that was the cause." A different set of values organizes the following narrative emphasizing the prevalence of guns: "The mass shooting was possible because semiautomatic weapons were readily available. Guns were in the shooter's home. He had had an extremely lonely and frustrating day, and if the guns had not been in sight, he might have kicked a wall or even a person. Had those guns not been in his home, by the time that angry youth put his hands on a semiautomatic, he might, just might, have calmed down." People sometimes organize narratives with diverse values in tension, such as "The constitutional right to bear arms was made centuries ago when it took a long time to load each potential shot. Since then much more lethal guns have become available, and people who shouldn't have those weapons readily available have used them for mass shootings." The tension in the latter narrative is between the value for freedom to bear arms expressed in an amendment to the Constitution and the value of protecting people given 21st-century realities. Whether a person narrates in terms of one set of values or another on an issue, like gun control, is not purely a personal matter. Instead, values develop in social life.

Values, Society, and Change

Individuals become members of their cultures by adopting values. Values are, however, dynamic, because as political, economic, cultural, and social realms of life change, so do values that organize activities and discourse. Values develop in relation to activities of people with different goals in different roles and relationships. Values are also sometimes in tension, such as when parents and teenagers narrate the perfect holiday, the ideal date, or a visit to an uncle in the hospital. As societies change, the values that guide people's actions, experiences, and understandings change, which in turn changes society further. For those reasons, people appropriate values rather than adopt them completely.

Those who are not already set in their ways, such as children, youth, newcomers to a society, new parents, professional apprentices, and digital novices, use narratives (among other means) to figure out what is going on around them and how they fit. Just as different cultures and religions have done for generations, each generation creates new values, albeit with varying degrees of change. For example, narratives about who counts as a role model for youth and which goals are worth pursing permeate the media, education, law, and the arts. Assumed values, such as those of patriotism, are also often hidden in narratives with imagery, like that of the ubiquitous display of national flags during difficult times (Billig, 1995; Scott, 1992). When defining values in social relations, one understands that the values guiding any single narrative involve the interaction of diverse personal, cultural, and situational factors.

Consistent with the use, relation, materiality, and diversity principles of dynamic narrating, values are in dialogue among people in a context. As discussed in Chapter 2, it is important to understand that each narrative—whether brief or extended—is a turn in an actual or virtual conversation among stakeholders (Bakhtin, 1986). Sampling relevant perspectives accounts for the interactive nature of narrative values. Toward that end, the following expressions enact different values related to conflict prevention, a major focus of urban schools in the United States before this became a focus of international security:

- A U.S. government report (excerpt):

  The United States has seen rapid proliferation of youth gangs since 1980. During this period, the number of cities reporting youth gang problems has increased from an estimated 286 jurisdictions with more than 2,000 gangs and nearly 100,000 members in 1980 (Miller, 1982) to about 2,000 jurisdictions with more than 23,000 gangs and more than 650,000 members in 1995 (Moore, 1997; National Youth Gang Center, 1997). All States and almost all large cities reported youth gang problems in 1995. . . . cities reporting gang migration said local crime rates or patterns generally were affected by migrants, primarily through increases in thefts, robberies, and other violent crimes. (Howell, 1997, pp. 1–2)

- A violence prevention curriculum in urban schools:

  Use words not fists when you have a conflict with someone.

- A narrative by 7-year-old Sylvia in the fall of third grade in a school using the violence prevention curriculum:

  I fot with my cousin George because of my bike; we hit each other.

- A story from Sylvia's teacher, Mrs. Morales (excerpt):

  They didn't like us in Puerto Rico because we were different . . . we got some help to talk it through.

- Sylvia's narrative in the spring of third grade:

  My cousin George needed my bike, but me too. So we fout with words and compromise.

As illustrated in the excerpts above from a study in public schools in a large city, perspectives around the issue of youth conflict differ in terms of the narrator's position of influence (Daiute, 2006; Daiute et al., 2003). The first excerpt, from an official report, narrates a situation in American cities during the latter part of the 20th century. This relatively impersonal narrative offers statistics pointing to increased youth violence in American cities during a certain period. The policy statement was among many that led to the implementation of school-based violence prevention programs during the 1980s and 1990s (Elliott et al., 1998). Numerous curricula provided contexts and guidelines to help young people identify conflicts and learn strategies, like "Use words not fists when in a conflict," for reducing the chance that conflicts would become violent (Educators for Social Responsibility, n.d.; Walker, 1996). In a school with such a curriculum, Sylvia's teacher, Mrs. Morales, an immigrant from

Puerto Rico, emphasized the values of talking about conflicts ("talk it through"), recognizing discrimination ("they didn't like us because we were different"), and the need sometimes for intervention ("we got some help to talk it through"). Over time, Sylvia, a child in the program, learned to conform her narratives about personal experiences of conflict to the values of the curriculum. The compilation of excerpts above offers insights for opening up a discussion about the interactions among values guiding narratives about social issues and other issues of inquiry.

Narrative research focuses on individuals' experiences, opinions, and activities around an issue, but individual expressions always interact—in part via values—with diverse others and activities. These interacting narrators are stakeholders as defined in dynamic narrative inquiry design, discussed in Chapter 2. The excerpts above are presented to indicate that Sylvia, like all of us, does not narrate in a vacuum. If young Sylvia and her peers are the focus of change in an educational program, researchers should consider students' narratives in relation to other narratives in the physical and symbolic realms where they live. Although a beginning writer, as illustrated by her phonetic spelling, young Sylvia was able to read values systems and switch values enacted in her narratives from the fall to the spring of her third-grade year. For example, Sylvia changed from including hitting in her fall story to replacing physical conflict with verbal disagreement after she had participated all year in reading, discussing, and creating narratives about the preferred ways of dealing with peer conflicts. When researchers seek individuals' perspectives, they must, as Chapter 1 explains, acknowledge that narratives (like all discourse) are authentic to contexts—the circumstances, purposes, interlocutors, and expectations of those contexts—rather than only to the individual as a singular authentic source. For that reason, considering Sylvia's narratives requires examining them in relation to the curriculum and other relevant contexts.

The sampling of expressions above, for example, narrates the situation of increased crime in American cities in the 1980s, a focus on gangs in that process, and a connection to migrants. The statistics in the first excerpt provide details of a narrative of increasing urban violence, but the shift to identifying a specific responsible group—in this case, migrant youth in gangs—should raise questions about values that may have guided the selection of the narrative details. Values also emerge in the curriculum statement "Use words not fists when you have a conflict with someone." This apparently clear directive embeds the value that individuals have choices when in conflicts and assumptions that subjects of this curriculum might tend to use fists. The approach of asking children to narrate personal experiences of conflict in the context of a curriculum designed to teach specific values about conflict also introduces values about narrating, such as the value that sharing potentially problematic experiences in school is appropriate. Such implicit and stated values in institutional narratives (like the national report and a violence prevention curriculum) are also relevant to meanings in practice and research.

Although diverse actors may or may not be addressing one another directly as in face-to-face interactions, values of a society or group, like those of the U.S. government, curriculum, teacher, and student above, are virtually speaking to one another as in social network environments. The implicit privilege and burden of those in positions of power, influence, and resources (such as those who create policies, mission statements, or curricula) is to express their values persuasively to "the people" and, of course, to solicit the people's opinions, while the implicit power and burden of the people is to take up, resist, or negotiate values. Those in relatively powerful positions, like parents, teachers, and policy makers, have pivotal roles to play between authorities like a national government and young people. For example, students interact with teachers, whose responsibility it is to promote or at least to present societal values, yet teachers are also individuals with personal experiences and cultural interpretations of the tenets their jobs require them to reproduce. The narrating process is, thus, one of negotiating and, ideally, transforming those values to the satisfaction of people who live by them.

This process whereby individuals do or do not take up others' values is **values negotiation**. Negotiating values may occur explicitly, as in conversations and narratives created in the same setting, or implicitly, as in narratives among those with mutual interests in a broader societal ecology. Values negotiation involves echoing values (taking up, performing values) expressed elsewhere, not echoing (contesting) values one would be expected to take up, and changing values in the environment. On this view, an individual may also narrate according to different values in different situations.

In her role as teacher, Mrs. Morales, for example, in the narrative above, emphasizes the value of getting help to resolve a conflict, which she might not emphasize in her role as friend or school board member. When comparing narratives by different people and groups who know and care about an issue, researchers can identify common, divergent, and new values in part by considering them together. As in the excerpts above, Sylvia expressed different values in the fall, before she learned that narrating fighting would be frowned upon ("we fot"), and the spring, when she wrote about her antagonist's point of view as well as her own, seeking help to address the conflict, and "talking it through." The violence prevention curriculum materials presented in Sylvia's class stated values explicitly, as also expressed in the teacher's narrative, which mentions "talking it through" and "using words." Some features of the teacher's story, however, contest the curriculum value that "people can usually resolve their conflicts" by focusing on how conflicts escalate, not emphasizing conflict resolution, and showing that resolving conflicts sometimes requires intervention of a person in authority. Sampling narratives by individuals (Sylvia and her teacher) with diverse roles (Sylvia as student, teacher as cultural guide) and the broader society (curriculum expressing educational values and government report pointing to the potentially violent children in urban public schools) provides a basis for values analysis.

The next section explains values analysis to consider how narratives by collectives and individuals do and do not echo one another.

VALUES ANALYSIS

Values analysis is a way of identifying collective and divergent meanings around an issue of research interest. This analytic strategy is based in the principles of dynamic narrating: Narrators use their stories to connect with and away from cultural norms in relation to others in diverse positions of influence, resources, and knowledge. Values analysis examines the guiding influences of narratives by participants in diverse roles—stakeholders/actors who have diverse interests, goals, and activities across a social system—as expressed in **cultural products** like documents, mission statements, news reports, curricula, and personal narratives. These mutually influencing actors may be in direct contact (which makes the research process easier) or virtual contact via participation in social institutions, the media, and popular culture. In addition to examining explicit interactions, researchers studying the important virtual social relations interacting with each and every narrative, like those among governments, media, and individuals, face logistical challenges. Values analysis is a way to manage at least some of the myriad dynamic factors in the narrative process, thereby providing findings sensitive to the richness of the genre.

A researcher doing values analysis examines values organizing relevant stakeholders' narratives and other pertinent expressions to identify shared and divergent meanings. Sampling an array of expressions—narratives and occasionally other kinds of expressions—by stakeholders around an issue provides material for identifying the values that narrators may be interacting with by echoing them, disagreeing with them, or transforming them. Values analysis examines expressions, by individuals within and across institutions, in contexts like community organizations, health care institutions, educational settings, informal interactions, and research settings. Documents such as mission statements, curriculum guides, transcripts of interviews, and YouTube videos express values in narrative or other genres, available for systematic analysis.

Values analysis identifies values in such cultural and personal products, considering whether and how values are performed, or not, across stakeholders. Researchers including diverse perspectives in their study designs gain insights about the complexity of narratives relevant to their research questions by doing values analysis to identify what is shared (performed), divergent (contested), or transformed (centered) in relation to research questions (Daiute, 2004). This approach extends **positioning** theory (Bamberg, 2004b; Harré & van Langenhove, 1999) by suggesting the sampling of diverse stakeholder expressions for **analysis**.

Values analysis is a way to acknowledge tensions between adopting and changing cultural norms in terms of issues of power, as well as interpersonal and intergroup relations. In the example from the curriculum study mentioned above, values related to cultural norms about peer conflict. The change in Sylvia's way of narrating conflict from the beginning to the end of a year in the violence prevention program indicates she conformed to the powerful messages shared in class while also expressing some of her own power by shifting expressions of physical conflict from autobiographical to fictional narrative writing.

Values analysis addresses questions like the following: How do individuals and cultural (or other) groups understand issues in their society? What values tensions (consistencies, contradictions, complementarities) are revealed across stakeholder expressions? How do actors in a system take up and negotiate diverse values salient at the time/space of inquiry? How does this change occur over time or space within or over an activity-meaning system? What do we learn about the contested or hot issues from this dynamic analysis of individual and collective narrating?

In summary, ideas guiding values analysis are that (a) narratives are developed in social-political relations, thereby requiring researchers to sample multiple relevant actors' expressions within a relevant system of activity and meaning, as illustrated in Chapter 2; (b) meaningful activities, like narrating, enact values (principles, norms, beliefs, ideologies, goals), implicitly and explicitly; (c) values are negotiated by participants with different perspectives (interests, authority/power, stakeholder groups, and so on), so sampling different stakeholders of issues of interest in the research often means including those of diverse roles, power, and influence; and (d) analyses examine the negotiation of values by identifying how diverse stakeholders **perform, contest, and center** values in relevant expressions (Daiute, 2004). Considering narrative values in a dynamic relational context of an existing practice or research design brings a profoundly important strand of meaning into view.

IDENTIFYING VALUES

Identifying values is a first step of values analysis. A sampling of narratives from a research project on immigration provides examples for practice identifying values for narrative analysis. Table 3.1 presents four narratives about a policy for undocumented youth brought to the United States when they were children: one by a national stakeholder, one by a representative of a university program to support students affected by the policy, one by a student organization, and one by a student offering her perspective. The excerpts were selected for an activity-meaning system research design to learn about how those involved understand deferred action (Daiute & Caicedo, 2012).

For information about the interacting nature of the narratives in Table 3.1, a very brief history of recent immigration policy in the United States is helpful. In 2001, the Development, Relief, and Education for Alien Minors Act, known as the Dream Act, was presented in Congress. The intent of the bill was to ease the pathway to citizenship for certain undocumented immigrants, especially minors who had been brought to the country illegally. In the summer of 2012, with the 2001 act still not passed, the administration of President Barack Obama introduced a policy to be implemented by the Department of Homeland Security—an institution created after 2001 (in part as a result of increased security measures after the terrorist attacks in the United States on September 11, 2001). Relevant immigration laws and policy reforms had been debated for more than a decade, as the lives of undocumented young people attending college, serving in the armed forces, and contributing in other ways to U.S. society were limited because they could not apply for scholarships, drivers' licenses, and employment requiring official status. Approximately 1.4 million "dreamers"— young people ages 16 to 30 brought to the United States before age 16 without official entry papers—are potentially affected by the policy (Immigration Policy Center, 2012), as are the U.S.-born children of undocumented immigrants, albeit indirectly.

One study focuses on urban community colleges, which are involved in negotiating citizenship, in part because many of their students are immigrants. The aim of the study is to learn about how young adults understand citizenship, how the threat of being deported affects daily lives and abilities to plan for the future, and how college policies and practices might make a positive

Table 3.1   Selected Expressions Related to the Deferred Action Policy Activity

Societal/national stakeholder:

"Secretary Napolitano Announces Deferred Action Process for Young People Who Are Low Enforcement Priorities" (Washington, D.C., June 15, 2012)

Secretary of Homeland Security Janet Napolitano today announced that effective immediately, certain young people who were brought to the United States as young children, do not present a risk to national security of public safety, and meet several key criteria will be considered for relief from removal of the country or from entering into removal proceedings. Those who demonstrate that they meet the criteria will be eligible to receive deferred action for a period of two years, subject to renewal, and will be eligible to apply for work authorization.

(http://www.dhs.gov/news/2012/06/15/secretary-napolitano-announces-deferred-action-process-young-people-who-are-low)

Local institutional stakeholder:

CUNY Citizenship Now!

"Taking Action on Deferred Action! Open Letter from Allan Wernick, Director of CUNY Citizenship Now"

If you qualify for President Obama's deferred action, you should apply. CUNY Citizenship Now! will provide free, high quality legal assistance to help you complete your application.

You can find information on the eligibility requirements for deferred action at www.cuny .edu/dreamers. Some Dreamers are worried that if they apply for deferred action, they'll be at risk of deportation because the program grants legal status for two years only. These Dreamers worry that if Romney becomes President, he will end the program. I believe that the risk is minimal and is far outweighed by the benefits of applying.

Anyone who qualifies for the Dreamer program who doesn't apply is missing the opportunity of a lifetime. It's true that a President Romney could reverse the policy, but I believe that is very unlikely. So unlikely that if a member of my own family qualified, I would urge him or her to apply. The Obama program will provide you employment authorization, the chance to get a driver's license and the ability to travel throughout the United States without fear. If you have an emergency that requires you leave the United States, you may qualify for USCIS travel permission. And, if you have lived in New York for at least 12 months, you will qualify for the lower in-state tuition at CUNY. The twelve months can be before or after you get deferred action status.

(http://www.cuny.edu/about/resources/citizenship/info4noncitizens/info4undocumented/DeferredAction/CUNYStudents.html)

(Continued)

Table 3.1   (Continued)

Ecological/everyday practice stakeholder:

United We Dream ("dreamer" advocate organization)

"Our Mission"

United We Dream is the largest immigrant youth-led organization in the nation, a powerful nonpartisan network made up of 52 affiliate organizations in 25 states. We organize and advocate for the dignity and fair treatment of immigrant youth and families, regardless of immigration status. UWD's current priority is to win citizenship for the entire undocumented community and end senseless deportations and abuses. We seek to address the inequities and obstacles faced by immigrant youth and believe that by empowering immigrant youth, we can advance the cause of the entire community—justice for all immigrants.

We're driven by and accountable to our thousands of members across the country who make up our sustainable and robust grassroots network. We believe we can build power by organizing at the local, regional, and national levels and aim to provide tools and resources to support our leaders and member organizations, as well as create meaningful alliances with other advocacy organizations.

In 2012, we successfully pressured President Obama and won the deferred action policy— providing protection from deportation and work permits for young people without papers—and leading a diverse immigrant rights' movement in our biggest success in over 25 years. In 2013 and beyond, our network has committed to relentlessly fight for our families and communities and win a roadmap to citizenship and fair treatment for all 11 million undocumented Americans. (Read our full platform for change here and our 20-point plan for immigration reform here.) As we've proven, we have the power to redefine what is possible and win.

(http://unitedwedream.org)

Individual stakeholder:

Dreamer youth contributing

"Citizen of the World," by Jacqueline Garcia

A beautiful country down south that Mexicanos adore saw a little girl cry and grow. She, so happy and full of life, was soon to learn what it meant to strive. At twenty-eight days old she was taken up North in a country where she was expected to succeed and always go forth. In 2012 she is 17, facing a challenge and chasing a dream; a dream she knows she'll reach if united she dreams. "You are not a legal citizen of America," she has been told but she knows that no matter what she is a citizen of the world. She believes to have the right to dream, fight and achieve, as long as she has the ability to dream. In any city, in a country, her citizenship of the world never expires for she dreams everywhere, achieves anywhere, and always inspires. "A citizen of the world I am" is what she tells to whom ever dares to tell her "In America, as undocumented, you have only the right to fail."

(http://unitedwedream.org/category/dreamer-narratives)

difference. Young people's narratives are the central focus. To include the broader societal, institutional, and group narratives with which students at community colleges in New York City interact, the activity-meaning system research design samples narratives by a government representative, a university official, an advocacy group of "dreamers," and a young self-declared dreamer.

As expressed in the excerpts in Table 3.1, the U.S. government administered the deferred action policy in the Department of Homeland Security. A U.S. government news release reported that "Secretary of Homeland Security Janet Napolitano today announced that effective immediately, certain young people who were brought to the United States as young children, do not present a risk to national security of public safety, and meet several key criteria will be considered for relief from removal of the country . . ." This excerpt and the rest of the brief news narrative on Table 3.1 mentions "certain young people," "young children," "risk to public safety," "relief from removal," "removal proceedings," "demonstrate," "eligible," "two years," and "deferred action." Beyond the mention of topics, the narrative is organized by values, including that certain children are worthy of protection; some children might be a risk to public safety; if not protected these certain children would be removed from the country; relevant youth must demonstrate that they meet the criteria set. The statement by the director of the CUNY Citizenship Now! project speaks directly to students who might qualify, stating values that deferred action is a good opportunity, mistrust about the process is understandable given what 2012 presidential candidate Romney had said about abolishing the policy, these students are worthy of free legal assistance, and so on.

Table 3.2 identifies values in the stakeholder expressions presented in Table 3.1. Examining the values stated for excerpts in Table 3.2 can help readers understand the definitions of values and values analysis above. Identifying values involves some reading between the lines, a process that speakers of a language do all the time, as they become members of cultures and groups, as well as when they narrate for different purposes for different others.

Some guidelines for determining "Is it a value?" include the following:

1a. There's a values statement, principle, norm, belief, or attendant assumption expressed in a sentence, such as the following from the website for CUNY Citizenship Now!: "Anyone who qualifies for the Dreamer program who doesn't apply is missing the opportunity of a lifetime" which expresses in a relatively literal way the value "What the Dreamer program offers is important and unique for this time."

Table 3.2   Identifying Values in Expressions by Stakeholders Around the Deferred Action Policy Activities

Using this table: This table is designed as supported practice for identifying values in narratives and related expressions. Building on the definition of values in this chapter and the values stated for the first stakeholder listed below, practice identifying values for the other narrative excerpts. These narratives are already segmented by sentence or thought unit, but each one of those sentences does not necessarily indicate a new value.

Remember: Values are stated in complete sentences expressing the explicit or implied norms, assumptions and/or organizing principles of the narrative. When values are difficult to identify, you can first focus on the topics that are emphasized (or seem to be required but are ignored), then, from what appear to be major topics, state values that the topics together express. As you find repeated values, you could number the values and state value numbers as you progress. Working in small groups could be helpful for generating, discussing, and refining values.

Societal/national stakeholder expression. Write a value that applies to any sentence (or thought unit) below:

"Secretary Napolitano Announces Deferred Action Process for Young People Who Are Low Enforcement Priorities" (Washington, D.C., June 15, 2012)

Secretary of Homeland Security Janet Napolitano today announced that effective immediately, certain young people who were brought to the United States as young children, do not present a risk to national security of public safety,
Value: People other than children present a risk of public safety.

and meet several key criteria
Value: Homeland Security has the values for establishing those criteria.

will be considered for relief from removal of the country or from entering into removal proceedings.
Value: Other people should be removed from the country.
Value: Those who came to the United States as young children deserve a kind of pardon, not necessarily full citizenship.

Those who demonstrate that they meet the criteria will be eligible to receive deferred action for a period of two years,
Value: Demonstrating criteria means one deserves to be free of the threat of removal.

subject to renewal,

Value: This is temporary permission, not a right.

and will be eligible to apply for work authorization.
Value: Those people are valued as workers.

(http://www.dhs.gov/news/2012/06/15/secretary-napolitano-announces-deferred-action-process-young-people-who-are-low)

Local institutional stakeholder expression: Write a value that applies to any sentence (or thought unit) below:

CUNY Citizenship Now!

"Taking Action on Deferred Action! Open Letter from Allan Wernicke, Director of CUNY Citizenship Now"

If you qualify for President Obama's deferred action, you should apply.
Value:

CUNY Citizenship Now! will provide free, high quality legal assistance to help you complete your application.

Value:
You can find information on the eligibility requirements for deferred action at www.cuny.edu/dreamers.
Some Dreamers are worried that if they apply for deferred action,
Value:

they'll be at risk of deportation because the program grants legal status for two years only.
Value:

These Dreamers worry that if Romney becomes President, he will end the program.
Value:

I believe that the risk is minimal and is far outweighed by the benefits of applying.
Value:

Anyone who qualifies for the Dreamer program who doesn't apply is missing the opportunity of a lifetime.
Value:

It's true that a President Romney could reverse the policy, but I believe that is very unlikely. So unlikely that if a member of my own family qualified, I would urge him or her to apply.
Value:

(Continued)

Table 3.2   (Continued)

The Obama program will provide you employment authorization, the chance to get a driver's license and the ability to travel throughout the United States without fear.
Value:

If you have an emergency that requires you leave the United States, you may qualify for USCIS travel permission.
Value:

And, if you have lived in New York for at least 12 months, you will qualify for the lower in-state tuition at CUNY. The twelve months can be before or after you get deferred action status.
Value:

(http://www.cuny.edu/about/resources/citizenship/info4noncitizens/info4undocumented/DeferredAction/CUNYStudents.html)

Ecological/everyday practice stakeholder expression. Write a value that applies to any sentence (or thought unit) below:

United We Dream ("dreamer" advocate organization)

"Our Mission"
United We Dream is the largest immigrant youth-led organization in the nation, a powerful nonpartisan network made up of 52 affiliate organizations in 25 states.
Value:

We organize and advocate for the dignity and fair treatment of immigrant youth and families, regardless of immigration status.
Value:

UWD's current priority is to win citizenship for the entire undocumented community and end senseless deportations and abuses.
Value:

We seek to address the inequities and obstacles faced by immigrant youth and believe that by empowering immigrant youth, we can advance the cause of the entire community—justice for all immigrants.
Value:

We're driven by and accountable to our thousands of members across the country who make up our sustainable and robust grassroots network.
Value:

We believe we can build power by organizing at the local, regional, and national levels and aim to provide tools and resources to support our leaders and member organizations, as well as create meaningful alliances with other advocacy organizations.
Value:

In 2012, we successfully pressured President Obama and won the deferred action policy—providing protection from deportation and work permits for young people without papers—and leading a diverse immigrant rights' movement in our biggest success in over 25 years.
Value:

In 2013 and beyond, our network has committed to relentlessly fight for our families and communities and win a roadmap to citizenship and fair treatment for all 11 million undocumented Americans.
Value:

(http://unitedwedream.org)

Individual stakeholder expression. Write a value that applies to any sentence (or thought unit) below:

Dreamer youth contributing

"Citizen of the World," by Jacqueline Garcia
A beautiful country down south that Mexicanos adore saw a little girl cry and grow.
Value:

She, so happy and full of life, was soon to learn what it meant to strive.
Value:

At twenty-eight days old she was taken up North in a country where she was expected to succeed and always go forth.
Value:

In 2012 she is 17, facing a challenge and chasing a dream; a dream she knows she'll reach if united she dreams.
Value:

(Continued)

Table 3.2   (Continued)

"You are not a legal citizen of America," she has been told
Value:

but she knows that no matter what she is a citizen of the world.
Value:

She believes to have the right to dream, fight and achieve, as long as she has the ability to dream.
Value:

In any city, in a country, her citizenship of the world never expires for she dreams everywhere, achieves anywhere, and always inspires.
Value:

"A citizen of the world I am" is what she tells to whom ever dares to tell her "In America, as undocumented, you have only the right to fail."
Value:

(http://unitedwedream.org/category/dreamer-narratives)

1b. There's a sequence of statements, phrases, or words that together imply a judgment about the topics mentioned, such as in the narrative "Citizen of the World": "'You are not a legal citizen of America,' she has been told but she knows that no matter what she is a citizen of the world" . . . "as long as she has the ability to dream. . . . In any city, in a country, her citizenship of the world never expires." The different meanings of *dream* and *citizen* combine to express a value something like "People who dream are human, and humans cannot be illegal." People may do illegal acts, but humans are humans and not acts.

1c. Something that is stated implies a value about what is not stated. For example, the sentence "Secretary of Homeland Security Janet Napolitano today announced that effective immediately, certain young people who were brought to the United States as young children, do not present a risk to national security of public safety" implies the value "People other than 'certain young people' do present 'a risk to national security of public safety.'"

2. Values are stated as sentences, as in 1a., 1b., and 1c. above. Because values are propositions about ways of knowing and living, stating a value requires a sentence with a subject (or topic) and a predicate (the action or implication of the topic). Another way to think of this is that, in English and many other languages, the sentence subject is usually the topic, while the predicate is the "So what?" of the topic. Values may also be related by topics, such as values about citizenship, values about education, and so on, and within those topical groups, specific values are stated more precisely. Grouping values by topic can be useful before or after identifying the specific value statements.

3. Discussing values with co-researchers or classmates helps with the process of identifying values. When you discuss draft values with co-researchers or classmates, do you agree about the values? Can editing the values statements help you gain agreement?

Because narrative inquiry considers the social nature of values, stakeholders' negotiation of values is an important aspect of the analysis. After identifying values across stakeholders (as with Table 3.2), a researcher compiles those values that are more and less prominent. This step then prepares the researcher for examining values negotiation—the performing, contesting, and transforming of values across stakeholders to reveal the shared and divergent meanings around an issue. Table 3.2 provides a template for identifying values, a necessary step before considering values negotiation. This table is useful for practice identifying values that account for each stakeholder position in the deferred action policy study examples.

Using Table 3.3 involves identifying the most prevalent values organizing a stakeholder position (across those sampled for that stakeholder) and those that may be evident although more minor. Values guide each or most expressions within a narrative (typically as sentences). The most and least prevalent values in a narrative and by stakeholders then emerge as researchers compile the sentence-by-sentence expressions. Major values are ones that organize an entire narrative and, as such, are enacted or expressed relatively extensively across the narrative compared to more minor or less prominent values. For the deferred action example, this process addresses the question, What are the meanings of citizenship expressed across stakeholders sampled to include the government, local university system, advocate group, and individual?

The next section briefly summarizes values analyses in four studies. These summaries further illustrate the nature and potential contributions of values analysis.

Table 3.3 Practice Identifying Predominant Values in Stakeholder Expressions for a Study of the Meaning of the Deferred Action Policy

Using this table: Once a researcher had identified values for a stakeholder position (as in Table 3.2), a next step is to compile a list of the major values expressed by each stakeholder. Drawing on information in this chapter and your work for Table 3.2, list the major values (up to four) and minor values (one or two) for each stakeholder to address this research question: What are the meanings of citizenship expressed across stakeholders sampled to include the government, local university system, advocate group, and individual?

Stakeholders and space-time dimensions	Stakeholder expressions	Major values	Minor values
Societal/national (United States)	Announcement of deferred action policy by the U.S. secretary of Homeland Security		
Institutional (large urban university)	Open letter from the director of CUNY Citizenship Now!		
Ecological/everyday practice	Mission statement of United We Dream, student advocacy organization		
Individual involved with and/or interacting explicitly or implicitly with the broader ones sampled (above)	Story submitted to United We Dream		

VALUES ANALYSIS IN PRIOR RESEARCH

Values analysis is especially useful in research addressing individual and societal change, such as research on learning, development, conflict, health, migration, technology use, workplace practices, human rights, and other processes. Values analysis has, for example, been employed in international research projects in a study on the development of children and youth participating in community organizations after the 1990s wars across the former Yugoslavia (Daiute, 2010), a study of the human resources institution in a country changing from a socialist to a capitalist economy (Ninkovic, 2012), a study of children's rights policy (Daiute, 2008), and a study with early adolescents involves in a vocational simulation computer program (Kreniske, 2012). Brief summaries of values analysis in these studies can aid other researchers deciding whether and how to employ this tool of dynamic narrative inquiry.

Negotiating Values in an Educational Practice

Values analysis in the activity-meaning system of a violence prevention program across nine third- and fifth-grade classrooms in urban public schools indicated that teachers identifying with different ethnic groups emphasized some different as well as similar values to those in curriculum (Daiute et al., 2003). The design for this study appears in Table 3.4, which outlines stakeholders across the issue of violence in urban schools, an educational program to address the issue, and narratives by teachers and children in participating classrooms. The excerpts above are from this study.

As shown in Table 3.4, the study design involved sampling statements about violence in urban schools, a review of violence prevention and related curricula, and a series of narratives by teachers and children in nine classrooms across two urban elementary schools (among other activities). Children's narratives of personal experiences of conflicts with peers and fictional scenarios of potential peer conflicts were elicited at the beginning and the end of the program implementation school years to determine whether and how the children appropriated values about peer relations.

As an example of this design, the study sampled different positions of power, including the school system that included a violence prevention program for 7- to 10-year-olds, the curriculum goals that teachers in the study were to implement, writing selections by literary authors outside the classroom, the teachers' personal stories providing a bridge between their curricular work and

Table 3.4 Stakeholders and Stakeholder Expressions for a Research Project on the Meaning of Conflict in a Violence Prevention Program

Sphere of activity	Example of a stakeholder	Example of a stakeholder expression
Broad societal sphere relevant	Educational institutions seeking violence prevention; curriculum developers	Statement of curricular goals
Participant role responsible for socially reproducing sociocultural values	Teachers	Teachers implementing the curriculum—Mrs. Morales
Individual cultural-personal role	Teacher as person in a broader context	Teacher's personal historical values interacting with the curriculum
Subject meant to take up the value(s)	Students identified as students and in terms of other relevant demographics	Students in the class—Mrs. Morales's student, Jeff

personal lives (to the extent that they would vary these), and children's writing in different narrative activities over the course of a school year.

A teacher's job is, in part, to convey the values of the system where he or she works. Each teacher, however, has his or her own history. Mrs. Morales, for example, a third-grade teacher in a public school, proudly identifies with a Puerto Rican heritage and recognizes the discrimination she endured for that claim as she grew up in a U.S. city where the many Puerto Rican immigrants experienced discrimination. Having volunteered to implement a literature-based conflict prevention and resolution program in her third-grade classroom, Mrs. Morales narratively performed values related to how conflicts escalate rather than to how they are resolved, as emphasized in the literary selections and teachers' guide to the curriculum (Walker, 1996):

I'm going to tell you a story first. At the end of it . . . you can ask me questions and I will answer them. . . . When I was about nineteen years old I was in college. . . . Yeah that was many moons ago [children laugh], actually it was twenty years ago [children try to guess how old the teacher is and they all joke good naturedly about this]. My college roommate Carmen and I decided to take a study [trip] to Puerto Rico and we were going to study there for a semester which is about four months. . . . Okay, so our plane ride there was great. We were anxious to get there because you know this was Puerto Rico. . . . We were also excited about the trip, right?

So our room, my room was shared with my roommate Carmen, but we also had to share the kitchen, the bathroom with other students that were there. There was a group of us from New York, there was seven of us, but the rest of the students were from Puerto Rico. Now I am of Puerto Rican descent, and I was born in Puerto Rico, but I had never been there since I was a baby. Okay, and we started to have trouble with the girl students who were living in the boarding house. [Student says "because they were different."] Well we all spoke Spanish, all of us, we spoke our New York Spanish, but we spoke and we understood. It's just that they didn't like us because we were from New York, and they didn't make us feel comfortable. They wanted us out, and in the middle of the night we actually had a fight. [Students say "oooooo."] It was not a fist fight . . . and we had to leave . . . because we were the newcomers. . . . (excerpted from Daiute, 2006, pp. 212–213. By permission of Oxford University Press, USA)

Mrs. Morales's narrative about her experience as a newcomer in her birthplace of Puerto Rico implicitly expresses a number of values. Among the values presented in the curriculum materials, Mrs. Morales emphasizes several in her personal story, while notably not expressing other values. Mrs. Morales's story echoes at least one value in the curriculum and the literary selection: that conflicts sometimes escalate when people are different.

When thinking about values that might be guiding a narrator's choice of characters, actions, feelings, settings, rising and resolving steps of conflict, and other details, one notices Mrs. Morales's focus on escalation in the second part of the story, against the background of the main character's positive experience in the first part of the story. Mrs. Morales builds the first part of the story with an anticipation of something that could change everything—a common narrative move: ". . . but we also had to share the kitchen, the bathroom with other students that were there." Mrs. Morales then emphasizes differences among the people in her story: ". . . group of us from New York . . . the rest of the students were from Puerto Rico . . . they were different . . . we spoke our New York Spanish. . . ."

In her narrative, Mrs. Morales narrates steps of increasing conflict, which have to do with differences: ". . . we started to have trouble with the girl students who were living there. . . . It's just that they didn't like us because we were from New York. . . . we had to leave . . . because we were the newcomers." Those narrative details reveal a value something like "Conflicts escalate when people are different" or "Conflicts sometimes occur when people are different" or "Some people who are bothered by differences create conflict." The actions in the story imply a second prominent value: "The last to come have to leave when there's a conflict." A final value implied here is that fights that aren't fistfights are preferable to ones that are, which we learn from the final sentences of Mrs. Morales's story: "They wanted us out, and in the middle of the night we actually had a fight. [Students say "oooooo."] It was not a fist fight." Mrs. Morales notably does not focus on the value to resolve conflicts, which is a major value in the curriculum materials. This approach differs from the one narrated by Mrs. Smith, a European American teacher in a third-grade classroom using the same curriculum across town.

In contrast to Mrs. Morales's focus on escalating actions, other teachers advanced their narratives with strategies for reaching out to people from apparently diverse backgrounds (Daiute et al., 2003). As you read Mrs. Smith's newcomer story below, note the details about the many efforts she, as the "different one," and subsequently other characters in her story made to connect with others:

> . . . I had just graduated from college and I was a teacher. . . . it is just as uncomfortable for teachers to come into a whole new class of 25 children that she doesn't know. So what I decided, I called up the woman who gave me the job, the principal of the school, and . . . I asked her if they had a summer program there and then I also asked her if I could come by and then maybe meet some of the children that I might be teaching, get used to the school, find out what kind of books that they might have. She said, "Oh my goodness," we have too many kids in our summer program, and in fact we're looking for a teacher . . . come the next day, we're all going on a trip and then Thursday we will start you with your class. So the next day I went. Okay, I didn't really know anybody, so we were . . . on . . . a yellow school bus. . . . Then I looked around and I noticed that I was the only white person on the bus. It had never happened to me before. All the children were, I think mostly . . . African-American or Hispanic. All the teachers were African-American or Hispanic, and I was the only white person, and somehow you know because in this country we are very aware of . . . I guess our race. I started to feel a little uncomfortable. . . . I was sitting on the bus and I said, "Okay, this is what I'm going to do is, I've got to start to feel comfortable." So I was sitting next to this little girl, and I just started to talk to her, and of course, I asked her her name. I asked her what grade she was in. I asked her what she liked to do in the summer, and then she asked me the same questions . . . and then

I started to talk to the other children on the bus. And then . . . when I got off the bus, I started to talk to the other teachers . . . and then I started to feel very, very comfortable. (excerpted from Daiute, 2006, pp. 213–214. By permission of Oxford University Press, USA.)

A values analysis of Mrs. Smith's story observes her point that even people with some power, like a teacher, might feel uncomfortable in a new setting and values of empathy for others. This comparison does not imply a judgment of whether Mrs. Morales's or Mrs. Smith's values are better; rather, it illustrates that narratives pick up in different ways on the values they are meant to convey. The difference in this study was that teachers identifying as African American and Latino tended to emphasize conflict escalation, perhaps to help their many minority students realize what they may be subjected to and how to be attentive to those steps, while teachers identifying as European American tended to emphasize conflict resolution, perhaps from a sense of having been in control of conflicts (Daiute et al., 2003).

Not surprisingly, students in Mrs. Morales's class echoed their teacher's value of paying attention to how conflicts escalate, while other teachers' students echoed their emphasis on conflict resolutions (Daiute et al., 2003). Values analysis in this study revealed a pattern with student narrations over the school year. In the fall of his third-grade year, Jeff, for example, wrote a brief yet culturally consistent narrative in response to the following prompt to write about a personal experience: "Write about a time when you or someone you know had a disagreement or a conflict with a friend, a classmate, or someone your age. What happened? How did the people involved feel? How did it all turn out?"

Like his classmates and other third graders, Jeff shared an experience in a value-laden way, as we would expect:

When I Had a Conflict

Once in my class in second grade Jarad said I was copying his answer in a mathproblem I said "I wasn't then he hit on my forrhead with a metal thing it was part of a belt. He had to go to the princeble and he got suspended for one week. Now he is on the fourth floor and he is in Ms. P's class.

Jeff recounted an event when a classmate accused him of "copying"; he defended himself, "I wasn't," and the classmate responded physically, "then he hit on my forrhead with a metal thing . . . ," leading to various consequences, and an ending indicating the separation of these two former friends.

Jeff's response to the same prompt to recount a personal experience in the spring of third grade began with a similar structure that played out narratively quite differently:

A Bad Kickball Day

Me and mark were captins. It was 21 21 and Mark's team got a home run so it was 21 22 and my team lost. Then he started to tease me about the game. Then I told on him and he got time out. He felt bad for him and me. After the time he came over to me and said "I'm sorry."

Jeff's spring third-grade narrative also recounted a conflict with a peer who acted aggressively toward him, although this time verbally, "to tease me," rather than physically as in the fall. As in the fall, Jeff narrated consequences, although this time he intervened directly, "I told on him," which led to disciplining by someone else, "he got time out," compared to the consequences in the prior more passive narration of consequences, "He had to go to the princeble and got suspended for one week."

These narratives illustrate how children as young as 7, like Jeff, narrate in relation to values. As listed in Table 3.5, values expressed in Jeff's personal experience narrative include, for example, that copying is not okay, that one must defend oneself in the face of such an accusation, and that the altercation may seem serious enough to elicit a response, but aggression is not okay and will be punished. Changes in Jeff's spring narration of a conflict with a peer indicate, moreover, that values can be malleable, albeit not conforming to a binary of "narrative" or "counter narrative." While Jeff's spring narrative maintained values about interactions around accusations worthy of response and punishment, he brought in other values, like the relevance of a verbal response (teasing), his own right to participate in the consequences (telling on a person who teases), the value of considering different perspectives in the disagreement, and the value of apologizing when one has teased a friend.

These values and changes in Jeff's narratives interact in particular with his teacher's story. Jeff echoes Mrs. Morales's value of detailed enumerating of steps in the escalation of conflicts among peers, verbal rather than physically aggressive responses to disagreements, and the defusing intervention of someone in power.

Jeff expressed diverse values across the school year and, most interestingly, in diverse kinds of narratives—with personal experience narratives echoing the curriculum values and his teacher's values increasingly over time, while the fictional narratives expressed fewer curriculum values over the school year. Jeff also wrote narratives in response to the following fictional prompt: "Three:

Table 3.5   Values Analysis Guide: Identifying Values Across Stakeholder Expressions

Using this table: Consider the values identified below for Jeff's narratives in relation to the narratives presented in this chapter and in relation to values identified for Mrs. Morales's narrative, as well as those stated for the curricular missions statement and the literary selection. Are all of the values for Jeff's narratives included? If not, which would you add or not? The curricular statement and literary selection are not included, but the values stated may be helpful for providing context for Jeff's narratives over time.

Curricular mission statement

Value 1: Conflicts escalate when people expand small annoyances or dislikes into attacks.

Value 2: Conflicts escalate when people are different.

Value 3: Conflicts can de-escalate when people talk about their annoyances, understandings, hurts, or other problems that escalated into fighting or harm.

Value 4: Conflicts should be resolved with words, not fists.

Value 5: Conflicts can always be resolved.

Cultural artifact: Literary selection—*Angel Child, Dragon Child* (Surat, 1990)

Value 1: People tease others when they don't know about or understand others.

Value 2: If not addressed, conflicts sometimes escalate from teasing to physical fighting.

Value 3: Talking or doing something together can help de-escalate conflicts.

Value 4: Sometimes someone else has to intervene to help resolve the conflict.

Value 5: Both participants must be involved in resolving the conflict—that is, both say "Sorry."

Teacher narrative about being a newcomer

Value 1: Conflicts escalate when people are different.

Value 2: Sometimes someone else has to intervene.

Value 3: Physical conflicts are not okay.

Value 4: Fighting with words is better, if there must be a fight.

Student's narrative: Jeff 1

Value 1: Peers, friends converse freely.

Value 2: Friends can disagree or have bad feelings about one another sometimes.

Value 3: Copying is not okay.

(Continued)

Table 3.5   (Continued)

Value 4: Questioning transgressions is okay.

Value 5: Physical retaliation is a response.

Value 6: Retaliation (verbal or physical) is not okay.

Value 7: There are consequences to retaliating.

Value 8: Retaliations can be punished.

Student's narrative: Jeff 2

Value 1: Friends do things together.

Value 2: Peers, friends converse freely.

Value 3: Friends can disagree or have bad feelings about one another sometimes.

Value 4: Questioning transgressions is okay.

Value 5: Retaliation (verbal or physical) is not okay.

Value 6: There are consequences to retaliating.

Value 7: Retaliations can be punished.

Value 8: Victims can act on their own behalf.

Value 9: Conflicts should be resolved.

Student's narrative: Jeff 3

Value 1: Friends do things together.

Value 2: Peers, friends converse freely.

Value 3: Friends can disagree or have bad feelings about one another sometimes.

Value 4: Questioning transgressions is okay.

Jama and Max were best friends. Pat moved in next to Max, and they began to spend lots of time together. One day, Jama saw Max and Pat walking together and laughing. What happened next? Continue this story about how the friends got along. What happened? How did they all think and feel about the events? How did it all turn out?"

In the fall, Jeff wrote a conflict-free narrative detailing interactions among the fictional characters Jama, Max, and Pat:

I think Jama is going to run over to Pat and Max and say "Hi"? Pat and Max wil say "I didn't know that you know Pat". And Max will say "Come on lets walk to school together They all said "Ok". When they got to school they played with each other.

In the spring, however, Jeff wrote a more psychosocially and linguistically complex narrative in response to that same prompt:

> Then Jama got jealos then the next day at school Jama said "Who was that boy talk to you yesterday". And Max said "He's my new neighbor". Then at dissmisal Max took Jama to his house because he want Jama to see Pat. When Max got home Max intraduces Jama to Pat and Pat to Jama. The next day they made a secret club and every Thursdays they meet at Max's house, on Sundays they meet at Pat's house, and on Tuesdays they meet at Jama's house.—Sometimes Jama still get jealos and they fight but ok.

The goal of the yearlong curriculum in Jeff's class with Mrs. Morales was to teach conflict resolution strategies, but it also involved recognizing and examining conflicts. Values emerging in the spring narrative, compared to the fall one, expressed friendly verbal interaction and social inclusion, "Come on let's walk to school together. . . ." Values about friendship are expressed with phrases like "Max got jealos . . ."; "Max intraduces Jama to Pat. . . . they made a secret club . . . every Thursdays they meet," which adds in the value of taking turns; and, interestingly, the observation that people may still "get jealos and they fight" but it's "ok." Jeff's autobiographical narratives include a combination of values consistency and variation across the school year as well as the child's use of the affordances of different narrative genres, such as the relative anonymity of fiction, to express, and perhaps to explore, less acceptable values.

Table 3.6 presents values expressed in Jeff's narratives across the different genres (autobiographical experience and fictional story) and across the school year. Values in Jeff's narratives range from "Friends do things together" to "Friends can disagree" to values about how people might deal with conflict, such as "Physical retaliation is a response" and "Retaliations can be punished." As one would expect from a child interacting in a classroom studying literature about intergroup conflict and strategies for dealing with and preventing conflict, the way Jeff narrated conflict changed over time, as indicated in the table with an X for the appearance of each value across genre and time.

One value expressed across all these writings is that friends converse with one another, while the other values appear in different patterns. Echoing Mrs. Morales's story, Jeff, her student, included the values that peers can disagree, peers can have bad feelings about each other, and verbal retaliation is a response. When looking at the values across Jeff's stories, one notices a pattern that occurred in the narratives of many of the 400 students in the related research (Daiute et al., 2003): Autobiographical stories in the spring

Table 3.6   Values Analysis Guide: Values Expressed in Jeff's Narratives Over Time

Value	Jeff's fall personal experience	Jeff's spring personal experience	Jeff's fall fictional story	Jeff's spring fictional story
Friends do things together.		X	X	X
Peers, friends converse freely.	X	X	X	X
Friends can disagree or have bad feelings about one another sometimes.	X	X		X
Copying is not okay.	X			
Winning is good.		X		
Questioning transgressions is okay.	X	X		X
Physical retaliation is a response.	X			
Verbal retaliation is a response.		X		
Retaliation (verbal or physical) is not okay.	X	X		
There are consequences to retaliating.	X	X		
Retaliations can be punished.	X	X		
Others can intervene to punish.	X	X		
Victims can act on their own behalf.		X		X
Conflicts should be resolved.		X		X

X= value present in the expression.

tended to include the values taught in the curriculum, such as "Victims can act on their own behalf" and "Conflicts are resolved," while fictional stories tended to include values that were not promoted in the curriculum.

The study identified values across stakeholders as shown in Table 3.7, which lists values in the left-hand column and various stakeholders across the top row. As the table indicates, the teacher performed some of the curriculum values in her narrative, such as how conflicts escalate, while she did not perform other values, like that conflicts can usually be resolved. Also interesting is that in the spring (rather than in the fall) the student performed values expressed in the curriculum and by the teacher's story. Relevant to the empirical study of how groups, individuals, and societies develop over time are the patterns of partial uptake (indicated in the table by "some") and contesting (indicated here by no expression at all).

Table 3.7   Values Analysis Guide: Identifying Stakeholder Positioning Around Values

Using this table: One way to identify common and different values by diverse stakeholders is to indicate whether they are major (predominant) across expressions, minor (some), or not expressed at all by some stakeholder(s).

Value	Curriculum mission statement (Walker, 1996)	Literary selection—used to illustrate intergroup conflict	Teacher's story about being a newcomer	Student's personal experience stories	Student's fictional stories
Value 1: How conflicts escalate.	Predominant	Some	Predominant	Some in fall; predominant in spring	None in fall; predominant in spring
Value 2: Conflicts should be resolved with words, not fists.	Predominant	Some	Some	None in fall; predominant in spring	Some in fall; few in spring
Value 3: Someone else intervenes to help.	Some	Predominant	Predominant	None in fall; some in spring	. . .
Value 4: Conflicts can always be resolved.	Predominant	Predominant	Some	. . .	. . .

Predominant = a major value for the stakeholder as sampled (accounts for much of what is expressed).

Some = a relatively minor value for the stakeholder as sampled (acknowledges the value).

. . . = not a value for the stakeholder as sampled (depending on the context, such values may be silent because contested or simply different from those of the other stakeholders).

The example from the study of values in an elementary school violence prevention program offered a range of findings about values expressed and negotiated across an activity-meaning system. Sampling and analyzing expressions—documents, literature, oral and written narratives—showed the values by each stakeholder, and the values negotiation analysis showed whether and how the different values were taken up, resisted, or changed. Analyses of the curriculum, classroom interactions, and hundreds of autobiographical and fictional narratives indicated that the 7- to 10-year-olds and their teachers used narratives to adopt, resist, or transform values of a violence prevention program. Eliciting a broad set of narratives was essential to reading the children's narratives. With interacting narratives like those by Jeff and by Sylvia (presented earlier in this chapter), a researcher understands not only that Sylvia changed her way of narrating conflict but also that she did so in relation to other narratives shared around her, not in any absolute way. Such flexibility indicated the social-relational nature of different narrating activities, in particular to mediate the narrative presentations of knowledge and self in relation to audience expectations. This process, thus, revealed a pattern of using narrating for conformity and change. Moreover, that children as young as 7 narrated in relation to values that were less as well as more explicit indicates the prominence of this strand of narrative meaning.

Values analysis in a very different setting with adults illustrates the portability of this narrative analysis strategy.

Values Analysis of Employment Practices in a Postsocialist Country

Discursive practices can be rigid as well as flexible during times of major societal change, such as during changes in political economic systems (Billig, 1995). During times of major change, values guiding who counts as an ideal person change dramatically, such as a narrative of a hero shifting from one who works for the greater good to one who works for individual gain. With the breakup of the Soviet Union and other socialist countries in the region at the end of the 20th century, governments, business, and other institutions established new systems with new values. An example of such a system is the human resources department in a corporation. Human resources departments serve as filters for corporations in capitalist systems, but such entities are relatively nonexistent in socialist and communist economies, where employee practices are organized in terms of national and union norms (Ninkovic, 2012). In a study designed to examine how people involved understand such changes, Ninkovic (2012) sampled the corporate perspective in official human resources documents and conducted interviews with human resources professionals, who, like teachers, held pivotal roles on behalf of their institutions; she also collected information on the professionals' own cultural and personal histories and their relationships with employees. To allow diverse values to emerge, the interviews with human resources professionals elicited narratives about experiences with friends as well as experiences in professional life.

Ninkovic collected human resources documents from companies in service and business industries (involving white-collar workers with relatively high educational achievement) and manufacturing or repair industries (involving blue-collar workers with vocational training) and conducted extended interviews with human resources professionals. To identify trends across the industries, Ninkovic sampled at least six of each kind of company, and to identify trends across those in the role of implementing professional values, by at least one individual from each company. Responses to the questions eliciting narratives were analyzed in detail.

The values analysis with 24 professionals in white-collar and blue-collar corporations elicited a wide range of values, some performing the new capitalist ways of being, referred to as "enterprising" values, some contesting those new ways of being with values more consistent with socialist times, not surprisingly primarily in the blue-collar companies, and in narratives about friendship.

This study of how values about the ideal person change from socialist to capitalist periods identified patterns of uptake, resistance, and change among the human resources managers in two different kinds of companies (Ninkovic, 2012). By sampling diverse positions rather than simply more individuals, this study showed that the values of the "enterprising person" emerged as the ideal in public policy, workplace policy, workplace practices, and human resources professionals' discursive practices. Nevertheless, given the opportunity to narrate in different realms of life and for different audiences, values of the enterprising person maintained certain values of the socialist era, such as the collaborative person. This ingenious study not only demonstrates the flexibility and precision of values analysis but, more importantly, also provides compelling qualitative findings about the relevance of narrating to political economic change.

Values Analysis in Research on Computer Simulation Game Use

Current global financial systems have effects inside countries even in the absence of revolution or war. One example of such a change occurring across the United States is the emphasis on vocational education. Phil Kreniske studied a remarkable instance of vocational education applied to middle school–age children participating in a community after-school program. Among a range of activities to enhance verbal and computational literacy among pre- and early adolescents living in low-income neighborhoods, one module involved computer-simulated training for the vocation of bank teller (Kreniske, 2012). As described in the research article, the simulation involved the game player as a bank teller having to decide whether or not to cash a check for a friend who has come to the bank in distress needing cash for a personal matter; the friend's account balance will not cover the amount of the check, and the player must decide whether to cash the check or to follow bank rules and inform the friend that the check cannot be cashed (Kreniske, 2012).

Interactive questions appeared in the simulation narrative, guiding the game player to decide whether to comply with the friend's request and other responses, each followed by a grading of whether, according to banking values, the player was correct or not. In addition to assessments of bank-related vocabulary, Kreniske's research design asked participants, before and after playing this simulation game, to write letters to a boss and to a friend about a real or imagined conflict at work. The letter format made the relational nature of the narratives concrete, and the values analysis of the narratives in the letters indicated that especially the older children (seventh and eighth graders) performed the bank values in their letters to the boss participating in the simulation game, while the value of appealing to a friend for understanding increased over time in the letters to friends. The research design and values analysis consistent with principles of dynamic narrating open an area of systematic narrative inquiry that enhances the conceptual nature of the kinds of developmental processes to measure and the scientific nature of assessing change.

This study design and analysis incorporated two types of audiences, the explicit feedback of the simulation game and addressees of letters framing participants' narratives about a conflict at work, presumably imagined, as the participants were sixth, seventh, and eighth graders. Interactive questions appeared in the simulation narrative, guiding the player to decide whether to comply with the friend's request or to follow the bank rules. The letter format made the relational nature of the narratives concrete and presented the opportunity to conduct a multilayered analysis.

Kreniske (2012) analyzed the ways participants addressed their bosses and the ways they addressed their friends, examined whether and how the participants incorporated the values from the computer simulation into their own narratives, and then analyzed how participants positioned themselves in relation to the computer simulation's value system. Each analysis offered critical insight into different ways that the narrators used narrative values to interact with diverse contexts. This values analysis investigated how participants used ultimatums when writing to their bosses and asked questions about perspectives more frequently when writing to their friends. An ultimatum was identified when a participant made a conditional demand using *if* or *or.* For example, KB24 wrote to his boss, "THE EMPOLYIES NEED A HIGHER RAISE AND YOUR BEHAVIOR STINK AND YOU ALWAYS FEEL SELF CONFIDANT TOWARDS THE OTHER WORKERS AND IF YOU DO NOT GIVE US A RAISE OR WE WILL GO ON STRIKE." Using the word "if," KB24 offers her boss an ultimatum—raise employee wages or the staff will strike. In addition, threats were coded as ultimatums. GG, another participant, used a similar formulation to express her desire for a raise. GG wrote to her boss, "If you don't think to give me more money I think am going to have to quit this job."

Coding for perspectives indicated by participants' questions checked for the audience's understanding. For example, KB24 wrote to a friend, "HE IS A STRAIGHT UP LOWDOWN PUNK. HE THINKS I AM THE BULLY ALL THE TIME. NOW DO YOU SEE WHAT I MEAN?" With this short question that ends the narrative, KB24 is checking to see if his friend understands the position he has presented. Like KB24, GG too asked her friend a question about perspective. GG wrote the following to her friend: "So I was just writing this letter to ask you what you think I should do. Love GG." GG uses this question about perspective to solicit her friend's advice.

Results indicated that participants were more likely to give ultimatums when addressing their bosses than when addressing friends. To determine how the computer simulation communicated values, Kreniske examined the simulation narrative. The simulation presented three options, denoted as *A, B,* and *C,* of which the participant had to select one. By choosing option *A,* the participant upheld bank policy and did not help the friend. This choice earned the participant the highest score, "*Great Job!*" The commendation emphasized the value that work rules supersede friendship obligations. With option *B,* the participant faked the boss's signature and committed forgery to help the friend. This resulted in the participant's being "*Fired!*" The reprimand reinforced the video game's value of following work rules over helping friends. By selecting option C, the participant chose to bend the bank rules and cash the friend's check. Participants who made this selection were put "*On Notice*" because they chose to value friendship over the rules of the bank.

In order to study how the participants incorporated the values from the vocational computer simulation, the researcher coded the narratives as either acknowledging or not acknowledging the simulation's value. Participants who did not write about the computer simulation's value were coded as not acknowledging. To be coded as acknowledging, a participant needed to write about the value of placing work rules over friendship obligations. Each narrative that incorporated the computer simulation value was then coded as performing, contesting, or centering (Daiute et al., 2003). A narrative coded as **performing** meant that the narrator agreed with the computer simulation value. For example, Vanessa valued work rules ahead of friendship in her narrative:

> Today one of my best friends came to cash her check she was in a rush because she needed to go to her brother's wedding and she needed to get their on time but their was an problem when I went to cash it I notice that she has past the limit by $50 I made her wait and she missed the bus now she is mad at me and her family to. I fill awful but if I did not do the right thing it would of cost me my job and it was my first day here to. But I am proud of myself it proves to mr that I can follow the rules don't matter in what situation I am in.

Vanessa adopted the computer simulation's values and stated that in the future she will use these rules. She suggested following the rules was important because "rules are rules." Vanessa understood the computer simulation's value of placing job rules over friendship obligations and incorporated this into her letter to a fictional friend. She both acknowledged and agreed with the value system expressed in the computer simulation.

Not all the participants who acknowledged the value system performed it. Bob contested the value of placing work rules over friendship in this example:

> I quit because this job made me lose a friend dat I new since middle skool so I do not want 2 wr0k 4 u any mor3 and I will see see u after u get off ITS PAY BACK TIME U heard

Bob acknowledged the value system but was angry that he had been forced to choose between his job and a friend. He disagreed with the computer simulation's value system and even vowed to seek retribution. Vanessa's and Bob's narratives are two representative examples of ways participants acknowledged the computer simulation's value system.

Finally, a narrative was coded as **centering** when students questioned the computer simulation's value system.

> The reason why am writing this letter is to ask why did I get fired. I think that it is a problem that you had fired me. I don't understand why I got fired I was just helping my friend for her wedding that she had to be to. I thought that it would be ok that I gave my friend some money I didn't know that it was a problem to you or anybody.

The narrator of this letter, GG, is questioning the value of placing work rules ahead of friendship obligations. She juxtaposes the idea of giving a friend some money with the response of the boss who had a problem with this action.

A values analysis is one method for examining how the relatively short inter-action with a vocational computer simulation influenced participants' writing and thinking. Participants called on their prior experiences and current cognitive abilities as they actively engaged with the computer simulation and the simulation's response to their choices.

Subsequent statistical analyses of the value codings indicated that participants across grades incorporated the computer simulation values into their writing differently. Compared with sixth graders, significantly more seventh and eighth graders incorporated the computer simulation's value. Some of the participants used their narratives to perform, while others vehemently contested or centered in relation the simulation's value system.

One explanation for this trend is that the participants' narratives reflected the communication patterns they experienced in their daily lives. Middle school students are accustomed to interacting with powerful others like teachers or parents. The use of ultimatums may have been a cultural tool these middle school students were familiar with in the context of conversations with authority. Therefore, these participants may have used ultimatums in the context of addressing bosses because the ultimatum was a tool they felt comfortable deploying in the context of a conversation with powerful authority figures.

Overall, Kreniske (2012) provides an initial impression of what students may be doing during and especially after playing a video game and how these interactions vary across the middle school age range. These findings indicate that middle school students may not be passively accepting the value systems of the games they play. In fact, middle school children actively engage the embedded value systems presented by digital contexts.

The research design and values analysis are consistent with principles of dynamic narrating, opening an area of systematic narrative inquiry that enhances the conceptual nature of the kinds of developmental processes used to measure change and the scientific nature of assessing change.

Values Analysis of Human Rights Policy and Implementation

Values analysis has been applied to examine how different states parties ratifying the Convention on the Rights of the Child followed through on their promises or not (Daiute, 2008). The analysis (based on the activity-meaning system design described in Chapter 2) was designed to address research questions about the interaction of international treaty making and the practice of children's increasing rights to self-determination. As discussed in Chapter 2, the study was motivated, in part, by scholarly and media reports that human rights treaties were not living up to their promise. The design for this analysis was to include stakeholders working in the international, national, and local spheres of activity to ensure children's rights. Documents from each of these spheres included the CRC treaty first ratified in 1989, national documents entered into the qualifications, and documents from local community organizations. Across the human rights documents sampled for this study, I identified values by each stakeholder actor and found that several specific rights were contested by national actors in particular. The values analysis showed that values ensured explicitly in the CRC, including children's rights to "freedom of thought, conscience, religion," "rights to birth registration, name, and nationality," "protection from punishment," "protection from armed conflict," and other rights that seems basic, like "freedom from discrimination," were contested by the nations that had signed the treaty through a formal process of appeals expressed as "Qualifications and Reservation" and confirmed in "Alternative Reports" by nongovernmental organizations (Daiute, 2008). Each of these contested rights was further in tension with other more important values promoted by the states, such as conformity to certain religions, history of armed conflict, and citizenship stratified by ethnicity or gender.

With these and other examples, we have established systematic, yet accessible, research designs and analytic processes for identifying stakeholders around an issue, ways to identify values inherent to stakeholder expressions, and three positioning categories indicating agreement, disagreement, or change to each value.

In summary, values analysis in four previous studies offers detailed accounts of meaning negotiations, in particular what is shared, diverse, and transformed in narratives by diverse stakeholders around an issue of interest. With analyses across stakeholders in educational, workplace, and multinational settings, patterns of common and divergent values emerge to offer insights about the social as well as the personal nature of narrating. That values of powerful societal stakeholders, such as curriculum developers and human resources departments, are performed by individuals may not be surprising. Also important, however, are the patterns of **contesting**, where individuals, presumably the least influential, do not perform the values of those who create the cultural and institutional norms. Of additional interest is the fact that across these studies, different narrative modes that individuals use, such as fictional and autobiographical and narratives addressed to different audiences, such as friends and employers, provide contexts for using narrative differentially to perform, contest, or transform values.

The next section lists steps in the values analysis process and offers guidelines to help organize that process.

THE VALUES ANALYSIS PROCESS

As detailed below, the values analysis process involves identifying narratives for analysis, ideally across relevant stakeholder positions in an activity-meaning system revolving around the issues of interest (as described in Chapter 2 and briefly above); selecting from among possible expressions by key stakeholders who are likely to interact more or less directly; identifying values expressed across these stakeholder actors; examining the values negotiation process across these actors—positions of performing (uptake of the institutional values), contesting (ignoring or denying or expressing values counter to the institutional values), and centering (creating some new form); and compiling the results of the values analyses.

1. Identify the context, participants, and narratives for analysis, ideally across relevant actors (stakeholder positions) in an activity-meaning system revolving around the issues of interest (as described in Chapter 2).

   1a. Review (revise or create) your research questions to ensure that relevant participants and narrative expressions around your issues of interest will be included in the database for values analysis.

   Remember the idea that actors across the system are interacting with various discursive expressions, as if in a conversation. Narratives, related documents, artistic productions, narrations, transcripts of interviews, transcripts of conversations, and other expressions could be relevant across stakeholders to address your research questions. Researchers' ideas about the necessary diversity across these stakeholders for values analysis are central. Table 3.8 is designed for you to use in making notes about possible stakeholder positions to include.

2. Select narratives and other expressions to enact key stakeholder actors for the values analysis relevant to your research question.

   Consider including narrative and other expressions characteristic of each stakeholder, such as policy statements, website mission statements, operations manuals (such as in workplace organizations), news articles, minutes of meetings, promotional materials, curriculum documents, teachers' presentations of documents, and students' engagements with those that (may) constitute values.

   Using the examples in this chapter as general guides to examining intersecting discourses, consider the ones that are or may be relevant to your research. Which institutions, groups, activities, and environments relevant to your research create and/or promote values (requirements of how to be, what can be said, or sanctions about how not to be, what cannot be said) in your context? What discourses are used? Which ones might you sample? Values analysis is a practical and flexible way to examine meaning in terms of influences, contestations, and change across a system of relationships and activities. Table 3.9 is designed for you to use in making notes about possible stakeholder expressions.

3. Identify values.

   3a. Identify explicitly stated values.

      When identifying values, you can mark the obvious ones, and then, perhaps, also check those that are less obvious.

   3b. Identify implicit values.

      Identify values expressed more implicitly by constructing statements that express connections among topics expressed across these stakeholders/actors.

      3b1. There's a phrase or word that states a value or norm, such as a situation, place, person, idea that is good, bad, beautiful, or some other judgment.

      3b2. There's a sequence of statements, phrases, or words that build to create an assumption about the value of the topics mentioned.

Table 3.8   Identify Stakeholders and Stakeholder Expressions in Your Study

Using this table: Begin with your (draft) research question or focus of your study. If you do not already have a research focus, you could redesign one of the studies discussed in this chapter. List stakeholders and stakeholder expressions relevant to your study. (Consult Chapter 2 for discussions about identifying stakeholders and stakeholder expressions.) After completing this table, proceed to Tables 3.9 and 3.10 to do a values analysis for your study.

Write the research question or focus:

State stakeholders, as relevant to your study research questions or focus	*Narrative (and other) expressions by that stakeholder*
Stakeholder 1 (global, societal, or broadly influencing): Stakeholder:	
Stakeholder 2 (next closest to the focal narrators—national, institutional, and so on): Stakeholder:	
Stakeholder 3 (ecological/everyday in terms of interacting in the actual practices of the narrator): Stakeholder:	
Stakeholder 4 (individuals, individuals from a relevant group, and so on): Stakeholder:	
Stakeholder 5 (other individuals, other groups, and so on): Stakeholder:	

Table 3.9 Values Analysis Guide: Identify Stakeholder Values in Your Study

Using this table: List each stakeholder (identified in or edited from Table 3.8) and the name or number of an expression by that stakeholder. You may have one or more expressions by a stakeholder. For each stakeholder/expression, list the major values (like those identified in Table 3.3). After identifying the values for each stakeholder, make a list of the unique values across stakeholders—that is, the list of values without repetitions (which will be noted on Table 3.10).

Remember: Values are stated as sentences indicating the guiding norms, assumptions, or organizing principles of the expression. If values are difficult to identify directly, list the frequent or focal topics and consider how a value might be linking or combining them.

Stakeholder 1 expression(s):

  Value1:

  Value 2:

  Value 3:

  Value 4:

Stakeholder 2 expression(s):

  Value1:

  Value 2:

  Value 3:

  Value 4:

Stakeholder 3 expression(s):

  Value1:

  Value 2:

  Value 3:

  Value 4:

Other stakeholders and expressions:

3b3. Values may not be literally stated as such in a narrative or related stakeholder expression, but when stating values for values analysis, write them as full sentences.

3b4. If there are topics mentioned prominently or frequently in the narrative or related stakeholder expression, and you think value judgments (beliefs, norms, so on) are being made about them, state the value you think is being placed on those topics. For example, in referring to undocumented youth as "dreamers," there's an implication that being in such a situation has positive value or at least should not be considered as negative, such as when referring to those youth as "illegal" or in the country "illegally."

Grouping values by topic may be helpful after identifying specific values, or before doing so. It is essential to state values as sentences (as also mentioned in 4 above in the section on "Identifying values"), but grouping values by topic can be helpful in the values analysis process, especially when testing the analysis for reliability.[1]

3b5. Values are sometimes most explicitly expressed in narratives by those in positions of influence, power, or speaking for some cause. For this reason, you may find it easier to identify values in stakeholders in the broader societal or institutional spheres of activity before you identify values by individuals. This top-down approach does not mean, however, that values of individuals or those in positions with little influence, power, or resources are less important, so checking carefully in a bottom-up way is also important. For example, if children, undocumented persons, or others in less influential positions are not expressing the values of those in more influential positions, they are likely to be expressing different values, or their silence on certain values may as likely mean disagreement.

4. Identifying values by sentence (or independent clauses if sentences are not clearly punctuated) or meaningful segments in any important visual materials can be helpful. In this process, researchers would segment sentences in writings or transcripts (meaningful segments of visual materials), then identify any value expressed (explicitly or implicitly) in each sentence/segment. There is often a value expressed or enacted in a sentence, although there may be more, and, of course, it is also possible that not every sentence indicates a value, as it may take several sentences for a value to become clear.

5. Examine the values negotiation process across these actors to address your research questions: positions of performing (uptake of the institutional values), contesting (ignoring or denying or expressing values counter to the institutional values), and centering (creating some new form). Table 3.10 provides a template for identifying performing, contesting, and centering.

   5a. Summarize each value (groups of values and the overall values) within and across stakeholder spheres, groups, and individuals to determine which are mutually taken up (performed), are not (contested), and are transformed in some way (centered as unique in some way).

   5b. Addressing several questions is helpful in this phase of values analysis. Which values are performed? Results of the violence prevention curriculum study discussed in this chapter indicated, for example, that values 1, 2, 3, and 4 were performed differently by different teachers in the program, performed differently by their students (who over time performed as their teachers did), and performed differently by students across the school year. Which values were not performed and thus contested? Mrs. Morales contested the value that conflicts can always be resolved, in part by emphasizing escalation and in part by favoring other intervention rather than having conflicting parties resolve the issue themselves. Which values are centered—that is, transformed? The students tended to introduce the value that it's okay to not be friends, to feel jealous, to walk away without continuing the conflict. The analysis of Jeff's narratives included considerable detail about the nature of communication, which is grouped as escalation, connection, or communication more broadly when related to values on a broader scale.

6. Compile results of the values analyses, referring to the questions in 5b. (above) to guide that process. See Chapter 7 when you are ready to summarize, interpret, and report on the values analysis (along with other analyses).

POINTS TO ALLEVIATE (SOME) CONCERNS ABOUT DOING VALUES ANALYSIS

Members of a culture and speakers of a language understand and act on values in everyday discourse. Values analysis involves building on those skills you already have and use in daily life. Clues in the language, like judgment words,

Table 3.10   Values Analysis Guide: Positioning Around Values*

Using this table: After compiling the list of unique values listed in Table 3.9, list the values in the first column below. After listing the values, indicate with an X (or other mark) whether each stakeholder sampled performed that value (either predominantly or some).

Values	Stakeholder 1	Stakeholder 2	Stakeholder 3	Stakeholder 4	Stakeholder 5
Value 1:					
Value 2:					
Value 3:					
Value 4:					
Value 5:					
Any additional values					

*Determine whether each stakeholder performs, contests, or centers each value.

being able to write a sentence stating the value judgment, and checking the value to see if it rings true to the narrative also help. Values are often implied in narrative discourse and other discourse forms as well. For this reason, identifying values involves applying your judgment, relying on what is expressed and what is not. If you find that identifying values is difficult, you may need additional information about the stakeholder, and noting questions about what you would need to know can be helpful. Also, it may not be necessary to identify all values; it may be sufficient to focus on major ones, like those major expectations in a physical or symbolic environment where your focal participants are narrating. Finally, the process of identifying values is iterative (not usually done in one smooth step). For this reason, in addition to repeating steps 2 through 4 above several times to make sure you have identified values and negotiation patterns thoroughly and consistently, you may have to add, delete, or group together similar values. In addition, depending on the nature of your research project and your desired publication context, you may want to do reliability checks, as discussed in Chapter 7.

CONCLUSION AND NEXT

Values analysis is, in summary, a way to consider interaction and changes of meanings in terms of culture, power, and dynamic societies. By selecting expressions from different perspectives participating in the creation and debate of meaning around an issue, a researcher can identify common, divergent, and changing values around the issue of research interest. While it would be fascinating to get all stakeholders in one room for a conversation—such as a president, a mayor, a superintendent of schools, a curriculum developer, teachers with different histories, and elementary school children—such an event is highly unlikely. Even if it were possible, power relations in that room would be incredibly oppressive to, for example, the youngest participants, and the situation would not resemble social interaction in actual life. Values analysis in an activity-meaning system actually resembles the implicit process of everyday social influence flowing in different directions, which might not occur with everyone in the room. With this analysis, researchers can gain insights about values that are in dispute or at least in flux for the less influential participants as well as the more influential. The values analysis design enacts theory about how meaning occurs and develops via interactions across diverse actors using cultural tools for purposeful higher-order thinking.

Chapter 4 focuses on plot analysis, a way to draw on the features of narrative to learn about how narrators are interacting with their environments and integrating those interactions into the very fabric of their stories. While values analysis focuses on organizing meanings of narrative across diverse stakeholders and/or diverse narratives by a participant, plot analysis focuses on the structure of individual or multiple narratives to provide insights about additional meaning in how an author/speaker uses narrative elements for meaning making. I present plot analysis after values analysis, which offers a broad view of the narrative process, but a researcher could embark on plot analysis before considering values and/or before a values analysis is complete. Plot analysis zeroes in on meaning in narrative structure and can be quite satisfying for learning about how participants in research are using narratives as lenses for understanding their worlds.

Note

1. When more than one researcher is doing values (or other) analysis, reliability checks may be required for publication or other purposes. Reliability training (making sure all analysts understand the identified values in the same way) and checking benefit from considering groups of values (on similar topics), as well as from considering the specific values.

4

Plot Analysis

Narratives *appear* to mirror life events. This appearance of art imitating life comes, in part, from the cultural organization of events as plots rather than as a copy of reality. What one recognizes as a story beginning, such as "Once upon a time," is not necessarily where the event began. The plot structure of a narrative maintains order to this means of communication, reflection, and art, while allowing alteration for narrator use. With some familiarity of narrative plot, a reader's pulse might quicken in anticipation about a beloved character's plight as the story progresses. A reader can become frightened or intrigued by what may seem like banal actions—the children walked to the woods; once there, they followed a lovely white bird—escalating toward some sort of danger, as in this climax of a fairy tale: They followed the bird all the way to a cottage of cakes, where they nibbled. Then Hansel and Gretel were lured inside by the old lady who promised more sweets and comfortable beds inside, and then they heard the door slam behind them! (Opie & Opie, 1980). This sequencing of narrative actions is meaningful, as are the words "woods" and "follow."

Allowing ourselves to play along emotionally and thoughtfully with the rising action of a plot is also pleasurable because we sense that the plot will resolve in some way that will relax us or, at least, offer closure. In this way, appearing to be objective accounts of past events—recounting *who, what, when, where, why*—plots are like lenses that guide perception, memory, and interpretation of the dramas of life. Without always being aware, narrators know which stories are worth sharing, which details to include, how to organize those details to capture the attention of their audiences, and which stories are gripping or fun rather than boring. Dynamic narrative inquiry draws on this observation that narratives of life experience make sense in part because of plot.

This chapter focuses on plots as tools for narrative inquiry. After defining plot, I offer examples of plot analysis from prior research and guidelines for the process in new projects. The focus then shifts to script and script analysis, an extension of plot analysis.

Plot is the structure of narrative, including characters (which may be human or otherwise), an **initiating action** or problem (sometimes also referred to as the "trouble"; Bruner, 2002), **complicating actions** that rise to a **high point** (climax, conflict, or turning point), attempts to resolve the problem, **resolution** of the problem, and sometimes a moral of the story or **coda**. Plot is the skeleton of a story, typically imperceptible under the flesh and dressing of the story. Sometimes, the bare bones of a story are repeated, like the familiar plot of conquering victors, "They came, they saw, they conquered," or the plot of a love triangle that ends well for two of the characters, "X meets Y, Y kisses Z, X says 'I love you,' X and Y go off into the sunset." The high point of the story is the focal center of the lens doubly pointed to something salient in life and back to the narrator him- or herself. Details like character names, dialogue, and characteristics of the setting are, of course, important and inextricable from a narrative, but the plot goes deeply into the meaning—in a way that can be examined.

Plot Elements

Plot involves certain lifelike elements, including characters, setting, complicating actions (usually with some in the past), a high point (turning point or climax), resolution, ending, and sometimes coda or moral of the story. These **plot elements** may appear with different elaboration, in different orders, and in different combinations. A narrative must, however, have some combination of elements to express a culturally relevant plot structure. In many cultures, a plot minimally includes character(s) and a sequence of actions, which could be presented as physical, "They came into town, set up a picnic in the park, and townspeople began to gather to figure out who they were," or as psychological, "They saw, they thought, they figured out what was going on!" Narratives may also include substitutes for plot elements, such as by imbuing a setting with humanlike qualities, "If the walls had eyes that day, what they would have seen! Nothing of the sort had happened like those events in the courtroom before that day. . . ." Because using plot elements is common across cultures to share life experience, paying attention to those elements is one strategy that researchers can apply.

Myriad scholars have studied plot and the manifestation of plot in literature, history, and social science, with a concentration of those scholars focusing on the workings of plot in everyday life (Bruner, 2002; Labov & Waletzky, 1967/1997). Literary study shows that plot elements may be included and organized in flexible ways according to cultural, personal, and sociopolitical norms (Bakhtin, 1986). Some narratives offer elaborate settings as backdrops for the main action and characters, while others set the story in time (Ricoeur, 1990). As illustrated below, some narratives develop with numerous complicating actions, while others disentangle a plot conflict with a series of attempts to resolve it.

Just as with sentences, which can be limitlessly novel yet understood by every speaker of a language because of their conformity to local grammar, narrators use plot structure to express and to explore different meanings. This process of watching, perceiving, and interpreting with plot is established in cultural development, so it is a reasonable foundation for understanding meaning in research. Examining plot elements in youth narratives brings the definition of plot to life. The young people who wrote the narratives below contributed to a collection of writings about conflict in young lives from the larger study about the effects of war on young people growing up in its midst (Daiute, 2010).

This narrative by 16-year-old Samii conforms to a basic plot, with a setting, initiating action (trouble or goal), complicating actions, high point (conflict, climax, or turning point), **resolution strategies**, and ending. Samii wrote this narrative in response to a community center activity to "write about a conflict with a peer":

> My friend was acting like she wasn't my friend any more and in school one day, she wanted to fight me. I felt really uncomforterble and I didn't want to have any conflict with her so I went to my counselor and she helped me out. At the end, me and her became really good friends again.[1]

Even seemingly unstructured narratives like this one employ plot elements. The narrative begins with an initiating action, a breach in the normal course of events, "My friend was acting like she wasn't my friend any more," followed by a temporal setting, "in school one day." The central conflict of the plot comes early in this narrative, with "she wanted to fight me." Complicating the action is the narrator-character's reflection "I didn't want to have any conflict with her," which leads to strategies for resolving the plot, "I went to my counselor" and "she helped me out." The story ends with "At the end, me and her became really good friends again." Especially interesting is that English was Samii's second language, yet she constructed a reasonable plot. Table 4.1 outlines basic plot elements in Samii's narrative.

As in Samii's brief narrative, the elements of plot do not always line up in the same way. Samii's narrative, for example, is relatively rich in stating

Table 4.1   Plot Elements and an Example

Plot element	Example: Samii's narrative
Setting	in school one day
Character—primary, plot-crucial secondary	First-person narrator; friend, counselor
Initiating action	My friend was acting like she wasn't my friend any more
Complicating action(s)	she wanted to fight me
High point (turning point, climax)	I didn't want to have any conflict with her
Resolution strategy(ies)	so I went to my counselor; she helped me out
Resolution/ending	At the end, me and her became really good friends again.
Coda	Not applicable to this narrative
Narrator stance	

resolution strategies, whereas 15-year-old Rudy in Bosnia and Herzegovina (BiH) focuses differently in his narrative responding to the same prompt in a similar research setting in another country:

> During the break at school, while I was waiting in the line for sandwiches, a boy from another class put a firecracker in my rucksack which was on my back. I didn't even notice that until other students started to laugh and move away from me. Then I realized that my books were burning, so I threw the rucksack onto the ground, and ran away because I was scared. I was very angry and scared because I didn't find it to be funny, but rather dangerous. The worst thing was that the other students either ran away or laughed; none of them defended me, nobody said anything to that boy.

Rudy's narrative includes some of the same plot elements as Samii's, but the differences lead to very different kinds of accounts of adolescent experiences of conflicts with peers. Rudy begins in a classic way with a setting, "During the break at school . . . ," and proceeds with the initiating action "a boy from another class put a firecracker in my rucksack." Complicating circumstances build with "which was on my back," "I didn't even notice," "until students started to laugh and move away from me," and so on, until the central high point of "I realized that my books were burning, so I threw the rucksack onto the ground and ran away because I was scared. . . . nobody said anything to that boy." The issue of Rudy having been in danger physically and socially remains unresolved in the narrative, but he does offer a final reflection or coda: "The worst thing was that the other students either ran away or laughed; none of them defended me." Table 4.2 compares plot elements in the narratives by Samii and Rudy, illustrating that the former is relatively rich in resolution strategies, while the latter is richer in complicating actions.

Evident in the comparison of Samii's and Rudy's narratives is how different people's applications of plot elements convey the meanings of events for them. The initiating action in one story is psychological—a reflection about how a friend had changed—while the initiating action in the other is a description of an aggressive act, "a boy from another class put a firecracker in my rucksack." The high points of the two stories are also notably different, with one being more psychological, "I didn't want to have any conflict with her," leading to the narrator's report of her strategy to resolve the conflict by going to her counselor. The high point in Rudy's narrative is, in contrast, defensive actions, "threw the rucksack onto the ground, and ran away," and mention of an accompanying emotional response. These differences in the plot high point, such as whether the narrator is focused on psychological aspects of a story or actions, indicate a central meaning of the story for the narrator and for someone understanding it. Although in daily life narrators do not plan plot organization, research indicates that a narrator's emotions, understandings, and social relations intertwine, contributing to meaning, implicitly guided by plot structure—conforming to the rules, learned in life, about what counts as a story.

Samii's and Rudy's narratives seem similar with their focus on peer relations and the adolescent narrators' responses to different kinds of problems with peers. If one rationale for narrative inquiry is to understand people's experiences of social issues, it is important, however, to analyze narratives beyond surface expressions to the interaction of the narrative with the situation. Both Samii's and Rudy's narratives seem commonplace before careful readings and rereadings assisted by a focus on how they organize plot. As shown in Table 4.2 and discussed above, these differences contribute to narrative meaning, meaning that goes beyond the fact that both stories are about difficulties in peer relations. Narrators, then, use plot to create possibilities within the frame of the mundane to interact with their environments, to reflect on them, and, sometimes, to act on problematic situations they narrate. As becomes clear later in this chapter, Samii and Rudy began life in the same place during a war before one moved away to presumably safer ground in the United States, thereby encountering different circumstances in her daily life, while the other remained in the war zone and the aftermath (Daiute, 2010).

Table 4.2 Plot Elements and Two Examples

Plot element	Example: Samii's narrative	Example: Rudy's narrative
Setting	in school one day	During the break at school, while I was waiting in line . . .
Character— primary, plot-crucial secondary	First-person narrator; friend, counselor	First-person narrator; a boy from another class; other students; nobody
Initiating action	My friend was acting like she wasn't my friend any more	a boy from another class put a firecracker in my rucksack
Complicating action(s)	she wanted to fight me	which was on my back; until other students started to laugh and move away from me; I was very angry and scared . . . ; nobody said anything to that boy.
High point (turning point, climax)	I didn't want to have any conflict with her	I threw the rucksack onto the ground, and ran away because I was scared.
Resolution strategy(ies)	So I went to my counselor; she helped me out	
Resolution/ending	At the end, me and her became really good friends again.	
Coda	Not applicable to this narrative	The worst thing was . . . none of them defended me
Narrator stance		

The next section expands beyond plot elements to address the cultural nature of plot as it matters ultimately for narrative inquiry.

Plots and Culture

Embedded in the cultural development of narrating is the concept of plot—the skeleton of meaning—*what happened* based on *what matters*. Because the plot structure—*what happened*—is a human invention, with some remarkably common qualities across cultures as well as important differences, it's *how* the story unfolds in a certain way that indicates some of *why* the story is meaningful. The how and why to structure a story is learned early in life and develops across the life span. The process begins in the most basic way as parents involve their infant in **joint attention**, directing the baby's gaze by pointing, sounds, affirmations, and other signals toward where to look (Tomasello, 2005). As children expand their participation in settings and activities beyond home, they gradually find the shared attention, point, and click into the story there. Even in the earliest phases, the object of joint attention is the high point of an unfolding story—the center of action—around which the relevant people, objects, and actions revolve. For example, as family members point to a pet puppy and teach the baby to pat it gently rather than pull its tail, a scene for joint attention is created. This shared gaze becomes the basis of other teaching as well, such as how to call the furry creature and when to leave it alone. Once a child learns to attend to a culturally shared focal point, jointly attending becomes a habit. Those who expand their horizons by involvement in unfamiliar activities and groups, whether in person or in virtual visits like the imagined visit to a party below, use plot structure (among other tools) to figure out what is going on in the environment. **Plot analysis** is a tool for understanding how participants do this in research discourse as in life.

Researchers have found that most children across diverse contexts of inquiry narrate with some version of a basic plot by around age 11 (Berman & Slobin, 1994; Labov & Waletzky, 1967/1997; Peterson & McCabe, 1983; Stein, 1982). Scholars have learned a lot about how narrating works from a seminal project that asked a wide range of people ages 10 to 72 to narrate their brushes with death or danger (Labov, 1973). As people acquire the ability to share stories in commonly structured ways, their interlocutors gain insights about their experience, because structure contributes to subtle yet important meaning. For this reason, individuals also learn to share experiences with alterations of plot.

Evidence of plot in narratives by people of diverse cultures, ages, and other characteristics suggests the humanity and utility of plot, while differences maintain cultural particularities. Plot allows for comparison around the common structure while not reducing differences in cultural details. The popular Ananse tale originating in West Africa includes elements similar to those in the narratives by Samii and Rudy:

Once there were no stories in the world. The Sky-God, Nyame, had them all. Ananse went to Nyame and asked how much they would cost to buy. Nyame set a high price: Ananse must bring back Onini the Python, Osebo the Leopard, the Mmoboro Hornets, and Mmoatia the dwarf. Ananse set about capturing these. First he went to where Python lived and debated out loud whether Python was really longer than the palm branch or not as his wife Aso says. Python overheard and, when Ananse explained the debate, agreed to lie along the palm branch. Because he cannot easily make himself completely straight a true impression of his actual length is difficult to obtain, so Python agreed to be tied to the branch. When he was completely tied, Ananse took him to Nyame. [The previous episode "to catch" repeats with appropriate variation for the leopard and the hornets.] To catch the dwarf he made a doll and covered it with sticky gum. He placed the doll under the odum tree where the dwarfs play and put some yam in a bowl in front of it. When the dwarf came and ate the yam she thanked the doll which of course did not reply. Annoyed at its bad manners she struck it, first with one hand then the other. The hands stuck and Ananse captured her. Ananse handed his captives over to Nyame. Nyame rewarded him with the stories.

Although oral, ancient, and from a different land than both Samii in the United States and Rudy in BiH, the basic plot structure of this Ghanaian tale turns in ways similar to those youth narratives. As retold in numerous different accounts, the Ananse tale is more lyrical and polished, developed and refined over generations, than the spontaneous tales of two adolescents growing up in contemporary troubled times and places. The Ananse tale includes characters—anthropomorphized protagonists Ananse the spider and Sky-God Nyame and secondary characters including python, leopard, hornets, and dwarf. Like the authors of the other stories, an Ananse storyteller includes an initiating action, Ananse's wanting to solve the problem of no stories in the world and a series of complicating actions, complying with his part of the bargain, to catch a series of other antagonists. The story culminates in the high point, "Ananse handed his captives over to Nyame," and the resolution, "Nyame rewarded him with the stories." The conflict in this Ananse tale is universal and spiritual, as could be expected of the cultural setting and history of such an epic. Nevertheless, that plot is generally available to relate such diverse narratives is its utility, in particular for making comparisons in research, while valuing each narrative for its own expression and context. Repetition of the plot to capture creatures to gain stories from a god in the Ananse tale, for example, may be echoing a local tradition of storytelling. In spite of surface and other differences, the function of plot seems a common quality.

Highlighting the dynamic nature of plot helps to define its form and function in research, as well as in life.

Plots Are Dynamic

Consistent with the definition of plots as structures that guide narrators' interactions in the world is the dynamic nature of plot. Plots are tools for relating to others and to the broader world. Narrators use plots to relate to social and physical environments. Although the primary feature of plot is structure, plots are also dynamic. Because of its role in creating a framework for events, plot is, in the most basic way, relational. Plot provides a relation between events in the world and people's perceptions of these events. Such perceptual and conceptual sensitivities are borne in culture and, in turn, are cultural lenses, at least in part. Plot provides an integrative framework among people who may share and compare accounts of events. In addition to mediating relations between people and environments, plot offers a stage on which narrators can depict relations—among characters, objects, actions, and meaningful life events. Entering into a new group or activity, for example, involves gaining insight about what matters there, who the central characters are, and the meaning attached to the development of character, object, and activity over time.

To appreciate the supportive function of plot in everyday life, imagine you have entered a room where a group of people you have recently met is having a party. Your attention is drawn to what appears to be the center of the scene, the person(s) involved, the actions of those people, and the progression of interactions until the interesting activity dissipates and moves elsewhere. Elements of plots guide what you understand as the story of that party and the one you may share with your close friends later on. Based on your history of hearing and reading, telling and writing stories, you intuitively pay attention to plot structure—setting (where the action is), protagonist(s) (who's making things happen), perhaps also antagonists (who's competing for influence), actions that seem to provoke excitement and resolve it. Not a mere observer, you react to what's going on, with personal curiosity or emotion, to certain participants, conflicts, or resolutions of the plot.

Most important, plots provide recognizable structures people use to communicate with one another. Organizing a story for one's parents and a story of the same experience for one's friends may involve different configurations of setting, character description, complicating actions toward the high point, the turning point, and resolution. A teenager telling his friends about the police raiding a noisy party in a quiet neighborhood emphasized the scene that led neighbors to call the police, humorous details of partygoers' scattering when they heard the cop car pull up to the front of the home, the storyteller's own close escape, and perhaps an ending allowing for heroism. For parents who heard about their child's brush with the law, the same teen might recount the more mundane details, such as about the meddlesome neighbors, the unfairness of the police, and a resolution depicting the narrator as a victim. With such variations, the teenage protagonist is connecting with different significant others and respecting what they have come to know as the bases of their relationships.

Plots are also material, as plot structure connects with the physical environment as well as the social. As mentioned above, the environmental details a narrator selects filter through cultural perspectives. Settings are grounded in physical space, and structure is flexible enough for narrators to adapt to diverse situations. In addition to variation for audience is variation over time, whereby memory of an event may change not only for the audience but also for subsequent information the narrator adds to the story. A plot structure is material as well, because the rhythms of rising and falling narrative action are not only conceptual. As described above, speakers, authors, listeners, and readers sometimes experience the drama of plot development in emotional sensations. Plots also sometimes convey meaning in patterns of repetition of structures and sounds, such as in the sentences of the Ananse tale. Plots are also material, and conceptual, as plot structure connects with the physical environment.

The next section guides a researcher's practice identifying plots and plot elements.

IDENTIFYING PLOTS

Identifying the plot offers a researcher a major insight into where the narrator was attending. The plot is not obvious from cursory readings but is a recognizable structure just beneath the surface of the story. Plot analysis is a systematic way to identify the deep structure of narrative meaning. Because narratives show rather than tell in any explicitly didactic way, deep structure defines meaning that eludes surface analysis alone.

Table 4.3 on page 124, presents two narratives about players in the sport of tennis. Identifying plots in these stories can help you define plot, raise questions moving forward, and, eventually, consider doing plot analysis.

Read the stories about two tennis players in Table 4.3, and follow the guide to identify plot elements. Read the narratives several times, then use the chart in the table to identify any plot elements you recognize. In no particular order, consider for each story the setting (spatial or temporal), characters (whether they seem major or minor in the plot), initiating action (event, thought, or other that indicates a problem or launch for the rest of the plot), complicating actions (subsequent physical or psychological actions that apparently follow from the

Table 4.3   Two Narratives for Plot Analysis

Using this table: Read these narratives several times, until you feel familiar with them. Then, for each narrative, identify sentences (or phrases from the sentences) you think express the various plot elements listed in the first column below. After that, think about and/or discuss how plot structure contributes to the meaning of each narrative and the comparison of the two narratives. Then, write the plot elements for each story in the appropriate column.

Tennis story 1:

The tennis player with the red, white, and blue patriotic sneakers strode onto the court. He walked to center court, smiling and waving to the cheering crowd, and he tripped! This was not a good omen for the impending competition with one of the other tennis greats. Perhaps to make his fall look intentional, he then knelt down on one knee, making a praying gesture as he looked skyward. While doing this, he bumped the beak of his cap, which then fell. At this point, the refs signaled time to start the game. He picked himself up, began with a scorching serve, and proceeded to win all sets.

Tennis story 1, parsed for analysis:

The tennis player with the red, white, and blue patriotic sneakers strode onto the court.

He walked to center court, smiling and waving to the cheering crowd, and he tripped!

This was not a good omen for the impending competition with one of the other tennis greats.

Perhaps to make his fall look intentional, he then knelt down on one knee, making a praying gesture as he looked skyward.

While doing this, he bumped the beak of his cap, which then fell.

At this point, the refs signaled time to start the game.

He picked himself up, began with a scorching serve, and proceeded to win all sets.

Tennis story 2:

The tennis player dressed in traditional whites came through the entranceway, left all his gear, except his racket and a ball, on the sideline, then proceeded to the serve line. This purposeful player stretched, bounced the ball a few times, and stretched his arms with a few racket swings through the air. This player won the first few games, then the set. Although never cracking a smile, he looked confident. That was, however, until his racket broke, after one fast volley. He quickly took another racket from his bag and resumed play. After a disappointing few games, he changed the racket again. This continued through several rackets. But he never regained his original secure footing.

Tennis story 2, parsed for analysis:

The tennis player dressed in traditional whites came through the entranceway, left all his gear, except his racket and a ball, on the sideline, then proceeded to the serve line.

This purposeful player stretched, bounced the ball a few times, and stretched his arms with a few racket swings through the air.

This player won the first few games, then the set.

Although never cracking a smile, he looked confident.

That was, however, until his racket broke, after one fast volley.

He quickly took another racket from his bag and resumed play.

After a disappointing few games, he changed the racket again.

This continued through several rackets. But he never regained his original secure footing.

Plot element	Example: Tennis story 1	Example: Tennis story 2
Setting		
Character—primary, plot-crucial secondary		
Initiating action		
Complicating action(s)		
High point (turning point, climax)		
Resolution strategy(ies)		
Ending		
Coda		
Narrator stance		

initiating action), high point (climax, turning point, or other shift in the narrative development), resolution strategies (attempts to address the initiating problem and/or complicating actions), resolution or ending (the resting place of the narrative), and a moral or final reflection.

Because plot features are regular, albeit under the surface of story, narrative analysts can use them to identify, for example, how seemingly similar stories, like the stories of youth conflicts and the tennis stories, might differ and might be similar. After identifying the plot elements and comparing them with the elements your colleagues have found, consider any contributions of the plot structures to narratives about tennis players, people under pressure.

Based on familiarity with plot, the next section focuses on plot analysis.

PLOT ANALYSIS

Plot analysis involves identifying the basic structure of narratives, allowing for comparison, and consideration of how narrators are using plot. Comparing narratives by an individual as well as across relevant groups in a study is also revealing, especially because speakers and writers interact with cultural norms as they organize and include details in stories. Plot will shift, for example, based on expectations in the context about controversial or hot topics, as in discussions about causes of war, poverty, race, or religion. Narrative speakers and writers are dealing with "the efficacy of a plot, one that reframes the division of our experience" (Ranciere, 2010, p. 115). With plot analysis, researchers can identify some of those diverse frames used by research participants and by researchers in field notes and reports. Researchers use narratives as well to present the methodological process, as Nathan did in his narrative research notes (Chapter 2).

Examples of plot analysis in prior research offer more detail about the nature and functions of plots, as well as the contribution of plot analysis to research.

EXAMPLES OF PLOT ANALYSIS IN PRIOR RESEARCH

Analyzing plots may not open all the meaning in narratives, but this process provides a reliable way to examine how narrators use stories in research contexts and thus the social and political phase of meaning that might otherwise remain elusive. Examples of plot analysis from prior research are presented in terms of the meaning identified with plot analysis.

Plots Interacting With Different Post-Yugoslav Countries

A study with 137 young people ages 12 to 27 who had grown up during and after wars addressed the following research questions: "How do adolescents across diverse postwar contexts narrate conflict?" "How do those adolescents use systematically varied opportunities to narrate conflict?" "What do we learn about adolescents' use of communicative complexity to integrate and transform societal narratives?" The practice-based research considered how young people positioned differently around a war make sense of their own experiences, connect to others' experiences, and relate those experiences to societal issues and their own goals.

In the context of research workshops from the spring to the fall of 2007 (Daiute, 2007), young people, their mentors, their teachers, and the research team created, shared, discussed, and inquired about stories of conflict in the present and future as a positive way to reflect on the past. The research workshop activities involved young people in the development of social history from the perspective of their transition to adulthood. In addition to this motivational and practical purpose, workshop activities allowed for within—as well as across—participant/context diversity, specifically about issues of conflict and development salient in the postwar period. To allow for such complexity, the features of narrative activities were varied systematically so participants could use their developmental capacities for relational flexibility—that is, the diversity of individual perspectives in relation to different narrating contexts and audiences. The hypothesis was that narrators would work with plot structure, among other things, as they interacted with features of the narrating context, such as expectations of present and imagined audiences, power relations among the narrator and the diverse audiences, and features of the physical and social settings.

The study offered participants a range of narrating activities, as discussed in Chapter 2 and listed in Table 2.3. Those different narrating activities are consistent with the relational qualities presented in Chapters 1 and 2. Because in a postwar context conflict remains a controversial issue, even when narrating mundane events of daily life, participants were invited to narrate from a variety of stances, including as more and less anonymous characters in stories of social conflicts. The research workshop involved writing autobiographical first-person narratives of conflicts with peers, third-person narratives of conflicts among adults in the society, and fictional accounts of community events. Such diverse narrating activities elicit perspective-taking processes in relation to the social worlds within and around narratives. The young authors were most personally exposed in the peer-focused narratives and less exposed in the adult-focused narratives, where most, in this study, assumed the stance of observers. Although the first-person stance allowed for a wide range of possible stories, it also exposed narrators to judgment by the immediate audience (researchers, community center directors, and peers) and distant audiences (reflections on the family and society). Recounting a first-person narrative may, of course, be easier and more interesting, self-focused, heartfelt, or authentic, but it also requires the author to consider carefully how he or she will be perceived. In this postwar context, for example, all youth who had been exposed to the media, attended public school, and engaged in public life knew that the Balkan countries of the 1990s wars were being judged for their war-related past, including "ethnic cleansing."

The young people's awareness of such distant audiences, as well as the more present ones who could directly censor war talk, for example, or exert pressure for resilient narratives, may have led to self-censoring in first-person accounts, where their thoughts and actions would be on display as authors, protagonists, antagonists, or bystanders. In contrast, narrating conflicts among adults invited the adolescents to focus on the generation who experienced the war and to express information that someone might withhold if it were to portray him- or herself negatively. The hypothetical community narrative activity offered the most opportunity, because fictional characters have more leeway to express knowledge and issues considered less than ideal or taboo. In this way, we invited adolescents to tell others' stories as well as their own and to narrate openly in autobiography and indirectly in fiction. The fictional community narrative shifts the narrator stance again with a more subtle invitation to narrate conflict by asking a participant to establish two characters "from different groups," albeit leaving open the nature of the groups and asking for completion after the turning point "someone came with the news that changed everything." The narrator is thus freed to express knowledge or subjectivity, such as the bitterness of those who experienced the war, without feeling that he or she might be perceived as personally expressing an unpopular "mentality of the past." The resulting narratives provide data the researchers can use to analyze variations of meaning within and across activities and to learn about the wider range of experience research participants express rather than limiting them to one expressive mode—or plot.

The written narrative mode is relevant for several reasons. Previous research in the United States and internationally indicates that adolescents have the encoding and decoding skills necessary for writing narratives. In addition, the use of computers for many of the workshop activities, including narrative writing, appealed to potential participants and the directors of organizations who recruited them. Moreover, writing narratives provides a medium for comparison to the more explicitly interactive ones in the workshop. Children and youth who are not literate or comfortable with writing have dictated their stories in previous research and can have that option in future research.

In response to one of the narrative prompts, "Write a story about a conflict you observed among adults in society," youth across the former Yugoslavia narrated conflicts about different issues and resolved those conflicts in different ways. Young people observed the adult social world to learn how it is organized. Those growing up in crisis situations were especially astute observers and raconteurs of the troubles in public life. It is thus not surprising that most participants in the research workshop responded to the request for a narrative describing adult conflict (79% to 95% across contexts), although some deferred with comments like "Older people in my community don't speak English so they can't get into conflicts with other adults" or "I have never observed conflicts among adults." Youth in BiH were most likely to write that no conflicts occurred in their society (21%), while denial of conflict occurred less in narratives by youth in Croatia (11%), by youth in the United States (5%), and not at all by youth in Serbia. Claims that adults do not have conflicts are interesting, partly because denial suggests reluctance to perceive and/or report conflict. In other words, whether speakers and writers narrate conflict events has to do with perceptions of conflict in society, as well as experiences of individuals. Interacting with their environments, young people across four positions of the former Yugoslavia portrayed very different landscapes in narratives of conflicts among adults.

After identifying the plot elements in each of hundreds of narratives, I focused on the high point or pivotal issue of the plot in each narrative and then in those narratives by youth in each country. This analysis and compilation led, for example, to findings that conflict issues and resolution strategies differed in narratives across the countries. Conflict issues and resolutions accounted for the full set of narratives, resulting in issues about social relationships, differences of opinion, politics, property/turf, physical altercations, character/emotion, and fate/silly issues. Strategies for resolving those issues included psychological, communication, intervention, physical, and collective action.

The conflict issue in a narrative by Feniks revolves around a difference of opinion about whether to focus on the past or the future. "Adults find it difficult to forget certain things from the past. . . . My opinion is that we shouldn't forget the past but that we must look forward to the future." The author's resolution strategy is a psychological one of compromise: "This problem can never be solved because it exists subconsciously." In contrast, this narrative by Narandjica in BiH is about a physical conflict on a bus:

> One of the conflicts occurred on the bus. I was going back home from school with some friends. The bus was crowded. On the second stop, the door opened and an elderly gentleman was trying to get off, but he couldn't because of the crowd and because in his way was standing another man who himself didn't know where to move! The man who was trying to get off swore at the man standing next to him, who just kept gazing confusedly, not knowing what to do. Then they started exchanging bad words, which was soon followed by hitting each other. The bus driver solved the conflict by pulling over and throwing them both out of the bus.

Many conflict resolution structures in narratives by youth in BiH were physical altercations (33.3%) addressed by interventions of secondary characters (30%). This pattern differed in the narratives from Croatia, where the majority of conflicts revolved around differences of opinion (22.2%) addressed with psychological strategies (38.9%). Yet another pattern dominated in Serbia, with a majority of narrative conflicts in social relationships (26.3%) resolved overwhelmingly via psychological strategies (63.2%). Conflict issues in narratives by youth in the United States were distributed more evenly across strategies, including differences of opinion, politics, property, and physical altercations (15.8% each), all addressed by the similar strategy of intervention by nonprimary characters (52.6%). Also interesting is the overall difference in total resolution strategies applied, with 73.3% of the narratives by youth in BiH including strategies to resolve the conflicts, whereas more than 136.8% of the narratives by youth in Serbia included resolution strategies, often more than one per narrative. As these results show, plot analysis involves identifying plot elements and the focal issue in particular of the high point of the story.

Because there was information from the broader activity-meaning system design of the study (see Chapter 2), I considered these narrative plot patterns in relation to background history, theory, and research questions in the study. Sampling social and political issues in the context, as with an activity-meaning system design or ethnographic study, provides societal narratives to relate to individuals' narratives, thereby facilitating the interpretation of patterns of plot. For example, differences in plot structure across narratives by participants in the different countries supported the plot analysis indicating that youth in BiH perceived the adult world as unstable and requiring assistance. Youth participants in Croatia narrated adult characters as annoying and requiring reflection, in Serbia as socially divided and psychosocially intense, and in the United States as requiring assistance. These differences suggest that young people are attuned to environmental circumstances, even in the adult social milieu. Surprising given previous theory and research highlighting adolescents' obsession with personal identity is the finding that they use narrating as a lens to focus more broadly on contentious issues in the local society, which do not always revolve around identity. For example, the resolution strategy in Narandjica's narrative of a physical conflict is the intervention of a secondary character, the bus driver, which resonates with the situation of the government in her country being under United Nations protection.

As shown in Table 4.4, participants in the research workshops did indeed use a range of plot elements and structures. The table presents their plot conflict and resolution strategies, which differed across three different narrative genres: conflict with peer, conflict among adults, and fictional community event. Most participants across the country contexts organized their peer conflicts around a wide range of issues (relationships, differences of opinion, physical altercations, issues of character, or silly reasons) and used predominantly psychological resolution strategies. In contrast, issues revolving around politics-infrastructure did not tend to occur in narratives of conflicts among peers but were prominent in narratives of conflicts among adults and in the fictional community narratives.

As shown in three narratives by 15-year-old Rudy in BiH, similar yet systematically varied narrative activities yielded different meanings. Rudy used three narrative contexts to interact with different dimensions of social life: his community, the workshop setting, and an imagined world. In his story about a conflict with a peer (presented above), Rudy progressed from being an unsuspecting participant to being attacked, frightened, and isolated.

As also shown in Table 4.4, unique conflict issues and resolution strategies appearing most commonly in the youth participants' adult-conflict narratives, compared in particular to their peer-conflict narratives, are issues of politics-infrastructure and the intervention of a third party to resolve conflicts. Adult-conflict narratives differed dramatically across contexts, and from the perspective of this analysis focusing on differences across narrative genres, one gains independent insights that participants used the scenario of conflicts among adults to address political conflict and the incompetence of the war generation. These young authors were not without sympathy for their elders, but they recognized the problematic nature of the history they inherited. For example, youth narratives of conflicts among adults often reflected on the problematic nature of a presidency that must rotate several times a year to give each ethnic group power,

Table 4.4 Most Common Plot Structures Across Narrative Genres in a Prior Study

Plot element	Autobiographical peer conflict	Autobiographical adult conflict	Fictional community conflict
Issue at high point			
Social relations	X		
Differences of opinion	X	X	
Physical altercations	X		
Politics-infrastructure		X	X
Character/emotion	X		
Fate, silly, no conflict	X	X	
Resolution strategies			
Psychological	X		
Other intervention		X	
Collective action			X

Source: Daiute (2010, p. 126).

persistent petty arguments about property boundaries, meddlesome neighbors, and the older generation's apparent need for interventions to resolve their conflicts, whether in the political realm, such as by the United Nations ensuring human rights, or in the social realm, such as by bus drivers stopping fights.

Young people across contexts used the fictional community context in similar ways but differed in how they narrated adult conflicts and, to a lesser extent, peer conflicts. Several questions motivated the inquiry, with multiple opportunities to narrate conflict. The fictional prompt set up potential for a range of conflicts and strategies to resolve them, either peacefully or not. Interestingly, although participants named groups that opposed each other in some aspect of local life, such as sports teams and political parties, they used the fictional story starter to identify bureaucratic obstacles, abuses of power, and democratic means to counter such abuses. Some, like Moira, focused on identity-group conflicts; many others did not.

Illustrating the different uses of plot structure across narrative genres are two more narratives by Rudy. Rudy's narrative of a conflict with peers, discussed above, reveals complicating actions and a high point where he was a victim, no resolution, but a reflective coda at the end of the story. Rudy puts plot to work in a different way in the following story of a conflict among adults:

> It happened at the crossroads when two drivers got out of their cars and, for some reason, started an argument (probably one of them violated traffic regulations). They stopped the traffic and nearly started to fight physically. The other drivers were yelling and cursing from their cars. A young man interfered and made the two men stop arguing. Personally, I was appalled by the incident and I was particularly irritated because they prevented the others from moving.

Although he also ends this story with a negative judgment, Rudy conveys the emotional tension of the participants: ". . . nearly started to fight physically," ". . . other drivers were yelling and cursing," and so forth. Rudy enters the story in two ways: first, apparently siding with the "young man [who] interfered and made the two men stop arguing," and then with his closing, "Personally, I was appalled. . . ."

With these two brief narratives, Rudy demonstrates his own abilities to feel, project, and judge the morality of a situation. He also astutely observes how adults "prevented others from moving," which resonates with the local political situation. Lest we think him too serious, negative, depressed, or defensive, Rudy crafts another stance in a fictional story.

> The news was that the mayor appeared and told the people who were present that the city administration donated a certain amount of money to the Center so it could obtain necessary equipment such as computers, video recorders, and other technical devices. Everybody was extremely excited and happy. Eventually, they threw a big party attended by the mayor himself.

This story performs positive intentions and actions. After distancing himself from the powerful mob of the school yard and voicing the heroism of a bystander in the chaos of a city street, Rudy uses this fictional story to foreground the generosity of the most powerful man in town, the mayor, to make people happy. Thus, although not explicitly about power, these three stories mediate such relations across a broader system than is evident in any single narrative. As discussed in subsequent chapters, when we consider the range of workshop activities as mediators of living history, we gain insights about young people's understandings of the environments where they find themselves.

Across the fictional stories, "the news that changed everything" is bad, most entailing political obstacles to the building of a community center. For the most part, the narrative plots turn on a range of political issues and strategies to resolve them. Many of the political issues involve abuses of power, such as "the Mayor . . . said he had bought the land from a man and had been planning to build a house," "air strikes started!!!!," "the man took the money [for the center construction] and ran away from the country," "cancelled because they didn't like everyone in the community," "both sides got involved in a bad argument which ended in cessation of any type of collaboration," "was being built on land that does not have the ownership status resolved," "the center would be owned by a foreign company and that no Croats could go there anymore," "a loud factory that would pollute the environment instead," "the government didn't allow immigrants into the U.S. anymore," and another participant's choice of symbolic character, "with time the Greens . . . wanted their capital and their success only for themselves."

Many obstacles revolve around bureaucratic issues, such as "the building did not meet the standards of the local community," ". . . does not have a building permit," and "property illegally purchased." Many others recount competing needs for resources or a general lack of resources: "the money was supposed to be spent . . . for reparation of a dam destroyed in recent bombings," "the state has to finance more profitable endeavors," and "12 million KM [Bosnian currency] was received to build a new embassy." Some of the political economic issues interact with issues of conscience, such as "the Fiat factory participated in the project only because of a tax reduction, not out of genuine concern for the community" and "participants lost their motivation." Some obstacles evolve as twists of fate: "Fire . . . nothing could help—the fire was gigantic," "found dinosaurs under the foundation of the building," "the construction site was a landfall," and "foreign nationals found a massive graveyard."

Along with conflict, the narrative genre presses for resolution tying together the major elements of the plot. As also shown in Table 4.4, the most common resolution in the fictional narratives across contexts is collective action. Examples of strategies for overcoming obstacles include collective political strategies, such as "they signed a petition and demonstrated peacefully . . . since the elections were close," "two years of signing petitions, demonstrations, appearances of their representatives in the media, filing complaints, seeking for public support on the Internet and other media, the City finally decided . . . ," "citizens decided to strike," "they tricked him [the mayor] into signing a document about donating the land for the youth center because he was drunk," "demonstrations were organized," "in the end, by strike, they won," "they agreed that everybody was going to give 10 percent of their salary," "they went up against the mayor and they won and the mayor went to prison for discrimination," and "environmentalists required a more sincere approach." Some strategies are pragmatic, like "they were trying to redirect the fire digging trenches," "they began collecting money," and "some generous people from the Balkans decided to help." Other responses are passive, such as "fortunately a representative of the construction company managed to negotiate terms with the owner" and "the lady from the local government office said she will try to find another location for the project." Of course, there is some giving up, as in "Nothing happened—everything remained the same," and "minorities were offended."

This story by 18-year-old Lolita in Serbia illustrates the plot structure of a political conflict with a collective-action resolution strategy:

Marija and Marko

They had run out of funds and the construction of the foundations had to be delayed or perhaps cancelled if they did not succeed in finding additional support. Marija and Marko, their neighbors, were disappointed. Another failed hope. Nothing again. . . . They decided to talk to the neighbors and to take initiative. They agreed that everybody was going to give 10 percent of their salary (surprisingly enough, everybody was willing to do it). If somebody couldn't afford it, they might have contributed the amount they could. They raised considerable funds and the municipality agreed to make a contribution to the full amount. The building had been finished. It is now an orphanage. Apart from several people who are employed there, the children are being helped by the neighbors who contribute things they no longer need.

Lolita identifies the political economic issue, "the construction of the foundations had to be delayed or perhaps cancelled if they did not succeed in finding additional support," with a corresponding political-resolution strategy, "They decided to talk to the neighbors and to take initiative. They agreed that everybody was going to give 10 percent of their salary." Their effort prevails with political acumen: "They raised considerable funds and the municipality agreed to make a contribution to the full amount." Lolita's approach is similar to that of most of her peers, although some differences emerge across country contexts.

A somewhat different strategy for overcoming obstacles to the hypothetical yet realistic building of a community center to benefit future children is 19-year-old Adin's psychological approach in his narrative from BiH:

> The only bad news that could come at this point is the prohibition of the construction of the Center. The participants would feel awful and that would eventually lead to protests.

Adin includes protests as an eventual strategy but expresses it as a potential consequence of feeling "awful" rather than as actual action. A cross-context difference worth mentioning is the relatively large percentage of young narrators in the United States and BiH who wrote stories without conflicts or, more typically, who claimed that no conflict would occur in such a situation.

The purpose of the review of plot analysis above is to offer information and a research narrative about the nature and contributions of plot analysis with a relatively large research project (a more comprehensive review of the study is available in Daiute, 2010). Plot analysis can also be applied richly to interview studies with fewer participants, as described in the next section.

Plot Analysis of Narratives of Transition From Military to College Life

Another example of plot analysis comes from a study of transitions to college by U.S. veterans of the Iraq and Afghanistan wars (Messina, 2013). In this study of veterans' experiences attending college for at least three semesters after returning from military service, Vienna Messina embedded narrative prompts in an interview about participants' transitions to college life. Among other topics, the researcher asked about particularly memorable events showing the difference between military life and college life. The researcher elicited these narratives as a way to invite a range of experiences and to learn about conflicts facing these students. Plot analysis of these narratives offered invaluable information about participants' peak concerns and goals in military and college life.

Having selected evocative narratives focusing on the transition from military to college life, which were high points in the one- to three-hour interviews, the researcher applied plot analysis to those excerpts. As in the research example above, the analysis involved identifying plot conflicts and resolution strategies in the evocative narratives—2 narrative excerpts for each of 12 interviewees. After identifying the 24 narrative high points, Messina grouped the similar conflicts, examined those conflicts again in the context of the narratives, re-sorted the groupings if necessary, and named the common issue of each group.

The common conflict of the military context (5 of 12) was a conflict attributable to the exigencies of war and its resultant threats to life. For example, one participant focused on the suffering and impending death of an enemy combatant, another alluded to the harm becoming stateless caused a beloved family member when he was displaced in a previous war, and others focused on the demand that soldiers show no weakness, becoming inured to enemy deaths, and the need to disobey an officer who ordered comrades to take an unnecessarily risky action. Less frequent were conflicts revolving around negative personal consequences of failing to respect officers, deceptive practices by military recruiters, and the need to negotiate with a superior officer for a higher performance evaluation.

The following example illustrates a transformation due to the exigencies of war (all names are pseudonyms):

> He was squad leader, . . . He's there, really, 'cause he's been there before and when you get back from deployments, you get new people in. And he, like, that's his job: babysitting the new people—while we get trained by the real—I mean it was RIDICULOUS. He's been deployed like seven times or something RIDICULOUS like that. And he had—I mean it was RIDICULOUS. He ended up with barely any breaks in between. He was just in country, Afghanistan and Iraq, for years. And, um, we were getting ready to pull away and we were—I was "hearts and minds" guy, I was, I think I'm a pacifist or . . . um, I'm not really a pacifist, but I'd like to be . . . as close as I get. And, um . . . he said if he could line up every man, woman, and child in that country against the wall, he'd put a bullet in the back of each one of their heads, so that he could come home. And I was, like, "Sergeant Morton . . ." I mean, I really respected this guy; I really liked him. And I was like, "Sergeant Morton, I . . . you know, I look up to you—I can't believe you're saying this, you know, that, that's how you feel." He said, "Yeah, that's how I feel." And I couldn't believe it—and I understand it now. I, five months in after Nick Robertson got killed, and I would kill every single Afghan. I didn't, I would kill every—I would even kill the interpreter that was my friend. If it saves American lives, you have to make a line somewhere in war: which lives matter? You have to make a line in war. Your lives matter; theirs do not. That's it. (quoted in Messina, 2013, pp. 149–150)

As in many of the narratives of conflicts in military life, the high point in this case is a turning point: "And I couldn't believe it—and I understand it now." The speaker narrated a life-changing experience in terms of the circumstances of war.

Conflicts in the academic context were most often (6 of 12) linked to negative assessments of other actors in the academic environment, with examples including faculty's lack of caring, administrators' lack of direction and accountability, fellow students' lack of collective responses to injustices, and other students' lack of seriousness. Fewer participants focused on self-doubts about succeeding in academia, lack of preparation for academic life, or, in a rare positive light, their own recognition of the care and attention of some academic figures.

Identifying the high points and issues they revolved around offered information about common and diverse issues beyond the literal topics or themes. Messina's analysis of resolution strategies indicated that individuals' actions to resolve conflicts occurred most commonly in narratives of military life, while psychological state resolution strategies predominated in the academic. Notable in conflict resolution strategies in the narratives of military life compared to those of academic life was that participants had completed military service and had opportunities to reflect on those events for at least the three semesters they had been in college (the minimal period for participation). This distance from active duty may explain these college students' reliance on psychological state strategies leaving their narratives open. The plot analysis overall indicated relative uncertainty in narratives of academic life, both in the nature of conflicts and resolution strategies.

The next section summarizes the plot analysis process.

THE PROCESS OF PLOT ANALYSIS

A plot analysis identifies the basic structure of a narrative and, as such, can apply to a single narrative, many narratives, groups of narratives, interviews, letters, or other time-marked discourses. Plot analysis identifies the structure of a plot—most simply beginning, middle, and end—comprised of setting, character(s), initiating action, complicating actions, plot conflict/turning point/ climax, resolution strategies, ending in some combination. The following steps detail the process of plot analysis:

1. Read each narrative, then read it again. When you think you are familiar with the narrative, take a first step at identifying what seem to be its major movements by identifying what you perceive as the beginning, middle, and end sections, and more specifically the plot elements. What can help with this (but is not necessary) is to parse the narratives—to separate the sentences or independent clauses, especially if there is no punctuation or inconsistent punctuation. This guides focus on each part (sentence or group of sentences) of the narrative for how it contributes to the plot. Table 4.5 provides a template for a plot analysis.

Table 4.5	Plot Analysis Guidelines for Your Example or Study

Using this table: Select narratives from your study, narratives you wrote in your work on Chapter 1, or published narratives (citing the sources). Follow the plot analysis process in Chapter 4 to identify plot elements. Write phrases or sentences indicating elements in the column for the narrative(s) you are studying. After that, consider how the plot structures, individually and in comparison, add to the meaning of the narrative and any additional narratives that would be appropriate to collect for your study.

Plot element	*Example:*	*Example:*
Setting		
Character—primary, plot-crucial secondary		
Initiating action		
Complicating action(s)		
High point (turning point, climax)		
Resolution strategy(ies)		
Ending		
Coda		
Narrator stance		

2. Identify the plot elements, including the following:

2a. Setting.

2b. Characters: Major actors in the narrative—protagonist, antagonist, other relevant characters (who may emerge later on in the process, such as in resolution strategies).

2c. **Initiating action:**[2] This action motivates the plot, which the narration then follows through (albeit with inexperienced narrators sometimes in a minimal way). This plot motivator is also referred to as the *breach,* the *trouble,* or the *engine of the plot.*

2d. **Complicating action(s):** Actions building from the initiating action you noted in 2c, above.

2e. **High point:** The pivotal conflict of the plot (character motivations in conflict with another aspect of the story); the turning point or climax where complicating actions reach an apex and then begin to recede to resolution strategies.

2f. **Resolution strategy(ies):** Attempt(s) to resolve the main plot issue; can be more than one suggested or attempted strategy and need not be an ultimate resolution.

2g. Final resolution or ending: Settles the plot conflict or problem in some way, beyond attempting to resolve it.

2h. **Coda:** A reflection on the entire narrative, once completed, typically from the perspective of one outside the events, unless otherwise stated; could also be a moral of the story.

2i. **Narrator stance:** The perspective or point of view crafted in the narrative by the author/speaker; created by the combination of plot elements, such as high point, resolution strategies, and coda, as well as narrative qualities of significance, character, and time (discussed in Chapters 5 and 6). Based on the narrative plot (at this point), especially high point, resolution strategies, and coda, what appears to be the narrator's point in this narrative?

3. Make an outline of major plot elements (such as character[s], initiating action, complicating actions, high point, resolution strategies). Notice, in particular, the major—plot-central/plot-turning—issue or conflict enacted in the high point.

4. This analysis focuses most basically on plot structure, developing, in particular, with the initiating action, high point, and resolution strategies. (Chapter 6 builds in a focused way on the element of character in combination with other narrative qualities discussed in Chapter 5.)

4a. Compile, in particular, the issue(s) expressed in the high point (plot conflict/turning point/climax) across the relevant set of narratives (and/or single narratives) in this plot analysis.

4b. Also compile the resolution strategies.

5. What similarities and differences do you observe across the high points? Table 4.6 displays a summary of such an analysis for Samii's and Rudy's narratives, with a column for a new analysis.

6. What similarities and differences do you observe across the resolution strategies?

7. What patterns of plot structure among the major elements (initiating actions, complicating actions, high points, and resolution strategies) do you see? What do these differences and similarities indicate about what the participants are communicating with their narratives, beyond the specific details of the stories?

8. What observations from this plot analysis address your research question?

As illustrated above, plot analysis is appropriate for revealing within- and across-person differences in attention and meaning, even when there are relatively few participants. Studies with a greater number of participants are likewise appropriate for an analysis of collective scripts.

A summary checklist of the plot analysis process appears in the appendix.

Table 4.6   Analysis of Plot High Points and Resolution Strategies

High point and resolution strategies	Samii's narrative	Rudy's narrative	Your narrative
High-point issue			
Affiliation issue	X	X	
Other?			
Resolution strategies			
Other intervention	X		
None		X	

FROM PLOTS TO SCRIPTS

Script analysis builds on plot analysis to identify an overall structure in terms of the shared meaning it conveys. **Script** is a collective narrative based on the combination of plot elements and logical connections. While plots are like lenses, scripts bring contours of images into view. Plot analysis can be applied to single stories, and script analysis requires multiple narratives to render collective images among groups of narratives organized around similar plot structures.

Scripts are commonly used plot structures, including similar elements and connections between the elements. Scripts are shared ways of knowing, interpreting, acting in the world (Nelson, 1998). Scripts are implicit shared orientations that organize people's perceptions and actions, because they are the naturalized interpretations of events, constructed over time as people explain to each other "what happened" and "why it's important to discuss." Scripts may be common cultural ways of narrating certain kinds of events, also referred to as worldviews, master narratives, or dominant narratives. Scripts smooth over plot elements. Scripts are derived from plots with a focus on the logical connections among plot elements and the meaning indicated by that smoothing. Because scripts are, moreover, collective meanings, they are defined with groups of narratives, while any single narrative can be analyzed for plot. Scripts may also become frozen in circumstances where people feel they must perform certain ways of explaining situations rather than contest or transform public scripts. Nevertheless, nonconforming narratives may emerge from a script analysis, thereby offering information about more and less commonly accepted ways of narrating events and experiences of events.

Scripts are developed and used collectively. Powerful people and institutions promote their scripts—renditions of reality in speeches, writings, and actions expressing their political views, justifications of wars or rationales for reforms, with powerful resources like the media and state-sponsored education programs. While plot analysis ends with a structural description of elements—initiating actions, high point, resolution, and so on—script analysis ends with a description generated from the overall flow, such as a hero/heroine narrative or a victim narrative. A victimization script is unlikely to include resolutions enacted by the main character or at all. A heroic script, in contrast, is likely to include numerous or purposeful strategies for resolving the problem in the story.

Individuals become socialized to their families and cultures via scripts of how to act, what counts as a good person, and other norms of how things go, and groups maintain their practices and ideologies through scripts (Nelson, 1998). Scripting begins in infancy, with the routines that parents and other caretakers use to organize children's mealtimes, special events, and strategies for obtaining support. First words are learned in relation to bedtime rituals, mealtime protocols, play, and other cultural practices (Nelson, 1998). Throughout the life course, scripts continue to serve as frameworks for learning beyond basic language acquisition, extending to sharing experience and knowledge in school (Daiute & Nelson, 1997), which may be quite different from how it is done at home (Heath, 1983).

Scripts are thus excellent analytic tools for studying the complex intersecting individual and collective meanings in research discourse. This dynamic narrating approach adds a method for identifying whether and how scripts occur, rather than assuming that they rely on general common themes or explicit word usage. Scripts may be predicted by the context, but script analysis ideally involves a process of identifying plots, identifying common plot structures, and then naming the resulting scripts for the issues central to the plot. Script analysis builds on a natural process of cultural development whereby language enacts knowledge and meaning as people across the life span experience meaning in the routines of everyday life.

SCRIPT ANALYSIS

Script analysis is an extension of plot analysis. A script analysis involves identifying the combined plot-logic organizing a narrative: conflicts, resolutions, and causal connections among those major plot elements. Of course, we read the young authors' scripts with our own, with questions like, "What scripts do I (researcher) think organize(d) this narrative?" and "What sociocultural forces shape the narrative?" In other words, reading scripts means zooming back from literal statements in the narrative and reading between the lines to gain insights about how a narrator is communicating with the context via the organization of the narrative and other details. Particularly interesting for understanding how groups of young people understand events are the "patterns of similarity" and "difference of conflict" scripts.

SCRIPT ANALYSIS IN PRIOR RESEARCH

Three Scripts Organizing Narratives of Conflict

A script analysis of narratives described above identified three scripts, common for the most part in relation to the political economic local/national circumstances. The plot analysis indicated that conflicts and resolution strategies differed; examination of the common and diverse patterns of plots across narratives of conflicts among adults by youth living in postwar BiH, Croatia, Serbia, and a refugee community in the United States, in particular, revealed three scripts that differed dramatically across the study contexts (Daiute, 2010). This extended analysis, which looked at regularities in the overall plot structure and named the common structures, revealed three major scripts: tensions abound (in public life), moving beyond difficulties, and reflecting on societal divisions.

Youth in BiH narrated conflicts among adults in terms of tensions as they escalated mostly in public life but also in some private settings (hotel rooms and homes)—yielding a script I called "tensions abound." The range of tensions among adults on public transportation, at events to honor war victims, and in other public settings, like school trips, also persists across the narratives. The "tensions abound" script, organizing conflicts around interpersonal tensions, the escalation of those tensions, and their ongoing nature, includes specific types of conflict characteristic in adult-conflict narratives by youth in BiH.

This narrative by Ema focuses characteristically on conflicts among adults in public transportation:

> It is truly difficult to use our public transportation and not to see everyday conflicts between nervous citizens, retired people, drivers and conductors. Usually the problem starts out of nothing, maybe as a result of general unhappiness and stress in people, and then it escalates into something big. In a typical situation everyone is screaming, pushing each other. Conflicts like this one are never resolved, they just serve as a pressure relief.

Ema echoes tensions in conflicts on public transportation. After identifying "nervous citizens, retired people, drivers and conductors" as participants, the author mentions possible causes, "maybe as a result of general unhappiness and stress in people," and escalations, "then it escalates into something big. In a typical situation, everyone is screaming, pushing each other." Ema concludes by summarizing the tension-filled nature of such events. As narrator, Ema situates herself as an observer, entering the narrative by attributing psychological states impersonally with the observations "It is truly difficult to use our public transportation" and "Conflicts . . . just serve as a pressure relief."

That youth in BiH would perceive conflicts among adults in terms of ongoing tensions, in some cases attributed specifically to tensions of the war, is consistent with the local circumstances of human destruction, political division, and protracted economic difficulties. Nevertheless, as in these examples, participants in

BiH also reflected on those tensions for themselves and their readers. Thus, rather than characterizing youth in BiH as victims of trauma because they echo tensions in their society, their narrative performances suggest that they may be using the activity to manage those tensions and to make sense of them.

A script summarized in the name "moving beyond difficulties" was common in narratives in Croatia, which makes sense in a context that has recovered relatively more from the war, certainly in economic terms, than the other contexts. Young authors in Croatia fluently observed difficulties resulting from profound problems such as mental illness among wounded war veterans to petty antagonisms such as arguments about wayward chickens. Nevertheless, although participants in Croatia offered great and sometimes humorous detail to highlight how ridiculous the conflicts among adults can be, they also crafted plots with communication among former antagonists to move beyond the past.

As shown in the following narrative by Anamaria, young people understand local conflicts but also distance themselves from them:

> My two neighbors always fight over a piece of land. The problem is that the hens that belong to one of them always go to the piece of the land that belongs to the other neighbor and she always calls the police and makes a fuss about it. One day, while I was coming back from school, I saw them having an argument. I mean, they are adult women and it is not nice to see them fight and shout and call themselves names. Everyone who was passing by laughed and turned their eyes. Ugly! After the long lasting fight, the conflict was covered up. But every day these fights happen again. Sometimes I feel embarrassed to be their neighbor.

The narrator moves beyond this recurrent conflict by distancing with judgments ("it is not nice . . . "; "Everyone . . . laughed and turned their eyes"; "Ugly!") and a clear personal statement about her embarrassment to be their neighbor and distancing from the situation.

This process of seeing how plot structures across a group of narratives convey similar messages is iterative—that is, involves (a) comparing results of plot analyses; (b) examining the logical connections among plot elements, such as whether there are explanations among a series of resolution strategies, as well as whether resolution strategies are present or not; (c) returning to examine whether and how common script patterns occur within a group of narratives; (d) naming the emerging scripts for the common narrative purpose (i.e., displaying societal tensions or moving beyond war); and (e) identifying narratives conforming to one, another, or none of the common patterns. For the 101 narratives of adult conflicts in the postwar study described above, I removed all the identifiers, mixed the stories across contexts, identified several scripts from the narratives, then re-sorted the individual narratives into groups with common scripts. Interestingly, this revealed that a majority (but not all) of the narratives by participants in BiH conformed to the "tensions abound" script, a majority of the narratives by participants in Croatia and the refugee community in the United States conformed to the "moving beyond difficulties" script, and a majority of the narratives by participants in Serbia conformed to the "reflecting on societal divisions" script (Daiute, 2010).

As such, a script analysis identifies in an empirical way what some scholars refer to as "master narratives" or "dominant discourse" but also the important diverse ways of organizing experience. Script analysis has also been done successfully in an entirely different setting with a focus on migration, as presented below.

Scripts by Immigrants Who Made It and Those Who Did Not

Another study employed script analysis as a method of identifying collective orientations toward immigration. Examining whether and how **narrator perspective** on a specific issue changed perceptions of life-transforming and dangerous processes, Sladkova (2010) interviewed prospective émigrés from Honduras and people who had not succeeded in immigrating, due to any of numerous obstacles, about their reasons for migrating, expectations, and experiences in hindsight. A script analysis indicated a difference in the nature of the migration story depending on whether the participant had reached a U.S. destination or not. Although participants in both groups recounted numerous violent circumstances along their journeys, those who made it to the United States explained hardships from the perspectives of those less fortunate, while those who failed to get to the United States told tales of personal suffering. These kinds of clear and reliable findings are difficult to find with numerous participants, unless the research is organized by design and analysis.

THE PROCESS OF SCRIPT ANALYSIS

Script analysis goes beyond identifying event structure to including the logical connections provided and the overall intent of the narrative. Because scripts are shared patterns, conducting script analysis requires compiling scripts identified across single narratives. Script analysis requires more than a few narratives, preferably by individuals or groups that you posit might differ in ways related to narrating, at least in relation to a specific issue. In addition to realizing why participants might be organizing narratives in different ways, researchers doing script analysis expend this effort because they are willing to be surprised about the nature and extent of common scripting.

The following steps detail the process of script analysis:

1. Begin with a plot analysis of narratives in your data set. Identifying scripts requires at least two narratives, as this concept is defined by collectivity.

2. After identifying the plot elements of each narrative, try three strategies for identifying the script:

    2a. *Smoothing the plot:* Describe the collection of plot elements, such as the relatively long sequence of complicating actions in tennis story 1, and a turning point, followed immediately by a resolution. In contrast, tennis story 2 establishes the confident character with a sequence of descriptions, a turning point, and several resolution strategies with no ultimate conclusion. The comparison of these two scripts for the narratives may be roughly the "victorious clown" in tennis story 1 and the "confident crumbler" in tennis story 2.

    2b. *Making logical connections:* After identifying the plot elements of each narrative, identify the logical connections among the plot elements in each narrative. What are the causal ("because," "since") and other logical connectors ("then") across the major plot events? What organization is implied in these logical connections?

    2c. *Applying master narratives (cultural or expected or identified from skimming):* After identifying the plot, focus on the turning point and resolution to identify possible classic scripts, like hero/heroine story, victim story, victory over odds, and others relevant to the context, the task, and the culture in which the study is occurring.

3. Identify common and diverse scripts across groups of narratives in your study, by groups of participants or by individuals in different narrating activities, such as over time, narrative task/genre, and so on. Questions guiding script analysis at this point include the following: What common patterns occur in narratives within and across locations in a system? What differences occur across the organizations? How do you characterize script, in terms of its approach to the issue?

4. Map these common and diverse scripts for each narrative (or other cultural product) you are analyzing (mission statements, legal agreements, news articles, websites, interviews, narratives, researcher memos-to-self); identify common structures across a group of individual narratives.

5. Discuss the collective nature of scripting in terms of power relations, persuasion, and individuals' management of pressures to narrate certain knowledge and interpretations and not others.

A summary checklist of the process of script analysis appears in the appendix.

CONCLUSION AND NEXT

In summary, plots are tools that guide experience and sense making in everyday life and consequently in research. Because plots hinge on trouble, a sudden turn of events, a breach in the norm, surprise, drama—the same intrigue that makes gossip a staple of human life—plot is the essence of story. For these reasons, plots are telescopic lenses—we use them to organize our stories. Somehow, intuitively, people in social life, good storytellers and even just okay ones, conform to basic plot structures when narrating. Just like travelers on stepping-stones and children who jump within the lines while playing hopscotch, narrators communicate something they know or sense will grab the attention of their listeners: "Did you hear what happened to X?" "Wow, was I surprised when I was on the train yesterday . . ." Once there's some attention from an audience (or an anticipated attention in narrative writing, video, or other virtual production), the narrator makes the story go somewhere. The structure of this "somewhere" involves complicating actions (to create suspense or at least ongoing interest), building toward one apparent point, sometimes then reversing it—and after the point is reached, progressing toward an ending (stories can't go on forever) by resolving the plot, tying together loose ends, and calling it a story.

Plot and script analyses are useful for identifying meaning in narratives gathered for any research project. These analytic strategies, as explained above, provide insights into narrator meanings via a systematic theory-based process. Plot analysis is an advance in narrative inquiry because it offers a way to identify subtle yet important differences in the experiences people share with their narratives. Plots are like lenses narrators use to focus on what intrigues them, concerns them, or functions in another way in a context. Noting the resolution indicates further the narrator's orientation to the high point—whether before or in the process, there's a sense of resolution about the high-point conflict or climax. The overall selection of plot elements and organization of them, as illustrated in the examples in this chapter, provides a basis for establishing patterns of meaning across narratives by an individual, group, or groups determined by the research design. For these reasons, plot analysis indicates the interactive focus of a person's use of the opportunity to narrate experience. The high point of a narrative indicates the author/speaker's focus, question, or concern. In the study across postwar Yugoslavia, plot analysis showed dramatically that participants used different narrative genres to express different issues in their environments and their relation to them, indicating, in particular, the liberating function of fictional narrating. Beyond that, differences by narrators across the country contexts showed that plots of victimhood and responsibility—characterized, for example, by a lack or paucity of resolution strategies in the former situation and numerous resolution strategies in the latter situation—indicated a collective orientation with the present and prior plights. These orientations become a phase of the meaning of narrating about growing up in specific difficult circumstances.

Chapter 5 focuses on the surface expressions of narratives with strategies that research has shown highlight the individuality of narrator meaning, or significance. While plot and script abstract away to meaning expressed in narrative structures, significance analysis examines evaluative devices, as explained and illustrated in Chapter 5, to get to the nuances of meaning, indicating why the narrator is telling this specific story at this specific time.

Notes

Narratives by Rudy (pages 117, 133, 133), Narandjica (page 130), Lolita (page 135), Ema (page 144), and Anamaria (page 145) are from *Human Development and Political Violence* by Colette Daiute. Copyright © 2010 Colette Daiute. Reprinted with the permission of Cambridge University Press.

1. This narrative comes from the Daiute (2010) study described in Chapters 1 and 2.
2. Plot elements shown in boldface in this list are the most important for comparative plot analysis, as illustrated in the tables.

5

Significance Analysis

Significance analysis focuses on individuality and diversity in narrative discourse. Because narrating experience is a social process, a person's perspective is unique yet always relational. People share their experience in ways conforming to certain sociocultural patterns (as discussed in previous chapters), while also expressing individually unique perspectives—the focus of this chapter. Narrators use natural techniques to individualize cultural ways of sharing experience, indicating in particular the significance of the narrative to the author.[1] **Significance analysis** builds on prior sociolinguistic, developmental, and narrative research examining dual phases of meaning in discourse—evaluative meaning and referential meaning (Labov & Waletzky, 1967/1997). The **referential phase of meaning** is the explicit statement, also referred to as content or theme. The **evaluative phase of meaning**, also referred to as individual inflection or style, is implicit. The philosopher J. L. Austin (1962) explained, "The uttering of the sentence is, or is a part of, the doing of an action, which would not normally be described as 'just saying something'" (p. 5). It is this discursive doing that dynamic narrative inquiry extends into research methods, with significance analysis as a major strategy.

Since Austin made his observation, scholars have studied "uttering" as "doing" with the evaluative phase of spoken and written language (Labov & Waletzky, 1967/1997). Evaluative meaning is expressed in the "small words" (Bamberg, 2004b), such as "really," "sort of," "then uh," and the rising intonation indicated by "!" in the sentence "I was really scared when the light went out, and then uh I sort of froze!" Those small words are powerful indicators of the author's meaning. Evaluative devices are indicators of what a person wants to *do* with a narrative.

The *way* a story is told offers clues to *why* it is told. This insight is invaluable to researchers. Significance analysis involves attending closely to the seemingly small and meaningless expressions, which are actually big and meaningful because they point outside the narrative text to activities, relationships, problems, and solutions. As shown in Chapter 4, plot analysis indicates authors' interactions with social and environmental situations. Significance analysis goes further, focusing on how authors evaluate those situations in narratives. Because significance individualizes meaning shared within a sociocultural group, significance analysis offers researchers a tool for attending to particulars, nuances, even quirks in ways that highlight person and purpose in narrating.

This chapter begins with illustrations of significance in action, then defines significance, explains significance analysis, offers examples of significance analysis in prior research, and outlines the significance analysis process.

SIGNIFICANCE IN ACTION

Significance embellishes plots, so when people are narrating personal experiences—the kinds that researchers are often keen to study—significance plays an important role in meaning. Building on the sociolinguistic tradition (discussed in relation to plot in Chapter 4), researchers have found that narratives about challenging situations also offer insights into cultural values, practices, and problems (Berman & Slobin, 1994; Labov & Waletzky, 1967/1997; Peterson & McCabe, 1983). Researchers can read meaning in the way narratives are told, as well as in explicit statements. No less important for narrative researchers is that people like to recount stories of danger and survival. Narrative researchers have examined spontaneous and elicited accident and injury stories because such stories are common fare of everyday narrating. Stories about accidents and injuries tend to include a lively mix of referential and evaluative meaning and integrate physical, cultural, and psychosocial aspects of experience, so, like other narratives of poignant experience, they rely quite a bit on **evaluative devices**.

To define significance and its relevance to narrative inquiry, I offer a series of injury stories as exemplars. Several people I know were hit by cars recently, and each was left with persistent back pain as a result. As told, two of their stories were similar. For this discussion of significance, I slightly adjusted the original narratives to illustrate the nature and use of evaluative devices (appearing in boldface in the examples below). Given the common occurrence of injury stories in life, the following one told to me by Chris might sound familiar:

I was hit by a car one morning. At 20 years old, I had **never** had back pain. My previous injuries were **emotional**—breakup, father leaving, grades, other stuff. The car bumped me and I fell to the ground. At first, I checked and was alive. Then, the **pain** started. I took aspirin but it did**n't** help. The **pain** continued. Now, I am one of those back **pain** people.

This narrative reports an accident, offers a little context, and notes some consequences. The narrative conforms to cultural expectations about human clashes with technology and human survival. This brief factual account sounds like those told to police or insurance claims officers investigating an accident. When interacting with friends, family, and researchers interested in a more personal story, however, people embellish basic plots to express the significance of an event.

Speakers and writers also elaborate stories with exclamations to release residual emotions and to seek understanding in the aftermath. To do so, injury stories are usually elaborated, like this one by Alex:

> I was hit by a car one morning. At 20 years old, I had**n't ever thought** about back pain. My previous injuries were **well, I guess sort of like** emotional—breakup, father leaving, grades, other **stupid** stuff. The car **really just** bumped me and I fell to the ground **hard**. At first, I checked and was alive **and still kicking!** Then, the **pain** started. I took aspirin and that was it, **or so I thought**. But, it was **not, no such luck** for this once **lucky** guy. The **pain** continued. **I tried many different things**. Now, I am one of those **fogey complaining** back **pain** people. But I'm **now only** 21, **you dig!**

Alex's use of *negatives* including "n't," "not," "no," *hedges* including "sort of," "just," "no such luck," and *qualifiers* including "stupid," "hard," "lucky," and "fogey" combine to express a persona unfazed by an accident that could have been devastating. Alex heightens the drama of the story by using quite a few evaluative devices, especially in the second half of the narrative. This specific combination of negative words, hedges, and qualifiers serves to minimize the apparent impact of the accident and to maintain the author's somewhat self-mocking attitude. In this way, Alex uses an injury story to present himself as resilient in the face of adversity, a posture perhaps crafted for an audience of peers.

Another version of the event, like this one shared by Bree, employs a different set of evaluative devices, conveying a very different reaction to being hit by a car:

> I was hit by a car one **beautiful sunny** morning when walking my **new puppy**. At 20 years old, I **had not thought** about back pain **but knew others suffered a lot**, like my mom. My previous injuries were **mostly** emotional **feelings**—breakup, father leaving, grades, **some other minor** stuff. The car bumped me **seemingly pretty softly** and

I fell to the ground. At first, I checked and was **thrilled** to be alive. Then, the pain started. I took aspirin and I **thought** to myself "that was it." But, it **most certainly** was not. The pain continued **day after day, month after month**. Now, I am one of those back pain people, and I can **relate** to them, **finally**.

Bree's use of *psychological state expressions*, especially affect, including "suffered," "thrilled," "relate," "thought," and *qualifiers* including "beautiful," "sunny," "new" invokes emotion and compassion for others more than a self-focus. While Alex uses the narrative to minimize personal vulnerability, Bree uses the narrative to qualify personal vulnerability in relation to others.

Considered together, these injury narratives demonstrate how authors communicate significance. Differences across these injury narratives illustrate the way significance markers build on plots. The words in boldface in the narratives and presented in Table 5.1 are evaluative devices—specific kinds of expressions (words, phrases, graphic markers like "!" representing speech intonation) that linguists have discovered people use regularly as means for indicating the significance of narrated events, why each speaker or author is sharing an experience at that time (Labov & Waletzky, 1667/1997; Peterson & McCabe, 1983).

This chapter on significance analysis is not, of course, only about narratives of accidents and injuries but is about how the evaluative phase of narrating expresses the significance of a narrative to the person sharing it—an invaluable quality for narrative analysis. The next section defines and explains significance in more detail.

WHAT IS SIGNIFICANCE?

Significance is the implicit—evaluative—phase of meaning in discourse. Identifying the evaluative phase of meaning is especially relevant to narrative discourse, where there's more rich illustrative detail than in non-narrative discourse such as the essay. Like good professional writing, which "shows rather than tells" (Strunk & White, 1999), narrative discourse enacts meaning and does so in ways that researchers can appreciate analytically.

Evaluative language interweaves two major strands of meaning. One strand of meaning comes more *from* the world, in language acquired over a lifetime in one or more cultural contexts. The other phase of meaning directs interactively *toward* the world, between the author and audiences.[2] These dual narrating activities occur with precision available to researchers seeking to acknowledge

Table 5.1   Significance Markers Across Three Injury Narratives

	Chris's basic narrative	Alex's story	Bree's story
All markers (evaluative devices) in order of appearance	never	hadn't ever thought	had
	thought	well	not
	emotional	guess	thought
	pain	sort of	beautiful
	not	like	sunny
	but	stupid	new
	minor	really	knew
		just	suffered
		hard	a lot
		still kicking	mostly
		!	feelings
		pain	seemingly
		tried many different	softly
		so I thought	thrilled
		no such luck	thought
		lucky	most
		fogey	certainly
		complaining	day after day
		you dig	month after month
		!	relate
			finally

the dynamics of individual and collective meanings. The referential phase of meaning is what one notices, in explicit statements with nouns, verbs, the words defined in dictionaries, while the evaluative phase of meaning is what we notice less, in implicit expressions with small words, the words between the nouns and verbs, some in the dictionary, others seemingly mistakes or beside the point (Labov & Waletzky, 1967/1997). Compare Alex's "The car really just bumped me" to Chris's "The car bumped me" and Bree's "The car bumped me seemingly pretty softly." The differences in the evaluative expressions affect the meanings the different speakers portray about dealing with adversity.

Referential and evaluative phases of meaning serve different interlocking purposes—one tells the story and the other hints at the purpose of the story. Meaning inextricably involves both. The evaluative phase also builds on literal meaning and plot. Research on oral and written narratives about salient personal events, like involvement in life-threatening accidents or crises, conflicts with friends or loved ones, and other provocative situations, has shown that from early in life (McCabe & Peterson, 1991; Peterson & McCabe, 1983) people use stories to make sense of the social and physical worlds around them (Nelson, 1998), to make sense of who they are (Bamberg, 2004a, 2004b), and to present themselves in ways that connect with, distance from, or try to change situations (Daiute, 2010).

The study of evaluative meaning builds on pragmatics (Austin, 1962), as expressed in the quote about "the uttering of the sentence is . . . the doing of an action" at the beginning of this chapter. Sociolinguists and psycholinguists have extended this work in areas including conversation analysis (Ochs & Capps, 2002; Schieffelin & Ochs, 1987; Schiffrin, 1994) and narrative inquiry (Bamberg, 2004b; Wortham, 2001). For example, one line of inquiry focusing on the uses of pragmatic markers relevant to understanding human behavior, in culturally diverse settings examines colloquial expressions like "aright" and "n'mean" as tools young people use to align with particular ethnic groups and, in that process, perform stances of power, conformity, and individuality in social settings (Reyes, 2005, 2011).

The observation that narrators use evaluative devices to enact personal perspectives is consistent with the explanation that narrating is a dynamic process of person-society relations. This also means that if each story presents an evaluation of a narrated event, if narrators use each story to *do* something in the social world, researchers must examine the range of different expressive moments as valid meaning. Each narrative communicates a bundle of meanings—experience, knowledge, opinion, and self-performance—for the time, place, and purpose of each telling or writing. Discursive events are also linked to a prior history of interactions that shaped how the author constructs a narrative account in the light of prior responses to it. In these ways, each narrative is connected to contexts, the literal narrative text and the author.

Researchers are, increasingly, identifying evaluative devices to understand narrative meaning. This increase is due, in part, to scholarly interest in sampling a range of diverse contexts with a range of outcomes, including learning, social relations, health, well-being in rapidly changing, culturally heterogeneous circumstances, like conflict, migration, education, youth organizations, families, social service, and religious institutions. When explaining that meaning is social, researchers must tap into the social nature of meaning. Rather than analyzing explicit mention of social categories and topics like "peer affiliation" or "rejection," researchers can tap into the social nature of narrating by examining the richness of evaluative devices. Researchers can, of course, ask participants about their motivations and reflections, but researchers should also acknowledge that much of the narrating process is spontaneous, occurring outside awareness and expressed, in part, with evaluative devices. This means that much of narrative meaning occurs during the telling or writing, so intent is often not stated explicitly. Interviews with research participants about what they meant in a specific narrative are, of course, possible, especially when the researcher has some preliminary analyses, like significance analyses, to help focus the conversation.

Based on the theoretical explanation of narrative evaluation, the next section defines and illustrates evaluative devices.

Evaluative Devices

Identifying even a few elements of evaluative language can help a researcher attend more carefully to what is being shared. Categories of evaluative devices include psychological state expressions, intensifiers, qualifiers, causal connectors, negatives/hedges, and valence (positive or negative).

- **Psychological state expressions** are typically verbs, but they may also be related nouns and adjectives evaluating in ways that are *cognitive* (e.g., *think, know, expect, realize*), with subcategories of social cognitions (*disagree, argue*), intentions (*try to, had to*), and perceptions (*see, hear, listen*); **affective** (*feel sorry, sad, cry, tear, happy, smile, want* [desire]); or **reported speech** (*she said*). Psychological state expressions bring persons or personified objects to life in particular ways, so they provide a dimension of consciousness.
- **Intensifiers** emphasize with devices including amplifiers (*very, too* [as in *too much*]), repetitions (*really really* sad, *day after day*), exclamations (*whew! go!*), and exaggerations (*biggest river I've ever seen, quieter than a mouse*). Intensifiers mark the significance of narrative elements (such as the high point or setting) or other evaluative devices, such as a psychological state expression, as in *thought long and hard*.
- **Qualifiers** indicate specific evaluations via the use of evaluative adjectives (e.g., *good, bad, big*), adverbs (*quickly, always*), and comparatives (*more, less*). Although qualifiers may seem like more than small words, qualifiers are judgments, the essence of evaluation.

- **Causal connectors** are evaluative because they build on assumptions about cause and effect, logical sequences and other culturally determined factors (e.g., *because, since, when, then, but, therefore*). Relations expressed by causal connectors are not predetermined, so stating them in narrative and other discourse involves opening the consciousness of a character, author, or narrator, depending on how the causal relation is expressed. Stating "She was different. She left town" differs from "She was different so she left town." The added meaning of "so" sets up a specific relation with implications for the narrative where it appears.
- **Negations** (*no, not, -n't* contractions, negative prefixes such as *unimpressed*) and **hedges** (*kind of, sort or, simply, just, only*) insert a barely noticeable evaluation that something is out of the ordinary.

Table 5.2 on page 158 outlines the different types of evaluative devices in the three injury narratives above. To become familiar with evaluative devices, review the categorizations in this table and make notes in the far-right column to describe your responses to these evaluations, the effect of the expressions for you, as an indication of the effect on the meaning of the narrative. Also consider whether and how you might have used, read, or heard these expressions in the past. The next section guides practice on noticing evaluative devices for significance analysis.

Noticing Evaluative Devices

Researchers wanting to deepen their understanding of meaning by identifying significance can select a sample narrative and make notes about aspects of the situation where the narrative occurred (such as place, time, others present, and purpose). I heard the following narrative in a coffee shop near a college I was visiting. From a conversation among four young adults, I understood that they were college students talking about how their parents' lives were different from their own. To practice recognizing evaluative language, consider the evaluative devices in this transcription of the conversation:

I was doing intake on my job in the emergency room one evening. I heard a noise and saw a group of men walking, then running toward me. I didn't know they were looking for me! I was alarmed when I first saw them, then really scared as they sped up, and ultimately terrified, when I heard someone say my father had done something. I'm a nurse at the hospital and these people could get me first, but I was more worried about why they were coming after me, so angry, for something about father. It's not that I

Table 5.2 Significance Markers in Three Injury Narratives by Types of Evaluative Devices

Using this table: Review the categorizations below and make notes in the column on the far right to describe your reactions to differences across the categories and consider whether and how you might have used, read, or heard these in the past.

Evaluative devices	Chris's basic narrative	Alex's story	Bree's story	Your responses to differences across and considerations of prior use
Psychological states				
Affective	pain emotional		suffered feelings relate	
Cognitive	thought	guess thought dig (understand)	knew seemingly thought	
Speech				
Intensifiers		ever well really just still !	a lot, mostly, pretty, day after day, month after month, finally	
Causal connectors	but	but now	but	
Negations and hedges	not	like no		
Qualifiers	minor	stupid hard lucky fogey complaining	beautiful sunny new softly	
Metaphors and sayings		still kicking you dig!	day after day	

don't love my father but why did he take part in the drug trade!? That was when I realized there is something called "war," and I am part of it, like everyone else.

This "emergency room narrative" begins with the mundane "I was doing intake on my job in the emergency room one evening"—the neatly packaged plot (character, action, setting) then progresses to express psychological states, "I heard a noise" and "saw a group of men walking, then running toward me." Rather than being objective descriptions of events, narratives express subjective stances via psychological states including emotions ("I felt scared"), cognitions ("I didn't know they were looking for me"), causal connections indicating the narrator's logical connections among the various statements ("because I heard someone say my father had done something"), and negations that highlight the narrator's subjective perspective by indicating the out-of-the-ordinary nature of the thought ("It's not that I don't love my father but . . ."). Because this narrative personalizes the discovery plot with psychological insights such as "heard" and "saw," building to "realized," the significance analysis could begin by identifying psychological states.

Table 5.3 on page 160 is a chart for listing evaluative devices in the emergency room narrative and grouping the different kinds of evaluative devices—steps in the significance analysis process. After rereading the emergency room narrative (above and repeated in the table), underline any evaluative devices you recognize. Consult the definitions above as necessary. Then list all the identified evaluative devices in the first column of the table. You may notice that these devices often slip by as you read for meaning, so identifying all the relevant words and graphic symbols may take several readings and/or working with a group of coresearchers or classmates. Use the third column of Table 5.3 to sort the evaluative devices into the categories in the second column. After completing this step and sharing your categorizations with others, use the final column of the table to make notes about how the different categories of devices contribute to the meaning.

After completing Table 5.3, you can begin to identify patterns in follow-up conversations with your coresearchers or classmates. Toward that end, you could address several questions: Is one kind of evaluative device used more than others? Does the author tend to use more cognitive, affective, or mixed psychological states? Which parts of the story does the author highlight with intensifiers? What becomes diminished or enhanced by the use of negatives, hedges, and qualifying adjectives? What effects do these different evaluative devices have on you as a reader? How do you feel about the event, character, or part of the narrative evaluated in this way? You may want to return to this

Table 5.3 Practice Noticing Evaluative Devices in the Emergency Room Narrative

Using this table: Read the narrative below. Read it again and underline evaluative devices. After a third reading, make any necessary changes in your underlining and then list the evaluative devices in the first column of the table. Consulting the definitions and examples of evaluative devices in the text and in Tables 5.1 and 5.2, use the third column to sort the evaluative devices into different categories as listed in the second column.

I was doing intake on my job in the emergency room one evening. I heard a noise and saw a group of men walking, then running toward me. I didn't know they were looking for me! I was alarmed when I first saw them, then really scared as they sped up, and ultimately terrified, when I heard someone say my father had done something. I'm a nurse at the hospital and these people could get me first, but I was more worried about why they were coming after me, so angry, for something about father. It's not that I don't love my father but why did he take part in the drug trade!? That was when I realized there is something called "war," and I am part of it, like everyone else.

List evaluative devices	Evaluative device categories	Organize the evaluative devices listed in the first column into the categories in the second column	Notes about possible functions of the devices
	Psychological states		
	Affective expressions		
	Cognitive expressions		
	Speech-dialogue		
	Intensifiers		
	Causal connectors		

List evaluative devices	Evaluative device categories	Organize the evaluative devices listed in the first column into the categories in the second column	Notes about possible functions of the devices
	Negations and hedges		
	Qualifiers		
	Other notable features		

activity after reading the section headed "Functions of Different Kinds of Evaluative Devices" below.

Based on the prior introduction of the concept of narrative significance—a strand of meaning that augments or sometimes changes literal and structural meanings—the next section discusses significance analysis.

WHAT IS SIGNIFICANCE ANALYSIS?

Significance analysis is a way to study an implicit strand of meaning in the author's evaluation of the narrative—why he or she is sharing a particular story at the time. Significance analysis identifies evaluative devices, including psychological state expressions (affective, cognitive, reported speech), intensifiers, qualifiers, causal connectors, negations, and hedges. Significance analysis also involves noticing the placement of those evaluative expressions, frequencies of evaluative devices, combinations of evaluative devices, and functions.

Researchers apply significance analysis to single or multiple narratives gathered in naturally occurring situations, such as conversations sampled during fieldwork, narrative excerpts from interviews or focus groups, and narratives elicited in a study protocol. Non-narrative discourse, especially certain types of letters or speeches that include narrative anecdotes, also contain evaluative language, although typically not as much or as centrally as narrative discourse. Narratives elicited with a research design, such as an activity-meaning system design (Chapter 2), participant observation during rituals or other practices, pre-post intervention designs, or other research contexts, can sample and elicit narratives to explore intra-individual, cross-individual, or cross-group comparisons in significance meanings around an issue of research interest. For example, varying narrating activities to include first- and third-person author/speaker stances or positive and negative experiences often reveals differences in how an individual understands and/or narrates a situation. Such differences are identifiable with significance analysis.

Because narrating is a dynamic process with meaning unfolding in time, speakers and writers rely on evaluative devices to share experience in the process of telling or writing. Repetitions, exaggerations, exclamations, psychological state expressions, and other devices imply how a person is feeling at the time of sharing. For example, Alex's injury story above conveys an image of someone tough, while Bree conveys an image of someone caring. Differences may have to do with people's different personal histories among those with whom they share specific experiences. Alex was sharing the story with a group of peers whom he may have wanted to impress with his resilience, while Bree shared hers with family members who sometimes criticize her for being uncaring. In addition, different self-presentations are performed not only because audiences differ across situations but also because people might perceive an event differently at different times. Alex, for example, shared his injury event several weeks after it had happened, thereby perhaps with diminished pain or surprise, while I heard Bree's narrative the day after the event. With an opportunity to edit written versions of their narratives, these authors may want to maintain significance markers indicating self-presentation while changing those having to do with how near or far they are from the accident at the time of telling about it. When some of the shock wears off, intensifiers, for example, may no longer seem relevant or expressive of the meaning.

Examining the three accounts of being hit by a car is useful for considering how patterns of evaluative devices indicate significance and the different purposes of such stories. Generally, while Chris stuck to the basics, Alex used relatively more intensifiers, negatives, and hedges, resulting in depicting a challenging event as not such a big deal for him. In this way, Alex's narrative suggests he used it to release tension and to present a resilient self in the face of danger.

Bree's narrative includes fewer intensifiers and more psychological states, in particular of empathy. In that way, Bree presented a stance of affiliation among characters in the narrative, with the possible effect of drawing in those who may hear or read it.

As well as possibly indicating an author's general orientation to an event, significance adds contrast, tension, or other interesting embellishments to plot. For example, Alex created tension by sharing a story about his clash with technology, yet the significance markers of the story yield quite a different meaning—one that minimizes the impact of the car. Bree, in contrast, chose significance markers creating a tension between physical vulnerability and emotional vulnerability toward others. Differences among Alex's, Bree's, and Chris's narratives foreground how uses of evaluative devices can express experience for effect.

Having identified evaluative devices and their patterning, researchers have material for considering narrative use. Toward that end, the next section discusses functions of evaluative language.

FUNCTIONS OF DIFFERENT KINDS OF EVALUATIVE DEVICES

As explained by Nelson (1998), everyday narrating involves using narrative to figure out what is going on in the world and how one fits. Building on this insight, dynamic narrative inquiry examines how different features of narrating—in this case significance—do that work. Defining narrative as performance implores us to consider purpose and function. The presence and patterning of evaluative devices provide systematic means for considering functions of narratives within this broader process of using narrating to interact. Extending Nelson's finding into research methods has led to identifying functions such as releasing tension (Spence, 1984), connecting with others and self (Bakhtin, 1986), and presenting a self-image (Oliveira, 1999).

Functions of significance are consistent with the principles of dynamic narrating (defined in Chapter 1). Relational dynamics, in particular, influence people's significance expressions when they are sharing specific stories for specific audiences. Significance analysis examines author stances around certain events—like narratives of car accidents, emergency room visits, weekend parties, family visits, and other kinds of experiences. Significance analysis offers insights about diversity of meaning within and across participants in research settings as in life. While people may use consistent patterns of evaluation over time, individuals' dynamic use of significance for interacting with specific issues is an important focus of this analytic strategy. Significance expressions depend on power relations, intergroup, interpersonal, or intra-individual factors in explicit or implicit author-narrative-audience interaction. When discussing health care issues, for example, a research participant may offer specific information related to a researcher's interests, but the way that information is narrated may enhance or alter the information. For instance, someone sharing facts about the delivery of a social service may use intensifiers to emphasize how "very very punctual" the social worker was or negatives ("wasn't late" or "lateness didn't bother me") to acknowledge the fact that the person did the job but something else might have been awry. Such nuances of meaning conveyed with evaluative language indicate communicative functions like humanizing, minimizing, qualifying, and connecting. Analyzing significance reveals implicit aspects of narrative meaning, raises questions for a researcher to explore further, and highlights narrative elements that are especially important to the person sharing experience.

Because evaluation is an indication of an author's juggling of personal feelings about an event, features of the event, and the audience for the narrative (actual and presumed), evaluative devices express important information about how the author wants to be perceived with the story as well as how the author feels about it. The patterns of evaluative devices, thus, indicate how a person wants to fit into a conversation, focus group, interview, or other interactive context. These relational meanings contribute to, if not wholly define, meanings shared explicitly in relation to a research issue of interest. The processes described below emerge from narrative research employing significance analysis. These examples illustrate contrasting functions of narratives with different significance patterns. The examples will show how speakers and writers use narratives for purposes of humanizing, minimizing, qualifying, intensifying, and connecting.

Humanizing

Psychological state expressions bring specific persons and symbolic characters in narratives to life as thinking, feeling, speaking beings. Whether and how characters' psychological states are expressed is an indication of author perspectives or intentions about how they would like characters and themselves to be perceived. The narrative by Chris at the beginning of this chapter did not personify an adversary in the accident, mentioning only "the car," which "bumped" the "I" character, presumably the author. The following version of that account includes the driver and something about his perspective (indicated in bold) on the accident. This version of an injury story highlights its use for humanizing.

> I was hit by a car one morning. At 20 years old, I had not thought about back pain. My previous injuries were emotional—breakup, father leaving, grades, other stuff. The car bumped me and I fell to the ground. At first, I checked and was alive. **The driver of that car stood over me, looked relieved, and asked "Are you okay?"** . . .

This narrative mentions the driver and employs evaluative devices that add the driver's conscious perspective. The narrative depicts the driver not only as a person with feelings but also as compassionate, indicated by the psychological state expressions "looked relieved" and "asked 'Are you okay'?"

Another version of the narrative dehumanizes the character with a different combination of psychological states:

> I was hit by a car one morning. At 20 years old, I had not thought about back pain. My previous injuries were emotional—breakup, father leaving, grades, other stuff. The car bumped me and I fell to the ground. At first, I checked and was alive. The driver of that car **just sat there, seemed to be sneering at me, as I lay on the ground. Was he glad to humble one of the increasing number of cyclists— a female at that!—from the streets of our city?**

The psychological state expressions "sneering," "glad," and "humble," as well as other devices, indicate the significance of the accident narrative to a set of presumed biases, in particular biases against an increasing number of cyclists and women. This narrative expresses a psychological state of disgust ". . . seemed to be sneering at me . . . ," intensifying the direction of disgust at women, ". . . female at that!" The narrative poses this orientation as a possibility while condemning the orientation toward someone who "lay on the ground."

The combination of evaluative devices can, thus, humanize a character— that is, present him or her in a positive or empathetic way. In contrast, the combination of evaluative devices can dehumanize a character—that is, present him or her in a negative or unsympathetic way.

Minimizing

People sometimes share difficult or threatening experiences to reduce their own and others' tension or to manage events by presenting them in a distant way—all purposes that create an effect of minimizing events in the narrated experiences. As observed near the beginning of this chapter, Alex minimized being hit by a car by piling on qualifying adjectives to convey irony and toughness, an expression that does the same ("still kicking"), and hedges that minimize events ("ever," "well," "just," "no," "still"), compounded by a lack of affect expressions, perhaps when sharing his tale with a group of male friends. (For studies showing such functional uses of narrating in context, see Bamberg, 2004b; Korobov, 2009.)

> I was hit by a car one morning. At 20 years old, I had**n't ever** thought about back pain. My previous injuries were **well, I guess sort of like** emotional—breakup, father leaving, grades, other **stupid** stuff. The car **really just** bumped me and I fell to the ground **hard**. At first, I checked

and was alive **and still kicking!** Then, the **pain** started. I took aspirin and that was it, **or so** I **thought**. **But**, it was not, **no such luck** for this once **lucky** guy. The **pain** continued. **I tried many different things**. Now, I am one of those **fogey complaining** back **pain** people. But I'm **now only** 21, **you dig!**

Identifying such a pattern of evaluative devices and the possible function of minimizing should not, however, lead to an assumption that the event was unimportant or insignificant for the author. To the contrary, if minimizing is a strategy for mediating challenges, via affective release, negating, mockery, or some other means, that is all the more reason to consider this as significant to narrative meaning in a research project. Having done research with people living in situations of conflict and marginalization, I have learned, for example, that people use narratives to minimize or intensify experiences of suffering to position themselves with or against assumptions and stereotypes in the local area. Such narrative moves do not, however, mean that that the event or related issue is insignificant to the speaker/author.

Qualifying

Differing from minimizing, qualifying in the following narrative adds descriptive words (adjectives "beautiful," "sunny," "new" and adverbs "softly," "a lot," "mostly," "certainly") that evaluate events, people, and settings in narratives to convey a specific meaning.

I was hit by a car one **beautiful sunny** morning **when walking my new puppy**. At 20 years old, I had not thought about my back pain **but knew others suffered a lot**, like my mom. My previous injuries were **mostly** emotional **feelings**—breakup, father leaving, grades, **some other minor** stuff. The car bumped me **seemingly pretty softly** and I fell to the ground. At first, I checked and was **thrilled** to be alive. Then, the pain started. I took aspirin and I **thought** to myself "that was it." But, it **most certainly** was not. The pain continued **day after day, month after month**. Now, I am one of those back pain people, and I **can relate** to them, **finally**.

Bree's narrative enacts a different kind of performance than Alex's by using intensifiers ("a lot," "mostly," "pretty," "most," "certainly," "day after day," "month after month") around positive qualifiers of the perilous event of being hit by a car ("beautiful," "sunny," "new," "softly"), perhaps to portray to her listeners a character generous in spirit even in an hour of personal danger. Some of these evaluative devices minimize the impact to Bree ("seemingly pretty softly," "minor stuff"), but the combined meaning of the evaluation is to emphasize the positive outcome and to empathize ("I can relate . . . finally") with others. This mixed use of evaluative devices highlights the speaker's personal qualities, interestingly turning the narrative gaze back on speaker.

Intensifying

Evaluative devices are often used for emphasis, to highlight a detail or plot element that is or is becoming particularly important to the narrator. Uses of *repetitions, exaggerations, adverbs of emphasis, exclamations,* and *fillers* are implicit material for accentuating meaning.

> I was hit by a car one morning. At 20 years old, I had not thought about back pain. My previous injuries were emotional—breakup, father leaving, grades, other stuff. The car bumped me and I fell to the ground, **stunned!** At first, I did**n't dare** move **at all**, **not even** to breathe. **Then,** I moved a finger, **another finger**, felt **around to** the **very** back of my head for blood, and, **whew! I finally** was **sure** I was **still** alive. That settled, I got up but **felt** a pain in my lower back. It was **sore**.

Whereas Bree used intensifiers of repetition ("day after day," "month after month") to emphasize how fortunate she had been, intensifiers in the narrative above point to a narrative element—the high point of the narrative—marked for special significance. Researchers have observed systematically that a clustering of evaluative devices indicates the high point (Labov & Waletzky, 1967/1997), as in the sequence "whew! I finally was sure I was still alive." Noticing the frequency and position of intensifiers can be helpful in identifying the high point from the author's perspective. Doing so indicates for the researcher the specific details a participant has emphasized among the myriad details in a narrative.

Connecting

Connecting occurs in subtle ways, such as by inserting evaluative devices like "ya know" and "n'mean" as shown in a study of Korean adolescents trying to gain the cachet of African American peers (Reyes, 2011). A narrative author or speaker might also connect to actual and imagined audiences by using very positive evaluative devices to perform an ideal self, or by using negative devices to evoke sympathy (see Chapter 6). Evaluative moves to connect with audiences may include moves to garner sympathy, moves to engender empathy, and self-aggrandizement (Labov & Waletzky, 1996/1997; Oliveira, 1999). Another way to connect is to include specific causal links among referential segments of narratives. Stating logical connections like "because," "so," or "then" belies assumptions about how the world works and thus is an implicit albeit recognizable evaluation of narrated events and characters.

Having read the preceding section on functions of significance, return to your prior work with Table 5.3. Consider how the different kinds of evaluative devices you listed might contribute to the meaning of the narrative. What does the pattern of evaluative devices indicate about how the speaker might have been using the narrative? What evidence do the patterns of evaluative devices provide for a reasoned explanation of how the narrator is using the story? How do those patterns of significance indicate humanizing, minimizing, or other reasons why the author/speaker might have shared that way?

When considering the functions of significance, keep in mind the ones discussed above. Also important to note, however, is that significance functions are not exhaustive, mutually exclusive, or defined in an absolute way. This means that others may emerge in future research. Also, because significance functions occur in relation to the narrative issue and context, they may be narrative-specific to the research situation. In other words, if, for example, people sharing experience understand that a narrative of suffering is expected, a narrative of resilience might be offered. In contrast, if a narrative of aggression is expected, some young people will go out of their way to narrate autobiographical accounts of passivity and compassion. With information about evaluative devices and their role in narrative meaning, researchers have a productive tool for examining such active meaning in new studies. Examples from prior research indicate the patterned nature and fertility of significance marking. Spontaneous narratives gathered in the field, culled from interviews, or elicited in relevant activities may be less sharply varied than the series of injury stories above. Nevertheless, significance analysis provides evidence researchers can point to when considering how a person was using a narrative in social context. Significance analysis is a promising approach for identifying otherwise elusive important narrative meaning.

The next section presents examples of significance analysis from prior research projects.

SIGNIFICANCE ANALYSIS IN PRIOR RESEARCH

Significance analysis in prior research has offered information about diverse personal stances and contributions of identifying those stances in narrative meaning. Presented below are examples from studies by researchers who offer empirical findings of significance analysis in research with people across age groups, languages, and cultural backgrounds in community and institutional settings. Significance analysis is especially useful for identifying individuality in collectives, which involves some examination of intra-individual differences as well. Several studies summarized briefly below offer insights about intra-personal diversity. Several other studies illustrate how significance analysis has identified differences across narratives by groups of people in different circumstances.

Intra-Personal Diversity

If the research design invites participants to narrate from diverse perspectives for diverse purposes and audiences (as suggested in Chapter 2), significance analysis can identify intra-personal perspectives—that is, diverse individual stances in different circumstances about issues of research interest. One such study involved narrative writing about events in history, which an elementary school class was studying, along with current events (Daiute et al., 1993; Daiute & Griffin, 1993). In a public school classroom, the teacher had implemented an open classroom model with students of a broad range of academic skills and ethnic backgrounds. Because the class was typically organized around projects that students would do collaboratively and individually—sometimes using computers, sometimes presenting their work at schoolwide events, and often involving teacher-student conferences—the research design was embedded in the normal course of instruction.

Within the framework of developmental theory (Vygotsky, 1978), the study addressed questions about the nature and effects of students' collaborative writing with an expert, the teacher, and with someone of more similar skills, a peer. In particular, the research design and analysis examined how the teacher would guide students' narrative writing about a series of historical and current events compared with how student pairs would work together and the nature of change in students' narrative writing after collaborating with the teacher and with the peer. Describing all the details of the study is beyond the scope of this chapter; the focus here is on significance as a measure of students' learning and development. The design features most relevant to narrative inquiry are (a) the sequences of narrative writing activities, which included writing five times individually, two times with the teacher, and two times with a peer (the teacher selected the student partners as potentially productive collaborative pairs); and (b) the analysis of evaluative devices and narrative structure in students' individual writings over time, which was a measure of how the different collaborative arrangements became part of their repertoire as narrative writers. To reveal processes and impacts of each collaborative situation on the 16 students' individually written narratives, the order of the nine writings was two individual, two collaborative (with teacher or peer partner), one individual, two collaborative (with teacher or peer partner), and two individual. (Of the 16 students, 8 worked with the teacher first, then the peer, and 8 the reverse.) The writing activities were framed as journalistic assignments, such as "Imagine you are a chronicler in the Renaissance. You have been hired to write a story about a meeting of merchants to discuss the city garbage and smells. . . ." and "Imagine you are a journalist for the Langston Hughes School Newsletter. You have been hired to write about the day Danny in Room 400 broke his leg on the playground." With audiences built into the activities as coauthors and readers of the class newsletter to be compiled and submitted to the library at the end of the study, the narratives were then available for study as social-relational engagements.

Narratives by fourth grader Shara were examined for significance and narrative structure (Daiute & Nelson, 1997). The teacher described Shara, who identified as African American, as a student whose literacy skills lagged behind her other abilities. Shara wrote the following three narratives among the broader nine in the series described above. She wrote one of these three before the intervention began, one after she had collaborated with the teacher, and one after she had collaborated with a peer (these were the first, fifth, and ninth narratives in her series). These three activities asked the young author to write a news story (or chronicle, as relevant to the time period) about a visit to a local museum reconstructed from a Venetian palace, activities at the after-school program, and the unveiling of a dome designed by Filippo Brunelleschi in Florence.

The analysis indicated that 10-year-old Shara wrote narratives conforming to basic structure during and after writing with the teacher, more elaborated narratives after writing with a peer, and a combination of structured and elaborated narratives at the end of the study. The following story is one of the more elaborated versions that Shara wrote individually. Important to point out is that the school, like many others at the time, promoted "invented spelling"— writing words as they sound rather than forcing correct orthography (Graves, 1983)—up through the elementary grades. Notice the many evaluative devices of all types in this narrative.

When they got there they saw a lot of broken stachus. we saw a lot of pichers from famus artist. then are guild gave the tore it was a little bit spcooky because the spirit of miss gardner was on the fourth floor in her will she said she did not want nobody to go on the fourth floor. we explored the museum there was a piucher called the rape of eropy. It was about a god who trured him selve in to a nice bull because if is wife saw him he would and on the roof there was a big piucher of all the gods.

This narrative conveys an engagement with the museum visit and artworks there, which Shara brings to life with psychological states, intensifiers, and other evaluative devices. To indicate the possibility of comparing these, Table 5.4 presents the numbers of evaluative devices in three narratives Shara wrote individually over the time of the study. The overall number of words in each narrative, evaluative devices by category, and the ratio of evaluative devices to words, or the density of evaluation, are relevant to comparing significance patterns across narratives of different fluency.

Another day, Shara shared a different event in the after-school program:

when we came back to the lh school it was time to go home then robin's mother fixst my walk man then I went to after school it fun there but im not to talk about that so what when I got after school I told rosa about my day she said that she wish she was in my class at 5:30 I went home

Table 5.4   Different Uses of Evaluative Devices Across Three Narratives by Shara

Evaluative devices	Museum visit	After school	Filippo's dome
Psychological states	5	5	1
Affective	1	2	0
Cognitive	3	0	0
Speech	1	3	1
Intensifiers	4	0	0
Causal connectors	1	2	3
Negations	2	1	0
Qualifiers	5	0	0
Total evaluative devices	17	8	4
Total words	107	65	78
Evaluative devices/words	0.16	0.12	0.05

Although also a narrative of personal experience, this account seems like a list of events, relatively unevaluated compared to Shara's story about the visit to the Isabella Stewart Gardner Museum.

On another day, Shara wrote the following account about the dome on the cathedral in Florence, full of historical details but with little of the previous evaluative detail.

> the dome of sting marry of the flower was build by filippo brunelesky it took about 10 years he sarted to build the dome when he was 24 years old. filippo travled to rome to and stued the coulmes and the archs and the masterpieces. When he came back he met a man named miclanglo he told him about the dome. Filippo died but the dome was build now the dome his still standing in florecs. THE END

As shown in Table 5.4, Shara used diverse types and densities of evaluative devices over the three narratives. As author, Shara managed the task of each writing activity in part with diverse uses of evaluative devices. She evaluated the two narratives of personal experience—the museum visit and interaction in an after-school program—more densely (number of evaluative devices to total number of words) than she did the narrative about the historical figure Filippo. More revealing of her stance as narrator are the different types of evaluative devices Shara used to bring the two personal experiences to life. Significance patterns across different participants were computed for comparison purposes.

Shara's perspective as a participant in research indicates the intra-personal range of her communicative stances. With significance analysis, the researchers learned that integrating interesting subject matter with personal experience seems to tap into a range of narrating abilities. The relatively richly evaluated narrative of the museum visit involved Shara in new, obviously challenging material about a historical period, about works of art ("rape of eropy"), about a local institution, and about how other people lived from the sensory experience of a virtual visit back in time afforded by the tour. Shara's inclusion of numerous historical facts about the 15th-century artists, paintings, the architect Filippo, and some of his projects in Florence reveals her acquaintance with the subject matter, perhaps less than had she visited Florence but also perhaps because she was able to use narrating to build on readings and role playing related to the period.

These narratives are from a larger study in a fourth/fifth-grade public school classroom where children wrote narratives with their teacher, with a peer, and on their own (Daiute et al., 1993; Daiute & Griffin, 1993). Based on the significance analysis over time, the researchers made the observation not only that Shara wrote considerably less after collaborating with the teacher ("after school" narrative) than before ("museum visit" narrative) but also that she wrote with more personal significance at the beginning of the intervention (0.16 evaluative devices per word) compared to after collaborating with others. Reported elsewhere are similar data for the collaboratively written narratives by Shara and her classmates (Daiute et al., 1993; Daiute & Griffin, 1993). The significance and plot analysis show, for example, that when Shara and others reduced significance expressions was also when they shifted the structure of their narratives to one more like the classic version—catchy opening stating the newsworthy event, introducing two major points with supporting details for each, and a reflective conclusion—that the teacher promoted in her collaborations with the students.

Another interesting finding relevant to significance analysis is that the majority of children in the study tended to include more evaluative devices (relative to how much they wrote) when they wrote individually and with a peer than when they wrote with the teacher. While this may not seem surprising, it offers several insights about the evaluative phase of narrating and for implications about meaning in research discourses. For children socialized in cultural backgrounds different from those of an American public school at the latter part of the 20th century, in particular in terms of culturally different patterns of narrating (Heath, 1983), collaborative writing with the teacher involved learning a new cultural way of narrating. The difference in children's uses of evaluative devices across collaborative contexts and time supports the theory that narrative texts interact with sociocultural contexts and that even inexperienced writers can use evaluation to express their points of view woven into referential phases of narrative. Although Shara, like most of her peers, was not yet a skilled writer, she, like more experienced narrators, chose what to express, what not to express, and how to connect her writing with the knowledge context, drawing on evaluative and referential language to interact strategically in each situation. Such variation in narrative meaning occurs among speakers and writers of all age groups.

Significance analysis has also been used with older youth in community settings.

Relational Flexibility of Different Groups in a Society

A study with 45 immigrant and U.S.-born adolescents in a large northeastern city identified different uses of evaluative devices in narratives interpreting a breach in peer communication in a text message (Lucić, 2012). While immigrant youth from many different countries of origin used evaluative devices differently when narrating about a miscommunication among participants projected to be from their same backgrounds and among U.S.-born and immigrant youth, U.S.-born youth did not employ evaluative devices to make such distinctions. The following brief description offers some highlights of the design, analysis, and results of this study, as relevant to the role of significance analysis in narrative inquiry.

Using a narrative vignette about a miscommunication among adolescent peers, Luka Lucic´ (2012) addressed questions about relations between immigrant and U.S.-born youth: Are there formal between-group differences in projective narratives of U.S.-born youth and immigrant youth? Are there formal within-group differences in projective narratives of these two groups of youth toward the members their own cultural group and toward the other cultural group?

In the vignette, two fictional characters, Alex and Kai, are depicted as engaged in an exchange via text messages. To embed narrating activity among diverse interpersonal audiences, the researcher varied the ethnic/cultural origins of Alex and Kai in two conditions of the study. Participants were instructed to read the following vignette and then answer several questions.

KAI, 10:59:31 a.m.:	Hey, when u r comin over? Let me know, cause I wanna plan
ALEX, 12:36:23 p.m.:	Like around 6 ill b there
KAI, 12:41:39 p.m.:	I thought that you were coming earlier? Why didnt you let me know?
ALEX, 12:42:59 p.m.:	Yea sorry for the late response I was sleeping
KAI, 12:43:34 p.m.:	You could have let me know yesterday?
ALEX, 12:44:28 p.m.:	I was going to but my phone was dead
KAI, 12:49:32 p.m.:	This isn't the first time you're standing me up like this
KAI, 12:52:36 p.m.:	Don't you have anything to say??

After reading the vignette, the participants were asked to narrate responses to several questions from two different relational perspectives—one with Kai and Alex imagined as being from their own birthplace of origin and the other with Kai and Alex imagined as from their own group and another birthplace of origin. The orienting questions were as follows: "What was Kai *thinking* and *feeling* while texting Alex but did not express in text messages? What was Alex *thinking* and *feeling* while texting Kai but did not express in text messages? What happened next? Did Kai and Alex resolve the conflict? How did they resolve the conflict?"

The vignette was like a small story, a narrative unfolding in a conversation, and the participants' written projections were narrative extensions into the conscious dimension of the story. The following is a response by a participant born in Japan.

> Alex and Kai are both Japanese
> youth living in New York City:

Kai was thinking that Alex is always irresponsible and delayed and it is selfish of him. He wants to plan ahead but cannot without knowing Alex's response. He finds it frustrating enough that he has been waiting around anxiously. Checking his phone every few minutes for an hour and a half waiting for a response from alex. To think that Alex was just sleeping and does not think it a big deal that he "blew him off" (in kai's mind) is even more infuriating. He feels anger and impatience and this impact their friendship and Kai's view of Alex. Kai also waited 5min before sending an angry text (12:49 text) even though he had his phone with him.

> Alex is a Japanese immigrant to New York City
> and Kai was born and raised in New York City:

Maybe he was thinking that alex has no concept of what is socially acceptable here—if a friend text you an urgent question you respond immediately, that is the polite way to treat a friend. Maybe he (alex) should spend more times with other American friends, it's not like they are family friends that he has an obligation to.

Findings indicated that immigrant youth used more narrative tools than did U.S.-born youth to make sense of the ambiguous situation in the text messages, not only from the perspective of their own cultural group but also oriented toward their American-born peers. Overall, immigrant youth offered different interpretations of the problematic text message when it was presumed to be an exchange between two members of their own immigrant background and when it was presumed to be between two U.S.-born youth. U.S.-born youth did not do that.

The researcher observed many requirements of a quasi-experimental study, such as varying the order of prompts, coding reliability checks, considering use of evaluative devices in relation to the overall number of words written, and statistical analyses of comparisons. For purposes of this discussion, the application of significance analysis is most relevant. As reported by Lucić (2012), immigrant youth used more logical/hypothetical causal connectors when narrating the interaction as among youth of their same origin than when the text messaging involved a U.S.-born youth with a same-origin peer. In contrast, a preference for affect expressions characterized immigrant youth narrations of interactions with U.S.-born peers. As shown in the examples by participant Hayette, these differences are illustrated with uses of evaluative devices including "but" and hypothetical thinking ("to think that . . . and does not think that . . . ," "even though"). The narrative above with Kai and Alex as a Japanese-born youth and an American-born youth is characteristically shorter than the one projected among immigrants by the same participant, and the density of affect expressions with intensifiers is greater, including emphasis ("no concept," "immediately," "urgent," "more" time) and affect ("acceptable"). The use of causal/hypothetical expressions in particular characterized the narrating meeting of minds, as those markers indicate knowledge and risk in spelling out logical connections and projections. The use of affective intensifiers for the projected communications with U.S. youth suggests an echoing of immigrant youths' perceptions of how their U.S.-born peers do or prefer to narrate. That U.S.-born youth narrated both conditions the same was in striking contrast.

The increased use of causal connectors for the same immigrant group of text messengers indicates a willingness to explain connections between events and characters' interpretations of events, thereby taking the risk of revealing a certain way of thinking. In addition, the relatively stronger ability of immigrant youth to use evaluative devices to differentiate narrative meaning in terms of the immigrant status of narrative characters, even though the immigrant youth were not native English speakers, is also remarkable in terms of the sensitivity of narrative devices and the usefulness of significance analysis potential in research as in life. In summary, Lucić's study offers invaluable evidence of how teenagers use narrating to become part of diverse cultures and use evaluative devices to do so.

A study discussed earlier in this book offers an additional contrast to illustrate how young people use evaluative devices to adjust narratives to circumstances in their environments.

Diversity Across Sociopolitical Situations

The study with young people growing up across four postwar countries of the former Yugoslavia (introduced in Chapters 2 and 4) found that 12- to

27-year-old participants who grew up during and after war used evaluative devices selectively across narrative genres as one means of conforming to and resisting sociopolitical requirements in their ongoing tense environments. In addition, although the 137 participants all began life in Yugoslavia, where their parents had been educated and their lives organized, they grew up during wars that ripped the country apart and in resulting countries with very different political, economic, and social organizations. Narratives by youth across the postwar countries (BiH, Croatia, Serbia, and a refugee community in the United States) were marked with different significance patterns, as illustrated with examples below.

As part of the larger study, young people were asked to write narratives of conflicts in everyday life. These and other narrating activities occurred in the context of workshops at local community centers devoted to youth development after the wars. Setting the narrating, letter writing, and other activities in purposeful context for the participants was the goal of creating newsletters of social history from young people's points of view. (For a complete description and results of the workshop, see Daiute, 2010.) Activities that yielded the narratives below included one using these instructions: "Write about a time when you had a conflict or disagreement with a peer. What happened? How did everyone involved think and feel about the event? How did it all turn out?" Focusing on the different uses of evaluative devices by 21-year-olds Thor, living in Serbia, and Juro, living in Croatia, reveals their skillful use of psychological states, intensifiers, and metaphors, which are very different across autobiographical and fictional narratives as enacted by the two young men. Thor's narrative about a disagreement at a gathering with his friends is quite earnest:

> A couple of days ago, there was a small gathering at my friend's place. As usual, there were several, carefully chosen people. The atmosphere was totally relaxed and cheerful. However, like everything else in life, even a good mood has an end, which happened when one of the friends started bullying one of the female friends who was very dear to me. We exchanged some really bad words and I almost left the gathering. I couldn't stand sitting at the same table with this friend. However, the host helped us calm down. The gathering went on, however, not as cheerfully as before the incident and I will never forgive this friend for doing what he did.

Another activity was to complete the beginning of a narrative describing a realistic but fictional community event: "Using the following story starter, complete your own version of the story":

_____ and _____ (fill in the names of characters from two groups) met at a ground-breaking of the new town center building. Everyone at the event had the opportunity to break the earth for the foundation and to place a brick for the building. It was an exciting community event and everyone was pleased that the new building would mark a new future. As they were working to begin the foundation, _____ and _____ (fill in the names from above) had a conversation about how they would like to make a difference in their town so their children could live happily together. All of a sudden, someone came with news that changed everything!

What was the news? How did everyone involved think and feel? How did it all turn out?

In contrast to his story above, Thor used tools of literary fiction, including reported speech, intensity, evaluative adjectives, and psychological states of feeling, in "Rockers and posers" to express very different experiences of conflict:

Rockers and Posers

An anxious guy came running. He was breathing so heavily that he could hardly speak. "Fire," he whispered. Both rockers and posers started to run, trying to rescue the people who were in vicinity. The fire was approaching us. They took to a safe place all the onlookers. They redirected their attention to a construction site. They were trying to redirect the fire digging trenches. Alas, nothing could help—the fire was gigantic. When the fire ceased, they came to where the construction site used to be. The sight was devastating. For the rockers, it was like a battlefield where their destiny was completed. For the posers, it was like a destroyed path. They went their own separate ways. They no longer hated each other, but they didn't love each other either. There's still hope.

Also more somber in his autobiographical narrative than in the fictional, Juro enacts preferences for cognitive orientations to differences of opinion among peers:

My friends and I were discussing the issue of how hard it was to be in college. I thought it was as easy as being in high school but they thought differently. I had a feeling that they felt the same way I did but didn't want to admit it. Now, being students in college, we have to say that it's hard and that we have to study a lot.

Working this all out via his own reflection, rather than, for example, through narrated dialogue among the friends as characters, Juro relies quite extensively on evaluative devices to express shades of meaning. For example, he uses feeling affectively in the beginning of the third sentence, "I had a feeling . . . ," as in having a hunch, while using "felt" to mean "think," ". . . they felt the same way I did," paralleling thoughts expressed in the second sentence, "I thought it was as easy as being in high school but they thought differently."

In this fictional narrative, Juro maintains his overall cognitive orientation compared to Thor's, while drawing in more affectivity for a dramatic move:

> The news was that the main investor wasn't able to provide the money he had promised and that the building process would be postponed for an undetermined period of time. The citizens felt betrayed. They had the right to protest; they chose this government and now the government didn't want to give them the money that was essential for the town. The citizens decided to strike and the government was forced to give them the money.

During the time of our study, Thor and Juro, both 21, were living in different postwar countries of the former Yugoslavia. Taking into account that Thor wrote more words overall than Juro, one finds that their frequency of evaluating narrative action is about the same: 0.21 by Thor and 0.22 by Juro. As shown in Table 5.5, however, Thor in Serbia and Juro in Croatia had different tensions surrounding them that would require strategic uses of narrative expression around issues of conflict.

Echoing the pattern of playing it relatively safe in autobiographical narratives of conflict—that is, conforming to current cultural norms, such as being in control to avoid escalating conflict, while expressing more counter-conforming views—both Juro and Thor do so in their fictional narratives. Thor's narratives indicate a preference for intensifiers, affective psychological states, and negations, while Juro's indicate a preference for cognitive psychological states followed by less than half with the same incidence affective psychological states and qualifiers. Intensity, affect, and negation emerged as relatively common orientations in narratives by participants in Croatia, and a relative cognitive and qualifying orientation was more common in narratives by participants in Serbia.

In addition to being a difference in style, these preferences enact the uses that narrating appears to have for these young people. Thor's relatively high emotional register of affect, intensifiers, and negations suggests an inclination to use narrating for release, while Juro's more qualified orientation suggests an inclination toward monitoring—whether the environment, self, or the interaction is unclear from this analysis but worth pursuing. Those differences are important

Table 5.5 Different Patterns of Evaluative Device Use in Narratives by Thor and Juro

Evaluative devices	Thor's autobiographical	Thor's fictional	Thor's totals	Juro's autobiographical	Juro's fictional	Juro's totals
Psychological states	7	11	18	10	8	18
Affective	6	5	**11**	2	3	**5**
Cognitive	1	5	6	6	5	**11**
Speech	0	1	1	2	0	2
Intensifiers	7	9	**16**	2	0	2
Causals	3	0	3	3	1	4
Negations	4	5	**9**	1	2	3
Qualifiers	5	3	8	4	1	**5**
Total evaluative devices	26	28	54	20	12	32
Total words	116	138	254	69	76	145
Evaluative devices/ words	0.22	0.20	0.21	0.29	0.16	0.22

Note: Numbers in boldface indicate particularly strong contrasts across participants' narratives.

to consider in any findings and interpretations. Thor employs the narration to restrain a negative emotional intensity, and Juro uses it to reflect.

Given such differences, consistent with those of other youth across Croatia and Serbia, the significance analysis offers evidence that evaluative devices are tools for using narrative to interact with life circumstances. Interesting in terms of significance analysis are the specific differences between the autobiographical and fictional narratives of each author and differences of those between-narrative strategies across the countries. While maintaining a politically correct orientation to others in the autobiographical narrative, Thor used the fictional context to express fear and victimization. Thor, who lives in the capital city of Serbia, known as being the major aggressor in the war, reserved for the fictional narrative his emotional orientation to what would be a thinly veiled bombing, which he experienced as a young teenager during the bombing of Belgrade. In contrast, Juro reserved for fiction his expression of betrayal due to corruption, which young people in Croatia try not to express, as their country was in the last stages of accession to the European Union. A detailed analysis of such pairs of autobiographical and fictional narratives by 77 participants in the same study as Thor and Juro indicates an overall reserving of political issues for fictional narratives, primarily achieved through uses of evaluative devices (Daiute, 2010).

As shown in examples from another study, adult narrators in a very different context also used significance to mediate circumstances of working in dangerous neighborhoods of Brazil.

Using Positive and Negative Situations

As originally discovered in narrations with young people in U.S. cities during the mid- to late 20th century, younger and older people from a range of ethnic backgrounds fluidly narrated events they or others deemed difficult, problematic, or bad experiences (Labov, 1973). Requests to share difficult experiences have proved to be quite rich in expression, effort, and insight.

An interview study with novice teachers in Rio de Janeiro asked the participants to narrate their best experiences and their most difficult experiences as early child-care teachers (Daiute et al., 2012). As one part of a three-hour interview designed to understand how these beginning teachers felt about the dangers of working in child-care centers in favelas, poor isolated neighborhoods with persistent serious daily crime. While resisting mentions of risks or dangers, the teachers used their stories of best and most difficult experiences to indicate how they managed to continue working in the favelas.

Comparing how the speakers evaluated positive and negative events is revealing of the relevance of significance analysis for research design and interpreting narrative meanings. Participants in this study indicated different significance in narratives of best experiences and most difficult experiences, also supporting the mediational function of evaluation in different sense-making processes. The narratives of difficult experiences included more evaluative devices of all kinds than did the narratives of best experiences. The best experiences were narrated more concisely around one central event that made an impression on the teacher—for example, that parents said their children had asked for her—with some evaluation ("feel," "strong," "positive," "too," "big," "trust," "asked"):

I think that the best [experience] was to have stayed with the group of students I was with last year and have accompanied this group. This way, I feel a very strong bond with the parents, a positive recognition in relation to the work that we are already developing, the children too, and . . . there is a strong big trust and especially during the period that I was away, the way girls talked, how the children asked for me, the parents asked, when I was about to come back they told the parents and they were, you know, celebrating that I was going to come back, I think that the best experience was this one, I think that pretty much for the children too.

In contrast, narratives of difficult experiences expressed relatively extensive evaluation from multiple perspectives, especially children's as refracted through issues with their mothers and fathers. Luar's narrative of her most difficult experience is an apt example of this finding:

Yes . . . there was a class in which I stayed that the children were very, like, aggressive, but today, I think that if I had to choose, I would choose two children from my class, one is a boy who is very caring, but who hits all the time, he blinks and is hitting someone and, like, we have spoken to his mother, found out that the mother gets beaten by her boyfriend, who in this case isn't even the father of the child, he is very caring, but he hits all the time! . . . And there's also another girl who, in the beginning of the year, we, like, she always arrived to the day care very hungry, very hungry! And she went and always took the same clothes, then we started to think that she, like, was in need, then we discovered that she had her house buried in those landslides that happened and in the beginning the family really was going through a lot of difficulties. . . . I think these two cases were the worst! (Translated from Daiute et al., 2012)

Such stories are more difficult to follow, in part because of the multiple character perspectives (discussed further in Chapter 6), but they also communicate quite directly with the use of intensifiers ("always" two times, "very" five times, "all the time" three times, "like" five times, exclamations [!] three times), among other evaluative devices.

The significance analysis in that study, combined with other phases of the analysis, showed that the teachers in the study used narrating to manage the many risks of working in dangerous favelas through their interactions and work with children and families, rather than in terms of personal threats. Because these teachers were novice professionals interviewed at their training college by professional researchers, they understandably would want to present as rational and in control as much as possible. Being asked for negative stories, thus, provided contexts for expressing intense affect, while stories framed as positive drew relatively reasoned expressions.

In summary, this prior research indicates that significance analysis of evaluative devices overall, by type, and by valence highlights the use function of narrating, offers a systematic way to identify the author's personal meaning of common events, and foregrounds certain kinds of narratives as especially useful for sense making. Reconsidering research designs in light of significance is worthwhile. Although it has not been used in narrative inquiry as much as content analysis or thematic analysis, there is increasing evidence that significance is an important and interesting aspect of meaning. Narrative inquiry research designs, like sensitivity to sampling across an activity-meaning system, as discussed in Chapter 2, can take advantage of the fact that narratives are imbued with especially rich personal stylistic tools for interacting with the narrating context. Those interactions, as discussed in this chapter with evaluative devices, bring an otherwise silent aspect of meaning into view.

As shown with the prior research examples, multiple narrating opportunities in a research design engage significance to express intra-individual diversity and intergroup diversities. Eliciting such diversities in the activity of narrating as well as in sampling relevant participants ensures that contemporary issues will emerge rather than assuming that categories like gender, ethnicity, age, and sexuality operate in stable and consistent ways within populations and individuals. When an activity-meaning system is in place to sample different positions around the issue of research interest, individuals have the opportunity to narrate for different purposes from diverse perspectives in relation to diverse audiences. As illustrated in the examples above, being invited to narrate best and worst experiences in autobiographical and fictional narrative genres and from first- and third-person perspectives (which will be a focus of Chapter 6) involves participants to use diverse patterns of significance around the issues of interest. Having multiple opportunities to narrate elicits complex significance—that is, the personal judgment phase of narrating. A systematic yet flexible analytic strategy, significance should offer new applications and findings for the future.

The next section outlines the significance analysis process.

THE PROCESS OF SIGNIFICANCE ANALYSIS

The process of significance analysis involves identifying evaluative devices in one or more narratives or narrative excerpts by an individual or groups. A summary of the steps in significance analysis follows:

1. Read each narrative, then read it again.

2. When you think you are familiar with the narrative or corpus you would like to analyze, take a first step to identify in a general way the evaluative devices. (See the subsection "Evaluative Devices" above and Tables 5.2 and 5.3 for lists of evaluative devices with examples.)

3. Focus on identifying one device at a time, all the way through, then checking after you have completed a first pass on all. For example, begin by identifying psychological states to get a sense of how the narrative expresses consciousness. Then focus on the next device, usually intensifiers, and so on. In a second round of analysis, review the narrative to identify any evaluative devices you may have previously missed. Then check your list of evaluative devices against the original narrative to make sure you identified each accurately. If you are working with paper and pencil or with transcription in a document on the computer, you can color code the different devices. When working with analysis software, like ATLAS.ti, NVivo, MAXQDA, or another data analysis system create "codes" for evaluative device categories in the pull-down menu options.

Table 5.6 is designed for you to use in identifying psychological state expressions, specifically affective, cognitive, and reported speech, in narratives from your research or experience, including the narratives of best and most difficult experiences written for activities in Chapter 2.

4. Identify frequencies of evaluative devices and different types of evaluative devices.

If there are differences in the lengths of the narratives you are comparing, include the number of words per narrative and compute the density of evaluation—that is, the number of evaluative devices overall or by type of evaluative device divided by the number of words. Insert these facts in the appropriate rows in Table 5.6.

After you have identified the full range of evaluative devices and categories of evaluations, you can systematically narrow to those features that are most representative among your focal participant(s) or those that indicate important similarities and differences across narratives or participants in relation to your research interest (as in Lucić, 2012).

5. Identify patterns of evaluative device expressions by individual, group, or some other factor relevant to your study. Based on frequencies, densities (number of evaluative devices per overall number of words in the narrative), and placement of evaluative devices of different kinds, observe similarity, difference, and change over context, time, or other qualities relevant to your research questions and design.

Notice the following: What are the patterns of frequency, density, and kind of evaluative devices per narrative, groups of narratives, and so on?

Table 5.6   Evaluative Devices in Narratives in Your Study

Using this table: Select narratives you have written, gathered in research, or identified in public or published sources. Complete this table with evaluative devices to learn more about the meaning of the narrative and embark on a significance analysis. Follow this step with any others that seem appropriate, such as identifying frequencies, functions, and considerations about how participants are using narrative to enact meaning.

Evaluative devices	Discursive event(s) 1	Discursive event(s) 2	Your "best experience" narrative	Your "worst experience" narrative
Psychological states				
Affective				
Cognitive				
Speech				
Intensifiers				
Causal connectors				
Negations and hedges				

(Continued)

Table 5.6   (Continued)

Evaluative devices	Discursive event(s) 1	Discursive event(s) 2	Your "best experience" narrative	Your "worst experience" narrative
Qualifiers				
Total evaluative devices				
Total words				
Evaluative devices/ words				

At what point(s) in the discursive event(s) (plot) is there evaluative intensity? This clustering can help you identify high points/turning points you found via plot analysis. How does this reading help expand your ideas about the meaning of the discursive event, the significance of the "story" for the storyteller? What do you learn that augments your other readings of the narrative(s)?

6. Identify functions of significance, first by paying attention to the effects of evaluation on you as a reader, and then by considering some of the common functions along with different kinds of evaluative devices that sometimes indicate these functions:

   Humanizing: Pay attention to psychological state expressions in particular, noticing the ones that are used, how those enact a character consciousness or other element, whether and how other evaluative devices highlight this humanizing or dehumanizing function.

   Minimizing: Pay attention to uses of negatives, hedges, or combinations of intensifiers that are deflated with other kinds of evaluative devices.

   Intensifying: Pay attention to where evaluative devices cluster in a narrative, if they do, and notice what is going on at that point in the narrative action and consciousness, how the plot builds toward and away from that point.

Connecting logically: Pay attention to causal connectors to consider the type of logical connections that are being made with the narrative.

What other functions do you notice based on significance patterns in your database of narratives and other discourses? What functions are suggested by the narrating context, such as what connections seem especially called for or silenced? Considering significance analysis in relation to values analysis would be helpful in addressing this question, if it seems relevant to the patterns of evaluative language and the overall study.

After this exploration, summarize the function(s) you believe add to the meaning of the narrative, support with your analysis, and include examples of full or excerpted narratives to support your observation of this function.

The following steps are also explained and supported in Chapter 7.

7. Summarize your findings. You can check evaluative device categories that seem prevalent in and across discursive events in the study. Which kinds of evaluative devices are used most in this discursive event? With what frequency, if applicable? What patterns of difference/similarity occur across discursive events of interest in your study (or across participant, across time, or other quality)?

8. How does the analysis of evaluative language help locate significance?

What patterns of significance marking relevant to your research design and question emerge?

What insights about experience and meaning making with narrative and narrating do you gain from significance analysis? What surprises you about the narrative meaning, if anything, after you have tried a significance analysis? What do you learn about narrative? What do you learn about how people use narrating? What insights can you consider with the significance analysis, such as about how participants in your study are using narrating to engage with your issue? What do you, thus, learn about the issue based on how people engage with it?

Also asking participants to reflect on these patterns enhances research interpretations about use rather than absolute meaning. While some may remember how they felt when writing, which would certainly be interesting to know, reflections among a group of these participants or ones with commonalities to why you selected these in the first place would be more relevant to your inquiry. You might ask questions such as, What do these narratives as a group (with groups you think you understand) indicate overall or uniquely by individuals about the issue at hand and/or about different ways of narrating in relation to that issue? Or, put more directly: What do you think these narratives indicate about these participants' approaches to the task and/or to the broader issues of the study? Summary notes addressing these questions will be useful for activities in Chapter 7.

9. What additional questions could you ask about narrative inquiry and/or your research interest?

10. It important to note that results of significance analysis can be summarized descriptively, such as with a focus on an individual's use of evaluative devices in a single narrative, or analytically, by comparing patterns of evaluative devices by an individual over situation and time or across individuals and groups.

CONCLUSION AND NEXT

Significance analysis is a strategy for studying expressive dynamics, diversity, and individuality in meaning making. A strategically placed *very* or emphasis with *!* in a written narrative or rising intonation in speech points to a personal perspective. A content analysis can identify topics being stated or that the researcher thinks relate to a topic of interest. Nevertheless, when examining complex or contentious issues in narratives, natural conversation, interviews, or mixed genres, much of the meaning is not expressed explicitly as a topic. This often leads to researchers' disappointment about not having "gotten at" what they are interested in, but delving deeper into the way we speak can open up the nuances, as discussed in this chapter.

Significance analysis adds to ways of appreciating the complexity of narrative meaning by focusing on evaluative language. Because evaluation occurs in natural language use, everyone who speaks a language has access to evaluative strategies available in his or her familiar culture. There is ample prior evidence that evaluative devices create material bridges between the narrative and the context of telling, reading, or imagining.

Evaluative devices play a large role in dynamic uses of narrating to express and/or identify meaning and intention. Researchers can draw on the evaluative phase of meaning and the referential meaning it complements for the systematic analysis of narrative significance. Significance analysis identifies the evaluative phase of meaning in narratives, in particular how the author uses evaluative devices to figure out what is going on the environment, how she or he fits. Qualitative differences in uses of specific evaluative devices to narrate similar events reveal dynamic uses of story for social interaction—presenting personae to others and oneself. Significance links an individual author as self, as narrator, and perhaps also as a character, actual audiences, potential audiences, and the unfolding referential phase of meaning in the narrative itself. In brief, evaluative devices carry the significance of a narrative. As discussed above, because evaluative devices indicate the significance of a narrative and/ or parts of it, significance analysis of narratives by individuals or groups captures a certain kind of personal meaning, agency, and intention of narrative use.

The next chapter draws on literary theory and narrative use theory to present analytic strategies focusing on character and time. Analysis of these qualities add to the overall picture of narrative meaning.

Notes

Narratives by Thor (pages 177, 178) and Juro (pages 178, 179) are from *Human Development and Political Violence* by Colette Daiute. Copyright © 2010 Colette Daiute. Reprinted with the permission of Cambridge University Press.

1. As defined in Chapter 2, *author* here refers to speaker and writer, the person creating the narrative, to reserve *narrator* for the character or omniscient voice guiding the narrative action and consciousness. *Author* stands, thus, for the speaking or writing person, as the originator and user of the narrative to interact.

2. As established in Chapter 2, corresponding with the use of *author* as narrating person, *audience* is used to refer to actual, potential, or imagined people who might hear, read, or know about the narrative (following Bakhtin, 1986).

6

Character Mapping and Time Analysis

Character and time are two fascinating yet deceptively simple literary qualities appropriate for narrative inquiry. Professional authors use narrative features for experimenting with artistic variations of meaning. Examining oral and written cultural masterpieces created over many centuries, literary scholars have shown how highly skilled authors play with narrative for social and political, as well as aesthetic, purposes. Literary qualities including **character** and **time** serve in this process to build on previous artistic traditions, probe the human condition, and invent new kinds of symbolic representations of life. Because social scientists and philosophers have worked in parallel with literary scholars to learn how people use narrative and its various features for interacting in everyday life, research methods can draw on an interdisciplinary integration across fields devoted to narrative discourse. Analytic strategies with character and time complement narrative methods with plot, evaluative devices, and values expressions, thereby augmenting the tool kit for studying narrative meaning.

This chapter focuses first on the concept of character, defining it and extending it as the basis for character mapping in narrative inquiry. With examples, I discuss interactions among diverse characters within and outside narrative texts, explaining how relations among characters reveal narrative meaning. Examples of character mapping in previous research provide a foundation for a process of character mapping in future research. The second part of the chapter considers time as an analytic lens in narrative inquiry. That discussion involves defining time in narrative, identifying time markers, and examining the patterning of time in narrative meaning.

CHARACTER

The first-person singular "I" **character** is typically the focal point of narrative inquiry, in large part because, as one scholar notes, "the kinds of narrative data

190

that [narrative study] bases itself on present a striking consensus: they are auto-biographical in kind (i.e., about non-shared, personal experience, single past events)" (Georgakopoulou, 2006, p. 122). Stated another way, the author of a narrative—the person who created it—is typically assumed to be and often seems to be the narrator. First-person authentic experience is, moreover, a premium that researchers seek. Somewhat tricky in that regard, "character" affords a means for sharing experience while conforming (or not) to inevitable social pressures about acceptable and unacceptable experiences to share about an issue. When focusing on characters in narratives for research, one learns that the "I" perspective in narrative discourse carries only some meaning and that secondary or even marginal characters do much of the work to express research participants' perspectives. One who steers clear of owning a seemingly undesirable experience or opinion sometimes shifts such expressions to non-"I" characters—"he," "she," "they," "my friend," "Sam," "the caseworker," "the cat," or others. Such moves should not be judged harshly, as they are the stuff of human relations, albeit rarely considered in the analysis of discourse in research.

The concept of character indicates that persons (and sometimes animals or objects depicted as actors) have symbolic meaning in narratives. That characters are symbols does not mean that the people they refer to do not exist in real life, or that they are unimportant. Instead, characters enter stories in creative ways endowed with the meaning that authors develop as a synergy of facts they remember and ideas or hopes they want to share. By analyzing strands of meaning related to diverse characters in narratives, researchers gain an analytic lens for mining nascent or controversial meanings that people do not claim with first person—"I." For example, beginning teachers participating in an interview about how they felt about working in dangerous neighborhoods expressed their students' problems more than their own.

In the following narrative excerpt from an extended interview about education in dangerous areas, Luar, a young teacher, narrated a "most difficult professional experience" (as requested) in the infancy early child-care center in Rio de Janeiro where she works (Daiute et al., 2012). Notice how Luar begins with "I" and shifts gradually to focus on others.

Yes . . . there was a class in which **I** stayed that **the children** were very, like, aggressive, but today, **I** think that if **I** had to choose, **I** would choose **two children** from my class, one is **a boy** who is very caring, but **who** hits all the time, **he** blinks and is hitting **someone** and, like, **we** have spoken to **his mother**, found out that **the mother** gets beaten by **her boyfriend**, who in this case isn't even **the father** of **the child**, **he** is very caring, but **he** hits all the time! . . . And there's also **another girl** who, in the beginning of the year, **we**, like, **she** always arrived to the day care very hungry, very hungry! And **she** went and always took the same clothes, then we started to think that **she**, like, was in need, then **we** discovered that **she** had **her** house buried in those landslides that happened and in the beginning **the family** really was going through a lot of difficulties. . . . I think these **two cases** were the worst!

Although the interviewers asked for Luar's personal experience, this teacher, like most narrators, included numerous characters beyond herself. The "two children from my class," for example, are actual children Luar found memorable and relevant to an interview question about a difficult experience in her professional life. As in this brief excerpt, speakers and writers express personal meaning through others' experiences.

Figure 6.1 illustrates this shift of character mentions from first person to third person. This figure offers an acquaintance with characters in Luar's narrative that differs from their order of appearance in the narrative. In the narrative, characters appear in relation to events and other elements of the plot. The figure, alternatively, offers a view of characters in terms of their roles as first-person, "I" perspective and third-person, "other" perspectives, and frequencies respectively. The purpose of this representation, as this chapter discusses, is to consider by looking closely at narrative character whether and how the author presents the consciousness of the narrative in terms of him- or herself in the first person or shifts focus to others. The figure illustrates this process graphically to suggest a way for researchers to identify focal characters and related meaning.

As shown with the analysis presented in Figure 6.1, Luar shifts the narrative action and consciousness from a first-person stance, plural "we" and singular "I," through others mentioned in the plural, such as "they" and most prominently third persons, "boy," "girl," "mother," "father." The increasing mention of third-person characters suggests that the researcher should pay special attention to the roles of those characters in expressing meaning related to the issues of interest. In other words, as Luar shifts her first-person "I" mentions from the character experiencing danger to the child and family characters in her charge, she positions herself as the professional child-care narrator. In literary terms, real and imagined others serve symbolic purposes as characters in narratives. With such a relatively major focus on third-person characters (in terms of frequency compared to first person), the author is mediating different aspects of the narrative. In this case, by focusing on others, Luar, the author, expresses what she knows and observes but may not want to claim as her own, given her professional role as teacher speaking with the research interviewers who are also teachers.

Figure 6.1   Character Map for Narrative of a Difficult Personal Experience

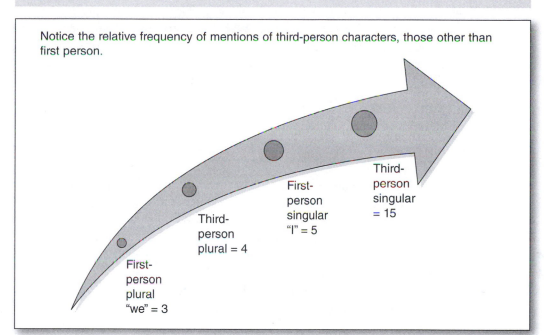

Notice the relative frequency of mentions of third-person characters, those other than first person.

Third-person singular = 15

First-person singular "I" = 5

Third-person plural = 4

First-person plural "we" = 3

This dramatic shift to third-person characters also suggests that research participants might symbolically locate some of their experience and knowledge at a distance, even though the presumption is that autobiographical narrating depicts carefully observed or deeply held realities. Third-person characters in narrative may serve to facilitate expression because they allow authors to hear their own ideas voiced by others and to reflect on personal experience from a distance. By zooming back from the "I" perspective—that is, loosening the assumption that people narrate personal experience as a direct outpouring of self—researchers can consider the relational patchwork of characters for insights about narrative meaning.

Consistent with the principles of dynamic narrative inquiry, defining the concept of "character" involves distinguishing among the author (person expressing the narrative), the narrator (the stance the author crafts as a gatekeeper of information), and characters depicted in the narrative. One of the fascinating things about narrative is the way in which these actual and symbolic perspectives overlap and do not. Because she was sharing her experience with others she knew, in a familiar physical setting, and from the perspective of her role as a professional, Luar crafted a narrator stance as an expert. From this expert stance as a teacher in an infant and early child-care center—the role for which she was selected to be an interview participant—Luar did not report experiencing fear herself. She did, however, recognize threats and adaptations among children and families for whom she is "teacher." Such recognition differs, moreover, from accounts that ignore or deny risks. Luar the person may have felt fear at some point, but as a participant in a study on teachers and teaching, she appears to have deemed it relevant to make her perspective as a teacher the priority. In that role, she did not claim fear of danger but distributed danger to others empathetically.

It is also clear that authors, characters, and narrators are not completely merged because people narrate in different ways across situations and across time. For example, Luar narrated from a critical stance in the sentence "Yes . . . there was a class in which I stayed that *the children* were very, like, aggressive, but today, I think that if I had to choose, I would choose *two children* from my class, one is *a boy* who is very caring, but *who* hits all the time . . . ," while several sentences later, the narrator assumes a more empathetic stance: "then we discovered that *she* had *her* house buried in those landslides that happened and in the beginning *the family* really was going through a lot of difficulties."

Also distinguishing author from narrator is Luar's initial choice of "I" as the narrating perspective from the later one as "we." That shift involves a broadening from Luar's personal stance to her professional stance as one among a group of teachers who discuss children and families in their charge. The concept of character interacts in this distinction between speaker/author and narrator. The author sometimes intervenes as a character, as above when Luar says "there was a class in which I stayed . . . ," while entering later with "we" to introduce evidence allowing for a comment on the action—the fare of narrators: ". . . these two cases were the worst!" Such observations emerge from analysis of character representations, where meaning is expressed in differences across characters. By reserving difficult experiences for characters other than herself, for example, Luar implied that those in the role of teacher should not dwell on their own difficulties but on those of others for whom they are responsible. Future research can, of course, delve into this interpretation further.

As discussed next, character mapping is an informative narrative analysis strategy.

CHARACTER MAPPING

Character mapping is a process of examining meanings across diverse narrative perspectives. Character mapping involves identifying characters, considering the relation of more and less central characters by identifying frequency of character mentions and charting character enactments to learn about their relative roles in narratives. With these analyses, researchers can reflect on diverse strands of meaning operating distinctly and together in ways that may otherwise remain implicit. A researcher doing character mapping asks, Who is the focal character? How do different characters express different and related meanings? Addressing these analytic questions has been helpful for identifying subtle or hidden narrative meanings.

Focal Character(s)

Examining patterns of character mentions reveals actual rather than assumed focal characters holding a primary strand of meaning. Rather than assuming that the focal perspective is expressed in the "I" character, a researcher studying narratives to identify focal characters and the narrative meaning they embody begins by paying close attention to the focal characters enacted by the author. Qualities of focal characters include that they may be mentioned often, they may be endowed with consciousness or agency via the expression of psychological states (see Chapter 5), and they may make comments about the overall narrative, whether those be complementary or counter to other strands of meaning. The process of character mapping zeroes in on the relative roles of characters rather than assuming the prominence of an "I" perspective.

An example illustrates the process of emphasizing non-"I" focal characters in a different context. The following narrative is from an impressive set of interviews with survivors of the November 2012 Hurricane Sandy. Connected with the Occupy movement, the organization Occupy Sandy mobilized volunteers to help victims across the affected region, as well as to memorialize their experiences (online at http://occupysandy.net/storyline). This story, "We're still here," was told by a woman I will refer to as Ada (a pseudonym) in Rockaway, Queens, New York, to Jordan Fletcher 19 days after the storm hit.

> . . . I was here for the storm, I was terrified. I didn't think we'd live through it. We have the big tree in front of the house, the wind was so fierce, I was sure that the tree was gonna fall on the house. Luckily it didn't. And ah, ya know, my boyfriend saw that water rushing in, he threw his bathing suit on, dove in the water, knocked off the sewer cap, turned off the main on the electric, cut open a dry well that was hidden under the linoleum, and came out and took a piece of boardwalk that floated down the block, a plank, and was trying to save the cars, keep the water away from his work truck, but there was no stopping it, then a big piece of boardwalk

came down and he shouted to me, "get out of the street, the boardwalk's comin!" Some of it ended up right here in front of the house. But they got that away already. But we were lucky, our house stood up, everybody's alive n' it's just a massive cleanup, still no heat, no electric. Ya know there's power in that box, they told me but, it's impossible to get, we're on three different lists for electricians. We're finally supposed to get one tomorrow. We used to come for the summers in '66 and ah moved down here in '73. Ya know, I never saw anything like this in all these years!

This transcription of an oral account makes a characteristic move of narrating personal experience from a first-person position to the perspective of others. Notice how Ada launches the story from the personal "I," extends to the narrator position "we," offers most detail with other characters, in particular one "he" and a list of his enactments ("[he] dove in the water, [he] knocked off the sewer cap, [he] turned off the main on the electric, [he] cut open a dry well that was hidden under the linoleum, and [he] came out and took a piece of boardwalk that floated down the block . . ."), finally returning to the "I" for a conclusion.

Such increasing mention of third-person characters suggests that the researcher consider the roles of participants' different characters as expressing meaning related to the research questions. In other words, Ada, for example, begins by positioning herself as the embodiment of fear and dread in the hurricane and a lack of public services to get life back to normal. She then shifts to detailed actions and intentions of another person battling the storm on Ada's and others' behalf, while the public servants mentioned are relatively passive. With character mapping, a researcher can document such a move. Such documentation does not prove that the experiences being described are literally those of the speaker but that the speaker is making sense of events, and perhaps experiencing them, through other characters. Narrating is, after all, a symbolic process, so such meanings are relevant to any research questions a social scientist may have about how people face adversity, about a specific public disaster, or myriad other issues.

Table 6.1 presents a preliminary character mapping for Ada's narrative. Similar to the organization of Figure 6.1, this table focuses on character roles as first-person singular ("I," "me," "my," "mine"), first-person plural ("we," "us," "our[s]"), third-person singular ("Ada," "boyfriend," "he/she/it," "him/her," "his/hers/its"), third-person plural ("they," "them," "their[s]"). In certain narratives, second person, referring to readers or listeners ("you can see," "ya know"), may be relevant for analysis. The names for these persons and pronouns are usually explicit—that is, stated in the narrative—but sometimes they are implicit as in the following sentence from Ada's narrative.

. . . **my boyfriend** saw that water rushing in, **he** threw **his** bathing suit on, dove in the water, knocked off the sewer cap, turned off the main on the electric, cut open a dry well that was hidden under the linoleum, and came out and took a piece of boardwalk that floated down the block . . .

Because Ada mentioned many of her boyfriend's actions, "he" became understood as the actor of many of the actions, that is, implicitly invoked again and again in the narrative, as is grammatical in English and other languages. Below the implied references to the boyfriend are inserted and italicized for the same segment of the narrative:

. . . my boyfriend saw that water rushing in, he threw his bathing suit on, *he* dove in the water, *he* knocked off the sewer cap, *he* turned off the main on the electric, *he* cut open a dry well that was hidden under the linoleum, and *he* came out and took a piece of boardwalk that floated down the block . . .

Consistent with the example above, notice in Table 6.1 the relatively frequent explicit and implicit references to the other—in this case the boyfriend, who, as considered below, is the character holding much of the narrative meaning—expressed by the author but more than the first-person character. A researcher focusing primarily on first-person experience might interpret Ada's narrative as expressing fear and abandonment by authorities, but an analysis focusing on the speaker's experience as distributed across characters

Table 6.1   Beginning Character Map for Ada's Disaster Narrative

	Character	Character mentions
First-person singular	I/me/my	7
First-person plural	we/our	6 (explicit)
		2 (implicit)
Third-person singular	boyfriend/he/his	4 (explicit)
		8 (implicit)
Third-person plural	everybody (in the neighborhood)	1
	they (public service)	2
	electricians/one	2

reveals a story of courage and pluck, in spite of abandonment by authorities. Such an analysis offers evidence, for example, that Ada's experience of the storm was, at least in part, one confirming her safety and trust in a loved one. Of course, such insights from an analysis of characters would combine with analyses of other narratives and other analyses for the ultimate interpretation.

From the perspectives of two very different places in the Americas, Luar's and Ada's focus on others when narrating personal experiences, as they were asked to do, turns out to be a common strategy. This theory of use guiding dynamic narrative inquiry offers insights about why this might be and how it matters in narrative analysis.

Speaking Through Others

The explanation that narrating is a cultural means for interacting in one's environment is foundational to dynamic narrative inquiry. According to this approach (outlined in Chapter 1 and applied in all subsequent chapters), narrative speakers and writers craft narratives interactively. On this view, the narrative is not a direct expression of all the author's relevant knowledge and experience but is instead the composition of facts and orientations he or she wants to share given the purpose (such as an interview question pulling for a narrative), the context (such as those present and imagined), and personal feelings about the events, purposes, and audiences at the time. When narrating contentious issues or issues that might present the author in an unfavorable light, that author can speak certain knowledge and experience through other characters rather than through the "I" character who is presumed to be the self. As a professional, Luar apparently found her way to narrate risk through others who would be vulnerable or dangerous. Similarly, Ada narrated the danger of the storm through the heroism of her boyfriend. There are numerous examples of authors speaking through characters in their narratives and stories.

Consistent with the dynamic narrative approach, a move that authors make is to use third-person characters. Such a move is like that of a ventriloquist (Bakhtin, 1986). How do we know that authors can be ventriloquists? Literary scholars and narrative researchers have begun to consider ventriloquation as a process of an author expressing meaning through non-"I" characters (Bakhtin, 1986; Wortham, 2001). Speakers and authors may locate meaning relevant to a conversation, interview, or written narrative in others, third-person characters depicted in a narrative. Authors use third-person characters as a ventriloquist uses a puppet, perhaps to perform but also to express certain affects and thoughts that they may not yet understand or may not want to express from the first-person stance. After expressing her fear, storm victim Ada, for example, considered the extreme danger of the storm through the actions and experience of her boyfriend.

Reasons for **ventriloquy**—diverting controversial meanings away from the narrating author—are numerous. Focal participants may be exploring meaning in the narrative process itself and, thus, through non-self characters. Issues being discussed may be hot, in that they revolve around contemporary issues of debate, taboo, or imposition that social scientists tend to study. Narratives thereby often embed a range of expectations and sanctions from the broader or immediate sociocultural context. College students involved in a focus group on romantic relationships would, for example, be aware of sounding sexist when sharing with same-sex friends troubles about their heterosexual romantic relationships, so they may tell stories of other friends' experiences, using others' words (Korobov, 2009). Research interactions, like those in everyday life, also enact power relations—whether between researcher and participant, among participants in collective interviews, or in other aspects of the context. A press to be authoritative, in control, and cooperative in interviewing as in social life (Brown & Levinson, 1987; Watts, 2003) pulls narrators to express personal experiences and interpretations to a positive, conforming, or happy ending, unless the negative is specifically requested. A dynamic narrative approach is sensitive to this possibility that narrating involves creating meaning in process, rather than primarily the sharing of stable memories or scripts.

As discovered in previous research where expectations about what can be said and what cannot be said are quite clear and sometimes oppressive, such as in postwar contexts, education contexts, and research contexts, the use of third-person characters to express ideas, fears, desires, and other psychological states is common. This and other examples of ventriloquy indicate that character focus is a source of personal narrative meaning making. As illustrated in Figure 6.1 and examples thus far in this chapter, much expression occurs with third-person characters.

Identifying the frequency of character mentions provides a hint to the author's focus, but there is more to defining the primary meaning of a narrative. Frequency is qualified by how character mentions combine with other narrative elements, in particular psychological state expressions of affect, cognition, and reported speech to construct character roles.

Character Roles

Narrative meanings are expressed in the roles that characters play in relation to one another. Authors orchestrate these meanings-in-character roles spontaneously, apparently conforming to values and expectations in the narrating context, as those might lead to the author's connection with the context. Examining how characters are enlivened (or not) with actions and psychological states indicates character roles and their contribution to the meaning of a narrative. Characters depicted with actions and consciousness have relatively active roles in narratives. In contrast, characters mentioned as bystanders or recipients of others' actions and intentions have relatively passive roles in narratives.

Character mapping identifies patterns of character-evaluative device pairings. As discussed in detail in Chapter 5, psychological state expressions of affect, cognition, and reported speech identify conscious energy in a narrative. As also discussed in Chapter 5, authors humanize characters with psychological states, allowing those to appear to be speaking for themselves. Specific characters and character relations brought to life with psychological state expressions create the consciousness of the narrative and, as such, add vibrant meaning to the plot. Significance functions other than humanizing may also occur with first- or third-person characters to convey narrative meaning. By identifying focal characters and the nature of their personification in the narrative, researchers recognize when participants enact roles associated with the research interest and question.

The meaning of risk emerges as an experience monitored by the author through the narrative stance. Character roles to consider for this analysis include the roles of third-person characters as sites of risk and the first-person character's role as a monitor of risk. Examined in this way, risk emerges as nuanced and mediated through personal stances. Given the highly charged nature of danger in the favelas and the professional role of teachers and others in those contexts (Vasconcellos 2011), it is not surprising that participants selected for this research focus might want to filter such issues through the device of "character" rather than discuss them as personally embodied. That experiences of risk and danger are apportioned in unexpected ways across Ada's narrative, as well, does not necessarily mean that teachers, other authorities, or survivors are never fearful of or directly subjected to dangers. Instead, voicing through others means that authors/speakers choose to narrate dangers as they observe them, at a distance, or as coming gradually into their own consciousness. Character mapping, thus, offers insights about the collective engagement of risk as experienced through others—in the study discussed above, teachers' focus on children and families for whom they are responsible in their work.

Table 6.2 presents an extended character map of Ada's narrative, with actions and psychological states for each of the characters in her disaster story. As shown in the table, paying attention to character's enactments of actions and psychological states indicates the characters' roles in the narrated landscapes of action and consciousness. Characters depicted with different psychological states, such as the "I" character's affect in Ada's narrative compared to the more cognitive states of the third-person boyfriend, play different roles. While the first-person character channels fear and dread in the disaster narrative, the third-person boyfriend character expresses an agency and intention to combat the negative effects of the storm. Another third-person plural character of public service is, in comparison, depicted as passive in the face of the protagonists' need. These diverse roles of victim, hero, and bystander work together to convey the complexity of a difficult situation still in process during the telling. More than a simple hero story with a happy ending, this narrative enlivened with a chorus of characters expresses meaning that no doubt would be different six months or a year later. Character mapping can help a researcher analyzing meaning as shared.

Table 6.2 Character Map—Focus on Roles in Ada's Disaster Narrative

	Characters	*Actions*	*Psych States*
First-person singular victim?	*I*	*was here*	*terrified* *didn't think* *was sure* *never saw*
First-person plural collective?	*we*	*used to come* *moved here*	*were lucky* *supposed to get*
Third-person singular hero?	*boyfriend/he*	*threw* (on suit) *dove* *knocked* *turned*	*saw* *trying* *keep* (it away) *shouted*
Third-person plural bystanders?	*everybody* (in the neighborhood) *they* (public service) *electricians*	*is alive* *got that away* *come*	*told*

Character mapping can also include the dimension of character position in the plot structure (as explained in Chapter 4), and including character-plot relations can contribute to understanding character roles. As shown in Table 6.3, the positioning of the boyfriend in Ada's narrative is also on the plot high point "get out of the street! The boardwalk's comin!"—additional support of this character's pivotal role in the overall meaning of the disaster story.

Table 6.3   Extended Character Map for Ada's Disaster Narrative

	Characters	Psych States	Position in Plot
First-person singular	I	terrified didn't think was sure never say	Setting Coda
First-person plural	we	were lucky supposed to get	Resolution
Third-person singular	boyfriend, he	saw trying keep (it away) shouted	High point
Third-person plural	they (public service)	told	Ending

The examples above illustrate the concepts of character, focal character, and character role in character mapping. The next section presents examples of character mapping from previous research.

CHARACTER MAPPING IN PRIOR RESEARCH

Character mapping is a relatively novel strategy of narrative analysis, and several examples offer information about its potential contribution to narrative inquiry.

Identifying Risk

An analysis of a three-hour interview with three beginning teachers in an integrated reform and education program to professionalize the infant and early child-care center educator role (Vasconcellos, 2011) showed the insights from character mapping analysis (Daiute et al., 2012). Parallel strands of analysis of referential meanings (explicit mentions, content analysis as defined in Chapter 5) and character mapping revealed the use of third-person characters to express meanings in relation to the research questions that were not expressed explicitly.

The teacher interviewees mentioned "danger," "risk," and related words like "gunshot" and "police" only 113 times, which in a 12,824-word interview about teachers' perspectives on working in the dangerous favelas is a very small percentage. Of the 113 mentions, it is interesting to note that 57% of the danger-related words mention "police" (17%), "danger" (10%), "gunshot" (10%), "action" (9%), "criminal" (6%), and "shoot out "(6%). Each teacher presented risk and danger words across the interview, but the words concentrate in two sections in particular: when the teachers responded to a question about the distance between their home and their work, and at the end of the interview, when they responded to explicit questions about their best and worst experiences and about risk.

Mentions of the teachers' personal distress rarely co-occur with mentions of danger or risk. Only 4 of 11 mentions of teachers' personal distress co-occur with mentions of danger/risk, and only 3 of 8 mentions of an individual child's distress co-occur with mentions of danger/risk. Such shifting away from personal risk is evident in the following narrative by Nadia:

> Yeah, I get used to it, right? I no longer get too scared, I just get very scared if my child is not home, then I get kind of terrified, but as for me, in relation to the work and there being a confrontation [violent episode like a shooting in the favela where she works] and in the case that I am in the nursery, right? I don't get so scared, in fact I try to stay calm, because children get agitated, right? (Translated from Daiute et al.,2012)

For insights about the patterning of mentions of risk, the researchers extended the analysis of the referential phase of meaning in the interview with an examination of psychological state expressions across the various characters in the teachers' narratives. This analysis revealed a collective engagement of risk. The most explicit expressions of favela dangers and risks occur when the conversation shifts to children and families. While the first-person accounts tend to be good or neutral, perhaps even controlled, the narratives where children, families, and especially fathers enter the narrative are the most explicitly horrifying stories. Analysis of the co-occurrences of dangers/risks and characters indicates that the participants frame danger and risk in relation to children, families, and the community. Of all mentions of dangers/risks, 42% appear with "community" (26%) and parents—"father" and/or "mother" (26%). When only the mother or father is mentioned in relation to risk, fathers are mentioned twice as frequently as mothers (8 versus 4, respectively, and thus not predominant overall in the discourse), even though fathers are mentioned less (33 times) than mothers (44 times) across the interviews. Mothers are also implicated in the web of violence and criminality that ultimately involves the mothers' relations to their children. While a father's death or imprisonment may be mentioned in relation to general dangers in the favela, a mother's crack addiction is expressed in terms of her lack of availability to the child.

Participants' narratives of their best experiences in their early child-care work were primarily first-person accounts, with an emphasis on the teachers' thoughts and feelings about specific times when they felt they had taken an active positive role in the lives of children and families and had been recognized for their role. Notice in this excerpt, for example, how Luar narrates a "best" experience:

> I think that the best [experience] was to have stayed with the group of students I was with last year and have accompanied this group. This way, I feel a very strong bond with the parents, a positive recognition in relation to the work that we are already developing, the children too, and . . . there is a strong big trust and especially during the period that I was away, the way girls talked, how the children asked for me, the parents asked, when I was about to come back they told the parents and they were, you know, celebrating that I was going to come back, I think that the best experience was this one, I think that pretty much for the children too very good for the day care as a whole. (Translated from Daiute et al., 2012)

Luar orients the narrative in terms of her psychological states, "I think . . . I feel . . . I stayed away, I was about to come back . . ." Not only an individual story, this one mentions other characters' speech, "the children asked for me . . . the parents asked . . ." Also demonstrating her sensitivity to the others involved, Luar broadens the perspective at the end of the account, projecting others' experience on her own, "I think that pretty much for the children too very good for the day care as a whole."

In contrast, the narratives of difficult experiences in early child-care work revolved more around the children's perspectives, often as refracted through issues with their mothers and fathers. Compare that process in Luar's narrative of her most difficult experience, presented and discussed at the beginning of this chapter. As already discussed, that narrative excerpt begins with the first-person perspective "I would choose . . ." but then shifts exclusively to the children's psychological states, "boy who is very caring, he blinks . . . girl . . . very hungry . . . she felt . . . ." The first-person "I" perspective also shifts to "we" as Luar explains the collective attempts in practice to interpret and to help these two cases that "were the worst!"

New teacher Luar, for example, considered the risks of living in the dangerous favelas of Rio de Janeiro through the experiences of children who are subjected to chaotic family situations wrought of the crime-ridden neighborhoods and women who are subjected to men often at the center of the drug trade ruling the areas. Speaking to other professional teachers and wanting to show her own professional acumen, Luar depersonalizes danger, yet those others in her story are clearly embedded in her personal meaning.

Based on a theoretical perspective that narrating is a sense-making process, the researchers considered, further, that the apparent minimizing of personal risk may be an adaptive orientation to living in such circumstances. It is as though shifting to others, others for whom the teachers are interlocutors, agents, protectors, allows the teachers to accept emotionally or to buffer the dangerous circumstances where they work. These novice teachers may have also been speaking from assumptions about expectations of the academic professors toward people who live on a daily basis with risk and danger. Although it is possible that Luar and her colleagues did not feel personally at risk, it is also likely that speaking as professionals in an interview with other professionals, they shifted expressions of vulnerability to others. Rather than identify with the favela and the attendant implications, the teachers might have wanted to identify with the interviewers (who are, after all, similar to them, in that they too had gone through academic studies), and offered self-expressions detached from the reality of daily life in the favela while working on behalf of those more subjected to unpredictability and violence there.

Another analysis with character mapping in a very different urban context revealed insights about selective uses of third-person characters.

Insights in Peripheral Characters

A study of social development of several hundred 7- through 10-year-old children participating in a literacy-based violence prevention program in their public school classrooms in a large northeastern U.S. city included character mapping analysis of the children's narratives of personal experiences of conflict (among numerous other oral and written, individual and collaborative activities analyzed in a variety of ways) (Daiute et al., 2001). The purpose of the research was to learn about whether and how children use narrative as a means to engage and advance their social development.

Third-person character psychological state expressions indicated significantly more use of third-party intentional state expressions (such as "started to . . . ," "meant to . . . ", an aspect of cognitive psychological states) by children identifying (in their own terms) as African American than by children identifying as European American or Latino. Over the course of a school year, teachers and children in nine third- and fifth-grade classrooms read and discussed high-quality children's literature in terms of a violence prevention curriculum focusing on mutual understanding in relation to social conflicts among people of different ethnic groups (Walker, 1996). Oral and written narrating was a major activity across the year, originally designed as a means of assessing children's internalization of the curriculum values about conflicts and conflict resolution, but then, as became increasingly evident, children used different narrative activities to mediate their understanding of curriculum values like "Use words not fists when involved in a conflict" with their own self-presentations in narratives of personal experience. One strand of analysis involved 224 autobiographical and fictional written narratives about social conflict by 56 children (15 African American, 16 Latino, 25 white). The analysis of psychological state expressions by different characters in the narratives indicated (among other results) that the African American children depicted the psychological states, in particular intentions, of characters other than the protagonist or primary antagonist in the conflict event (Daiute et al., 2001). The following narrative by third grader George illustrates this characteristic pattern of attributing psychological states to non-first-person characters:

Friends Fight

one day in Music I was working with Alexis. Tyronne got Mad a[t] Me Because I did not work with him. But then we came Friends. So I worked with Tyronne. but then Alxis got mad at me. But then I with both of them. We all became friends.

Characters in this narrative include the author/narrator "I" mentioned with actions "was working" and "did not work," "Alexis" with the psychological state "got mad," "Tyronne" with "got mad," and "we" with the psychological state "became friends." Because the curriculum was, in part, designed to expand children's understanding and consideration of the perspectives of other people, including antagonists in conflicts, this result that children did so was, of course, welcomed. That result was not, however, absolute, as the children tended to increase their humanizing of antagonists' perspectives in autobiographical and fictional narratives in different ways. That the psychological state expressions of third persons increased consistent with the curriculum in children's autobiographical narratives while not always consistent with the curriculum in fictional narratives suggests that the children were using the narratives strategically. They used the narratives that exposed themselves as authors (the autobiographical narratives) to connect with the curriculum, while they used the ones allowing themselves more anonymity as narrators (the fictional stories) to express alternative psychological states such as jealousy and dislike. The difference in the quality of character development by children identifying with different ethnic groups also underscores the use nature of narrating, as the African American children tended to humanize third-party characters even more than did children in the other two broad ethnic groups. Theory-based character mapping analysis offers reliable insights into such processes that have implications for our understanding of narrating and for methods of employing narrative analysis, as well as for social development more generally.

When thinking about doing character mapping in your research, consider the following questions: What characters are mentioned? How is each character developed with psychological states (which humanize the character), actions, and interactions? What is the focal character? What insights about meaning related to the question does the character mapping analysis indicate? How does the speaker/author use characters to convey meanings differently across the narrative, interview, or conversation?

With those questions in mind, you can review the character mapping process in the next section.

THE PROCESS OF CHARACTER MAPPING

Character mapping begins by reading generally for the psychological heart of a narrative, regardless of character, and then proceeds by listing all the characters, character mentions, and character roles—psychological and action states—associated with each mention. The following steps detail the process of character mapping:

1. Read the narrative(s) several times to become familiar with it/them.

2. Proceed to character analysis, using Table 6.4 as a guide for your notes. The table includes a listing of character perspectives in the first column, followed by three columns for each of two narratives you have chosen to work on: one for noting characters, one for listing psychological states of those characters, and one for listing actions.

   If you finish this preliminary analysis for psychological state expressions, you could create a new table for intensifiers or other evaluative devices to list in the columns headed "Characters and number for each."

Table 6.4 Character Mapping for Personal Experience Narratives by You and/or in Your Research

	Narrative 1			Narrative 2		
	Characters and frequency of each	Psychological states for each character	Actions for each character	Characters and frequency of each	Psychological states for each character	Actions for each character
First-person singular						
First-person plural						
Third-person singular						
Third-person plural						

3. Underline or make a list of the characters, noting names, nouns referring to specific characters ("child," "friend"), and pronouns referring to each character (as in Table 6.2).

4. Note the frequency, the number of times each character is mentioned explicitly (actually stated with a name, noun, pronoun) and implicitly (implied by a series of actions or psychological states, as in Ada's mentions of her boyfriend's actions and psychological states during the hurricane).

4a. Make a note about the character mentioned most, the character mentioned second, and third.

4b. What observation do you have about how the frequency of character mentions contributes to the meaning of the narrative? For example, in Ada's narrative the meaning that one must strive to overcome adversity is expressed in her boyfriend's actions and psychological states, while she presents her own perspective as one of fear, then moderated at the end of the account by the observation that although that was the worst storm she had ever seen in many years of being in Rockaway, she and others had prevailed.

5. Identify the actions and psychological states of each character, as shown in Table 6.2.

   5a. Are any characters associated in particular with actions or psychological states?

   5b. Based on any character-action-psychological state patterns you notice, would you say that certain characters are humanized as discussed in Chapter 5 and observed in the analysis of Ada's and other narratives?

6. If you have done a plot analysis (as shown in Chapter 4), note where each of the characters (or focal characters) is in the plot structure, as shown in Table 6.2.

   6a. Do any or all characters play a specific role in the plot, such as Ada's boyfriend in the high point?

   6b. If you have identified any character-plot element connections, what does this tell you? For example, Ada's story comes to a climax (high point) and then begins to resolve around the boyfriend's shouting to her to get out of the way because the boardwalk is coming down the street. This high point indicates that the meaning of the storm became one of collective agency in the face of danger and fear—a story of neither victimization nor heroism, but one of social survival made possible in particular by the boyfriend's active connection.

7. Review the specific set of characters, character mentions, character roles, and character positions in plots, and consider whether characters play specific roles in the web of meanings offered in the narrative.

   7a. What are some character roles? How does each role contribute a specific meaning to the narrative in relation to your issue of research interest or question? How do the character roles combine to an overall meaning? How does the meaning of the narrative expand beyond the first person?

8. Consider the role the narrator plays.

   Which characters does the author bring to life with psychological state expressions? Are the psychological state expressions more affective, cognitive, or mixed? How do the specific psychological state expressions portray that character? How do psychological state expressions sort out by different characters?

The prior discussion of the concept of character as a useful element of narrative meaning making adds another strategy to a researcher's analytic repertoire. In summary, character is a symbolic strategy, and character analysis builds on this notion for understanding the social nature of meaning. The next section highlights time as a foundation for analyzing meaning in time, thereby shedding light on another major narrative discourse.

TIME

Time is a major element of narrative. Events are marked for when they occur, either with tenses or with time-marking vocabulary. Narratives are often accounts of past events, or appear to be. Phrases like "Once upon a time," time markers like "yesterday," and tense inflections like "I stopp*ed* (by to see a friend)" suggest temporal settings of events, but time marking also expresses people's meaning. When recounting a remembered event, one narrates in past tense, "*Yesterday*, I stopp*ed* by to see a friend, and the strangest thing happen*ed*." That sentence includes three time markings, "yesterday," "(stop)ped," and "(happen)ed," so clearly the author made decisions about how to present those different pasts—two past time markers anchored in the narrative setting "*Yesterday*, I stopp*ed* by to see a friend," and another in the initiating action, "and the strangest thing happen*ed*." When narrating actual past events, authors would presumably narrate them as past, but not always.

Sometimes, to bring the past into the present, a speaker uses present or future **time markings**, as in "Last year on my birthday, he comes into my living room, offers a gift and leaves. I'm thinking, 'What will he do next?' Well, he returned and gave me a kiss!" Such presentations of past events with a mix of tenses—past ("Last year"), present ("comes," "offers," "leaves," "I'm thinking"), future ("What will he do next?")—out of the expected place indicate the purposeful use of time to convey complex meaning. From the perspective of a theory of dynamic narrating, time is a cultural invention people use to make sense of experience and to self-educate collectively. As a cultural invention, time is relational.

Time is relational in several ways. Time dimensions in narratives are relative to one another. For example, the sentence "*Yesterday*, I stopp*ed* by to see a friend, and the strangest thing happen*ed*" appears to occur in the same past time. There are, however, three past times in this sentence, which may have an impact on the meaning expressed in the narrative. For example, "stopped by" probably occurred before "the strangest thing happened," and both are embedded in the time frame of yesterday. The narrator may, however, then launch into another past time to provide background for stopping by to visit the friend, background for the strange thing that happened, or some other related event. Another relational fact is that "yesterday" might refer to the moment of telling the story, to the day after "yesterday" in the story, such as "When I arrived at my sister's house, she said 'Yesterday I stopped by to see a friend,'" or some other time relation. Time is also relative as past times compare with present and other time dimensions in narrative. The following continuation of the narrative a friend shared with me informally illustrates meaning in time.

> To answer your question about family relations, I'm telling you that when I arrived at my sister's house, she said "Yesterday a friend stopped by and the strangest thing happened." After she told the strange story, I began to think that the "friend" was thinly masqueraded as if he were me.

The myriad time markings interact with truth and imagination. All narrative time is symbolic, but past and present time markings imply actual experience, while the range of future, conditional, subjective, and hypothetical (possible) time markings are more clearly imagined times. Narrated past events appear fixed and true because they are reported as having happened. Future, conditional, and hypothetical events (or ones depicted as such) have not occurred, so they are imagined, although they are often overlooked in narrative analysis. Present tenses appear fixed in another way—expressing the narrating position. The result of this interplay of time settings contributes to narrative meaning. When narrated events are presented as conventional with completed events in various arrangements of past time and ongoing events in various arrangements of present, events that have not yet occurred can be thought of as imagined time. **Imagined time** is often presented in events marked as future, conditional, or hypothetical (with tenses or vocabulary).

Just as history is not an absolute time line, narratives are histories from specific points of view indicated in part with time markings. Narrative time is one among the range of tools people use to organize memory and intention. Narrators use time markings, like other tools, to interact in the world, as they experience moving through it, and as they make sense of the world. Time markings add depth and breadth to stories, as authors veer from linear progressions of events to an ebb and flow sensitive to narrative purpose. We have seen in Chapter 5 how an expression like "sort of" can slip unobtrusively into a narrative while creating a meaning like "it wasn't such a big deal to be hit by a car." Time words and tense markings, like a lurking "-ed" past-tense ending, do their own special work, such as conveying a sense of truth, when indicating an event occurred in the past. Specific time markings are not always connected in the same way with narrated fact and/or imagination, yet within a narrative or group of narratives, different times connect with different meanings. These relations might be, for example, that narrators use past time to convey truths or givens, present to convey intention, and imagined time to convey hopes and dreams. Alternatively, time relations might be that a narrator uses past time to express normalcy, present time to express questions, and imagined time to convey intention. Examining these time frames in narratives is revealing.

As described above, time is relational within a narrative, as a speaker/writer creates a narrator voice to order events in the speaking context, in the narrated event, and among characters. The use of time to organize activities, relationships, and intentions also occurs collectively in interactive processes. Since relational time refers outside a narrative to symbolic acts, time also takes on social meaning. If narrators in a focus group or conversation want to display solidarity, for example, they may agree by presenting events in past time—events marked as having occurred in the past and thus recorded and difficult to challenge. Because power relations operate prominently during group activities, nuances of time use, like the strategy of character ventriloquy, are fertile sources of meaning. As in the example above, the brief narration of the birthday party visit narrates a scene of last year's birthday in present time, perhaps to indicate that the visitor is still behaving strangely as in the example from the past. In these and other ways, time is a cultural, relational tool. A brief theoretical explanation of narrative time will be helpful for launching time analysis.

MEANING IN TIME

One literary scholar explains that narrating always occurs in a present—the time of telling or writing the narrative (Ricoeur, 1990). This present time is three-dimensional. With a look back in time, there's a "present of past things" (Ricoeur, 1990), often referred to as memory. Although a memory may be considered to be set, memory of any specific event can differ or present differently depending on circumstances of recall or sharing. The second dimension of the threefold present is "a present of future things" (Ricoeur, 1990). A projection into the future may be concrete or even stable if often repeated, yet it is imagined and fluid for that, as well as for demands of the narrating time. The third dimension of the threefold present is "a present of present things" (Ricoeur, 1990), which is the attention in the anchoring perspective of the narrating time. Even when a story is revised or edited many times, the author may have chosen a specific present perspective in which to anchor the story. Following this theoretical formulation of the threefold present in narrative, the time markings and verb tenses in narratives are clues to different domains of meaning. These time markings are useful tools for close study of narrative perspective about events, characters, ideas, and other elements for consideration. Past tense, for example, is typically used to convey events as having occurred, set in memory, probably true, and collectively agreed upon if in a group narration. Events depicted as future ("the time will come when war will stop") or hypothetical ("if tyrants were peacemakers . . .") might be desired, hoped for, or feared. The presentation of events as conditional ("I would tell you if I could remember") could easily indicate ambivalence or dread. Events presented as past craft certain truths or stabilities as actual time—actual because it is past—while events presented as future, conditional, or hypothetical craft possibilities or desires as imagined time. The simple and progressive present time lets the listener/reader experience the speaker/author most closely for his or her attention and, thus, intentional perspective in the narrating time.

Marking Time

Researchers who pay attention to time in narrative gain insights about meaning. All languages mark time in some way, indicating the importance of time in human consciousness and interactions. Many languages, including English, use tense markings—words and/or word endings that provide ways of distinguishing dimensions like past, present, and future. Another device in many languages, including African American Vernacular English, is aspect, words or word endings that indicate duration of time and a broader time frame in which the progress occurred. While past and present tenses and words mark (or appear to mark) actual time, another set of tenses and time markings indicates hypothetical time or imagined time—time that has not yet occurred. English includes several tenses to mark imagined time, most prominently future, conditional. English offers minimal marking for counterfactual events—that is, events that do not occur, such as "If I were you." This marking, called the subjunctive mood, is prevalent in Spanish, other Romance languages, and some languages from other bases.

Since every speaker of every language marks time linguistically in everyday language, it is well worth a researcher's effort to examine time, if not in detail, at least with rough outlines. Notice the movement of time from present to past in the tenses (in boldface) across the excerpt from above in this chapter:

To **answer** your question about family relations, I**'m telling** you that when I **arrived** at my sister's house, she **said** "Yesterday a friend **stopped by** and the strangest thing **happened**." **After she told** the

strange story, I **began to think** that the "friend" was thinly masqueraded as if he **were me**.

Destabilizing the idea that narratives primarily recount past events in some
ordered time progression, observe the fascinating moves with time in the brief
excerpt above. The narrative begins in the present with "to answer" (presumably in the now, present time of telling) and "I'm telling," shifts, perhaps pre-
dictably, to a past event, "arrived" and "said," two events that are linked in time
with "when"—"when I arrived at my sister's house, she said." The action
moves forward from there, "after she told," although not to the present because
"I began to think" occurred somewhere between the visit, the sister's telling,
and the time of telling. The excerpt ends with a fascinating trick of time, perhaps so important that it is the initiating action, "thinly masqueraded as if he
were me." The "as if . . . were me" construction—the subjunctive mood—is
common in many languages, including Spanish, French, and Italian, but used
rarely in English. The subjunctive is used to indicate, with a past time mark,
that something is not true or only possibly true. So the past "were" in this narrative is not past at all, or existing in any time. Instead, the past time marking
is used to indicate an imagined time, one that might have been possible given a
certain history or that someone might have thought possible but is not the case
or realized not to be the case in the now, the present time.

Interesting for the narrative researcher in this example are several points. The
first point is that noticing the flow of time relevant to what is marked as present
is important. For example, the established present "I'm telling you" is the reference point for the brief narrative above. Given that anchor, the events marked as
past serve different functions, some narrative—"When I arrived . . . , she said . . ."
and past before that "yesterday . . . she told the strange story. . . ." At the point of
the past telling of that story, the narrator realizes that something related to him is
going on with this move to the far past—in particular, that the far past suggests
that there's a masquerade and the story is about him, "as if . . . were me." Noticing
time, in this way, has been the focus of this discussion up to now. The next section
extends that focus to reading time for identifying meanings in research.

Distinctions among active time—such as past and present—and imagined
time are particularly relevant to identifying meaning in narrative. In that sense,
all narrative time is symbolic. The following narrative related to a study with
people living in rural areas of Colombia where the national trend toward globalization processes has completely changed the lives of the inhabitants. An
account of a bombing raid is typical of the situation and the strategy, seamlessly
interweaving past, present, and imagined time:

. . . the fighting began at 6 am when people were just beginning work on their [farming] plots. "The bullets came from both sides, so we had to return to the house had to protect children," says a resident of the region. Fear gripped people because the detonations increasingly felt close to home. Even so, in the evening, those assembled decided to go to sleep with the hope that the bombing would stop by sunrise. However, the sound of machine guns replaced the roosters crowing at dawn. Again, there was fighting all day. Guerrilla and army entrenched among civilians, throwing artillery above the houses.

One of these artifacts impacted the house of a villager injuring 6 people, including 3 children. The Indigenous Guard came to the site to evacuate the wounded. . . .

The wounded were evacuated by bike but M. V. C., age 11, failed to reach the nearest health post. "I picked up the girl, she was pale, with blood on her chest. She sighed and squeezed my hand tighter, then let go. Then I realized that I could not do anything for her. Then there was silence," said an indigenous guard.

A young girl had to die a girl to quiet the weapons. Only then both armed groups withdrew from the territory. . . .

As silence sits amid cries of M.V.'s family, the community . . . prepares a march to demand that all armed groups to leave, not to return, to let them live in their autonomy. "They recruit poor people to kill poor people. We know that the government and multinational companies are behind this, trying to leave us without territory and lifeless. So we want that this death not be forgotten, we want everyone to know that they are exterminating us. . . . We want you to know the truth" says a guard before returning with M.V.'s mother to give her some comfort.

Close examination of this narrative posted on the website of a community organization echoes other such events, enacting diverse uses of time, among other narrative strategies (http://www.nasaacin.org/contexto-colombiano/2682-que-todo-el-mundo-sepa-que-en-el-cauca-nos-estan-exterminando). Table 6.5 lists the past, present, and hypothetical time markings—time words, phrases, and tense markings—from this narrative. As the table shows, much of the narrative is presented in various versions of the past. The past in this narrative is the authoritative time, presenting numerous facts about the attack, punctuated with equally factual elements of life before the attack ("people were just beginning work on their farming plots" and "sound of machine guns replaced the roosters crowing at dawn")

Table 6.5   Past, Present, and Imagined Times in a Narrative of Attack on a Village

Past	Present	Imagined
fighting began	as silence sits amid cries	that the bombing would stop by sunrise,
people were . . . beginning work	community . . . prepares a march	that all armed groups to leave,
bullets came from both sides	they recruit poor people	not to return, to let them live,
we had to return		that this death not be forgotten
Fear gripped		We want you to know the truth
detonations . . . felt close		
those assembled decided to go to sleep		
guns replaced the roosters		
there was fighting all day		
Guerrilla and army entrenched		
artifacts impacted the house		
Guard came to . . . evacuate		
wounded were evacuated		
M. V. C. . . . failed to reach the nearest health post		
I picked up the girl		
she was pale		
She sighed		
squeezed my hand		
let go		
girl had to die		
armed groups withdrew		

The past tense paints a picture of the event as though in a film: "The fighting began, . . . bullets came from both sides . . . fear gripped people . . ." and so on as listed in Table 6.5. This picture of horror is only briefly punctuated by another past, "when people were just beginning to work on their plots . . . those assembled decided to go to sleep . . . the sound of machine guns replaced the roosters crowing at dawn. . . ." Against this landscape of action, present time expresses an awakening of the community's agency and intention: "As silence sits amid cries . . . community . . . prepares a march," ". . . We know that the government and multinational companies are behind this. . . . So we want . . ." Imagined time, mostly in the subjunctive, hypothetical tense used often, albeit selectively, in the

Spanish language, progresses onward to hopes and demands: "that the bombing would stop by sunrise ... that all armed groups to leave, not to return, to let them live" "that this death not be forgotten ... We want you to know the truth." As expressed in Spanish, "Que todo el mundo sepa," the imagined time indicated by "sepa"—that the whole world would know—gently speaks the point of this narrative.

The relativity of time is not only within its own formulation—that is, of time markings in narrative in relation to one another. When considering how these time markings imply truth and imagination, scholars consider those relations in terms of the prevailing forces determining human relations. Whether and how past events are considered past depends, after all, on the perspective of the person sharing experience, the designated narrator, characters, and the contexts where they occur. Practice noticing time in narrative can bring these ideas about the symbolic nature of time marking to life for narrative researchers. The indigenous peoples of the Cauca region have repeatedly been victims of such events. Their peaceful resistance and protests, as well as those by others on their behalf, obviously remain ignored, rendering this authoritative narrative all the more poignant. The cinematic use of past time and purposeful use of imagined time in this video narrative posted for all the world to view connects meaning within the narrative firmly with meaning around it.

Noticing Time

Using time marking is an everyday practice for everyone, which is why time analysis can offer important insights in narrative inquiry. Although marking time is a daily habit, researchers benefit from practicing noticing time markings in narratives. Table 6.6 on page 218 presents another disaster narrative. This time, the focus is on time markings.

Examples from a prior narrative study in an extremely challenging environment bring this ideological framing of time to light. After reading the narrative in Table 6.6, notice the time markings (verbs and time words) and separate them into columns indicating past time, present time, and imagined time. With that complete, reread the narrative, and discuss whether and how these time markings add to the meaning of the narrative. Questions to guide this discussion include the following: What events and kinds of events does the speaker indicate as past, ongoing, and imagined? How do these different placements of events in time suggest the speaker is feeling about the events? How do those different placements of events in time suggest how the speaker wants to be perceived in relation to the disaster?

Examples of time analysis in prior research will be helpful for this consideration of meaning in time as a potential strategy for future research.

Table 6.6   Noticing Time in the "Miracle" Disaster Narrative

Using this table: Identify the time markings in the "miracle" disaster story below. Underline each time marking on a verb, in a verb phrase, as a separate word or phrase, then list all the phrases in the first column. Next, place each of the phrases in the appropriate column for past, present, or imagined time. Remember that each general time may include variations, such as simple present (e.g., "She sees the problem"), present habitual (e.g., "Mother walks to work every day"), present progressive ("She is going to work now"), and so on. After this process, what do you notice about differences, if any, in the uses of each time for narrative meaning?

That's a miracle

by Meg Cramer (http://occupysandy.net/storyline)

I didn't think it was gonna be that bad to be honest, ya know, cause we were here for 40 years. And we had other storms and it was, and that's why I think a lot of people, stayed. They ah, I'm here for 40 years and we never had ocean water three quarters of a mile up. The next morning when the, what ya call it ah, all the water receded, I went out to see the damage to the homes, to my home to my mom's home and I look and my sister's car was moved 6 feet to the right, and I looked at the Blessed Mother statue, and she didn't move. Ya know, that's a miracle. And ah, ya know, we're alive, and we gotta be grateful. There's a lot o other people that were way off, way worse than us. Ya know. Gotta rebuild.

Time markings	Past	Present	Imagined

TIME ANALYSIS IN PRIOR RESEARCH

Imagined Time for Diversity in a Collective Narrative

Time analysis of a collective narrative commemorating a massacre in a community reveals a collective expression comprising different yet complementary perspectives across stakeholders—mothers, teachers, youth, community leaders, researchers (Daiute & Botero, 2012). A prior study examining the relational functions of time markings offers a window onto the use of time in situations where solidarity is essential yet people want to narrate experience and intention in different ways. Statements in the past and present appear to be agreements, while some differences emerge in imagined time. In particular, the young people and teachers express a moving forward that seems discouraged by the chorus, which expresses resistance to the modern way, which is robbing them of their lives, livelihoods, and traditions.

Posing the question of whether and how different stakeholders in the community might have been suggesting diverse voices within the overall chorus, the researchers did a time analysis. The varied use of tense markers in Spanish and the prevalent use of subjunctive mood in particular provide rich analysis of narrative time. The subjunctive in Spanish and other languages marks a verb as an event (physical or psychological) that could happen, one that probably will not happen, or a desired one, thus imagined. This symbolic use of imagined time for dreams that may not be shared by all in the group enables the collective narrative to remain so, while certain individuals can express hope or doubt or disagreement.

The different markers of time serve to help participants remember—memorialize—life as it was, as it was taken away, to pay attention to the moment, context, to reach out to others, to imagine otherwise, to caution, to disagree, to create a complex *tejido* of experience. The research team analyzed the 32 participants' contributions to the collective narrative as a whole and then by groups of participants by role (teacher, mother, community leader, student) for any different perspectives within the collective narrative. A little background will set the scene for this collective narrative.

Colombia has experienced almost 50 years of conflict over resources and control of the rich tropical land spanning the Pacific coast to the west, the Atlantic in the northeast, and the Amazon to the east and south. A mixing of diverse indigenous, African, and European peoples also creates cultural wealth. These riches have, however, been the center of conflicts among groups to control them, in a protracted and violent process with people in the midst of drug cartels, paramilitary groups, guerrilla groups, the government, and multinational corporations. Although everyone in society is affected, including the middle and wealthier classes, whose children are subject to kidnapping by guerrilla and other groups for ransom money, the major victims are indigenous peoples without the means to resist displacement by those intent on taking their lands. Lush lands that indigenous peoples have long cultivated with varied crops, fishing, and mining for subsistence rather than profit are being seized violently for use in corporate monoculture (the growing of single crops like palm or corn), for strategic positions in the conflict, for the building of highways to transport illegal and multinational goods, and for hiding places.

In just one of those events in 2011, helicopters flew over a village, reportedly in search of guerrillas, and shot relentlessly, killing women and child villagers (Botero & Palmero, 2013). In such events, hundreds of which have taken place over the past few decades, innocents are killed or forced to flee to overcrowded cities, where at best they can do low-paid labor and at worst they become dependent on and prey for groups colluding in their displacement. It is for these and other displaced people that narratives could be a restorative process not only personally but also for future generations, as well as to report events, like the narrative posted on YouTube. These personal narratives connect for sure with those of the communities, the nation, and the multinational process of globalization that has led to changes that are no longer isolated to Colombia. A comprehensive review of the recent history and social issues in Colombia far exceeds the scope of this chapter, but a story of collective narrating in one village offers a view into how narrating can play a role in research about how people perceive dramatic changes in their way of life.

Among other activities, narrating violent experiences can help to increase understanding as well as the ability to cope with the effects of violent events. Researchers have considered collective memory (Smorti et al., 2010; Wertsch, 2002), which corresponds roughly to scripts as defined in Chapter 4. There is still much to learn about the dynamic process of collective narrating, how it occurs, and where individuals diverge and introduce complexity or dissent into the collective.

Among the many activities and questions in the research about how Colombians make sense of the long-term conflict in their country and exert their will to improve the situation for their communities and themselves is "How do people use the cultural tool of **imagined time** to wrestle with and eventually manage their circumstances?" (Daiute & Botero, 2012). To address this question, community members, leaders, and researchers convened a collective event to remember the victims of a massacre in a village that had taken place just over six months prior (Botero & Palmero, 2013). The focus of the event was to speak supportively to the mothers of the children who were senselessly killed in this helicopter shooting aimed at others, whether or not those were valid victims.

Time analysis is particularly relevant to contexts where people appear to be diminished by globalization done for the benefit of the state, multinational corporations, and others with resources and power to claim lands long inhabited by indigenous peoples. In such contexts, there is increasing questioning, if not resistance, to symbolic as well as material aspects of the inevitable forward orientation of development. In fact, many participants in indigenous communities define development as returning to the past. The collective narration is interesting in many ways and, in particular for this study, for consideration of the uses of diverse time markers to add nuance to collective narrations.

"Memoria de G" is a collective narrative convened with 32 individuals in different positions—researchers, teachers, students, mothers. The narrative is collective in intention, process, and focus. The group convened on an anniversary of the killings with the intention to remember the event and those who were killed. The stated audience for the narration was the mothers of those killed and implicitly others in the community with whom everyone was claiming solidarity. In addition to these collective purposes and audiences, the narrating process was collective as participants contributed in the round with the intention that all would speak. Finally, the research question and process identified the collective— and diverging—foci of the narrative. Questions guiding the analysis included "What did people say was the problem? How do they use 'time' to explore what is possible, desired, uncertain but important to consider?"

For this analysis, *time* was defined as explicit statements in past and implied statements in imagined times (conditional and subjunctive), from the perspective of the present. The analysis of the collective narrative revealed diverse uses of time by diverse participants, indicating diverse kinds of contributions to the overall story. The mothers in the collective used past tense, almost exclusively, to share their experience, presumably from the position of truth, as they were the guests of honor. Mothers' contributions included statements like "I was in a day of recovering the land when the army arrived" and "together with other women we remained to resist" (Daiute & Botero, 2012, slide 19). Using present time, the mothers stated their roles and positions on the issues with phrases like "I am a peasant" and "I don't want to leave this land." The *mothers* used imagined time to express the need for faith, as well as resistance to being forced from their land because of violence. The teachers also used present time to narrate their observations from their positions, noting, for example, the problem of domestic violence, "child maltreatment" and "abandonment," which they know about because "children have problems in school." *Teachers* used imagined time to express hopes for "parents to spend quality time with their children" and for themselves to learn "strategies for dialoguing with young people" in the "midst of this conflict." Young people used present to state their positions "bear[ing] the cross of living in a 'red zone' [conflict zone]." *Young students* used imagined time to express very clear desires as those differed from the others': "Our parents' tools were the blade and the hoe, but many youth don't want to be like parents."

In summary, differences in orientations emerged across stakeholders' expressions of imagined time, while past time offers more consistent meanings. True to the purpose of collectively commemorating a terrible event, the past time was given as though in implicit consensus, while imagined time allowed difference, perhaps because of its subtlety. Participants in the collective narrative used a range of time markings to engage with memories, certainties, uncertainties, and hopes. The analysis is relatively unique in its focus on relational functions of time markings—relations among stakeholders narrating an event. The organization of the narration in these temporal terms offers insights about the givens of the past, the current intentions in narrating and in life, and hopes, admonishments, and possibilities in the imaged time. Revealing here is the use of time marking to maintain solidarity whereas the imagined time—in particular the subjunctive mood—is reserved for points of disagreement with the collective.

Solidarity expressed in that collective narrative socializes members of the community to understand what is going on around them, helps them to develop critical understanding of the broader political and economic processes leading to their displacement, and fosters a sense of resistance to such changes in their ancestral lives. At the same time, groups and individuals have somewhat different positions in the community—by role, such as teachers and mothers, by generation, such as children and elders, or in some other way. Because of the importance of such solidarity, some members may not want to break the narrative harmony, yet teachers, children, and community activists are likely to perceive possible reactions to such events and to solidarity itself differently.

From the perspective of dynamic narrative theory, researchers analyzing time marking account for authors' uses of past, present, and imagined time by people as characters in relation to their roles in the story, to one another, to narrated events. In this way, time analysis is also available for researchers to use to examine our own uses of time in the interview questions we ask and the prompts we use to elicit narratives. When we ask, "What happened?" for example, we implicitly prompt for the given, the consensus. When, in contrast, we ask, "What would you do instead . . . or next time?" we implicitly prompt for another kind of meaning, one that also defines the issues of interest as study participants use imagination to convey what may be divergent meanings. The interplay of narrative construction of fact and interpretation builds solidly on previous theory, yet, as a relatively new approach in narrative inquiry in the social sciences, requires ongoing application and development.

THE TIME ANALYSIS PROCESS

The process of conducting time analysis is a fairly straightforward one of identifying time markers and their functions in narratives to determine whether and how meanings otherwise missed may be expressed with time. The process involves noticing tense and time words as they are used to create narrative perspective, the landscape of consciousness (Bruner, 1986), and complementing action events, the landscape of action (Bruner, 1986). As illustrated in Tables 6.5 and 6.6 and discussed above with diverse examples and findings from previous research, time analysis involves identifying time markers, sorting them for various time periods, and considering their relative contributions to the narrative. Table 6.7 provides a framework for applying time analysis in your projects, with the process described in this chapter and outlined below.

Table 6.7   Template for Marking Time in Narrative for Your Research

Using this table: Select a narrative you have created, collected in research, or read in this book or another publication. Underline all time markings in the narratives. In the first column below, list all the time markings you can identify. Then list past-marked verbs, words, and phrases in the "Past" column, present-marked verbs, words, and phrases in the "Present" column, and future, conditional, and other not past- or present-marked words, verbs, and phrases in the "Imagined" column. After this process, what do you notice about differences, if any, in the uses of each time for narrative meaning?

Time markings	Past	Present	Imagined

The steps of time analysis are as follows:

1. Identify all time markings in a narrative or excerpt where you expect that marking time will offer additional insights to narrative meaning.

2. Using Table 6.7, list the past, present, and imagined (future, conditional, subjunctive) times in the appropriate columns, following the instructions in the table. After this process, what do you notice about differences, if any, in the uses of each time for narrative meaning?

3. Do patterns of past, present, and imagined time shape narrative meaning? If so, how? These patterns might be of emphasis (frequency) and/or of function (apparent purpose for the author).

4. Having examined and made observations based on the frequencies of different time orientations, you are in a better position to comment on possible functions of these time orientations in the narrative and the speaker using the narrating process. For example, one set of past phrases might establish how life was in the more remote past, another might offer details of a recent past event, two present-marked phrases might create a shift between the far past and the present, and four phrases might be in imagined time. Different from the others, the imagined time introduces questions, uncertainties, alerting the speaker to a dangerous possibility. Examining the definite past, present, and hypothetical time phrases together, consider the different functions they serve in the overall narrative.

CONCLUSION AND NEXT

Character and time are particular cultural inventions, so their literary formulations are especially productive for extending as strategies for analyzing narrative meaning.

Chapter 7 focuses on presenting the narrative analyses explored in this book. After considering the nature of presentations of narrative research with insights from narrative researchers generally and with dynamic narrating in particular, the chapter offers concepts and processes for compiling, reflecting on, and presenting narrative research.

7

Outcomes of Narrative Inquiry

The activity of research presumes there will be outcomes—new knowledge, new theory, new questions, airings of once-silent voices. Given the complexity of narrative inquiry, defining outcomes in a way that satisfies all those interested is a challenge. To address that challenge, this discussion of outcomes begins by considering tensions around the goals of narrative inquiry, the relevance of these tensions to principles of a dynamic narrative approach, and guidelines for presenting findings of narrative research.

Critiques of narrative inquiry and answers to those critiques by leaders in the field revolve around what count as appropriate goals of research. The thoughtful responses below address prior critiques of narrative inquiry and thereby direct (or redirect) researchers to the potentially important outcomes of their narrative studies. Each response to a prior critique rests on a different tension inherent in the complexity of narrative and the contribution of narrative research to knowledge, practice, or policy in the human sciences.

Tension swirls around the issue of goals and outcomes:

> There is a tension in narrative studies between generalizations on the one hand and the "unpacking" of speech and narrative form on the other. Our ultimate goals as social scientists are to learn about substance, make theoretical claims through method, and to learn about the general from the particular. (Riessman, 1993, p. 70)

Another tension has to do with the roles of researcher and subject as authorities:

> Narrative inquiry, from this point of view, is one of trying to make sense of life as lived. To begin with, it is trying to figure out the taken-for-grantedness. And when that taken-for-grantedness begins also to be

taken for granted by the researcher, then the researcher can begin to participate in and see things that worked in, for example, the hospital ward, the classroom, the organization. (Clandinin & Connolly, 2000, p. 78)

Tensions also emerge around relating the personal and political nature of narrative:

Looking at narratives-in-action, we may be better off to see how complicity and countering are activities that go hand-in-hand, making it difficult to specify "tout court" distinction between them. (Bamberg, 2004a, p. 353)

Finally, there is an ongoing tension wrought of defining *narrative*:

Narrative research is frequently described as a rich and diverse enterprise, yet the kinds of narrative data that it bases itself on present a striking consensus. . . . I put forth a case for . . . the sort of systematic research that will establish connections between their interactional features and their sites of engagement. (Georgakopoulou, 2006, p. 122)

These comments by leading scholars address diverse critiques of narrative inquiry at different times in the development of the method and from diverse disciplinary perspectives. Nevertheless, the comments all focus on the need to maintain tension rather than to reduce narrative inquiry to any single side of oppositions like qualitative versus quantitative, individual versus social, and narrative text versus context. Consistent with the goal of maintaining complexity in narrative inquiry, a dynamic narrative approach integrates the particular with the general, researcher and subject, master narrative and counter narrative, leading to outcomes that embody principles of relationship, diversity, materiality, and use. Readers of this book have, ideally, experienced these integrations by using the methods of dynamic inquiry to interact with narratives and meanings.

This chapter extends the research process to honor narrative analysis by suggesting concepts and strategies researchers can use to transform analyses into insights and research reports that contribute to knowledge in the human sciences. After a reminder of some anchors of the dynamic narrative approach, this path toward outcomes begins with ideas about how to generate observations from narrative analyses (from activities in Chapters 3 through 6), take the next step toward identifying patterns of meaning (patterns including similarity, difference, change, coherence, conflict/contradiction), and progress to stating findings that address research questions. The chapter concludes with an overview of several approaches for presenting narrative research.

The process of generating findings is reserved for this final chapter for several reasons. The narrative inquiry design and analysis strategies in previous chapters are conceptual, effortful, and, ideally, informative and interesting because they involve various ways of delving deeply into narrative meaning. As is common in research, steps in data analysis are iterative, and in the case of narrative inquiry, later analyses shed light on prior ones. Zooming back from detailed analyses to a discussion of the nature and kinds of outcomes of narrative inquiry, as in this chapter, the researcher can consider prior analyses anew, from the broader perspective of the purpose and questions of the research project. The next section provides a brief reminder of foundations of dynamic narrative inquiry, in particular for defining outcomes.

DYNAMIC FOUNDATIONS FOR OUTCOMES

As an epistemology and method that spans social sciences and humanities, narrative inquiry is what scholars have referred to as a "human science" (Riessman, 2007). A human science should involve an integration of scientific processes, such as analysis, and humanistic processes, such as gaining insights about individual and societal understandings, affects, and activities. Narrative studies contribute insights about human experience, varieties of experience, and attendant knowledge and activity. Based on principles of use, relationship, materiality, and diversity, outcomes of dynamic narrative inquiry address the tensions noted at the beginning of this chapter by offering insights about particular and broader experiences of individuals' and collectives' sense making about life's challenges and the role of narrating in that process.

Toward that end, few scholars of narrative claim to be seeking objective truths, many seek systematic research methods, and most work to maintain the voices of individuals in their studies. Dynamic narrative inquiry yields insights because the approach defines narrative as a cultural tool for interacting socially (with and for others) and personally (with and for self) to make a difference in the world. As a meaningful activity for social relations and development, dynamic narrating in research as in life involves analysis (figuring out what is going on in the world and how one fits), experiencing the world (describing experience and knowledge in the lifelike mode of narrative), and translating experiences into the cultural product of narrative. Because dynamic narrating builds on narrating in life, researchers using these strategies can work interactively with analyses and original narratives, keeping both in the mix while making observations about results and, ultimately, presenting findings.

Although not often the focus of narrative theory, narrating is also an analytic process. Using narrative as a cultural tool does not mean that narratives themselves make analytic claims. Rather, narrating is a process of reading other people's expectations, reading contexts of opportunity and danger, interacting with one's own relevant knowledge and motivations, and connecting with the environment. When a child has figured out how to share different accounts of an experience in different ways with different audiences, for example, such social sensitivity is the result of the child's analysis of the situation, expectations of others in the context, and knowledge of the appropriate way to present his own experience to achieve a certain purpose. When a physician shares her narrative about an operation to a patient's family members differently from the way she explains the operation to a medical intern, similar relational knowledge comes into play. While both the child and the physician are acting spontaneously because they have learned narrative in the context of everyday life, both are interacting analytically—in terms of what they have learned about narrative structure and function.

The approach in this book has bridged spontaneous analysis in life with scientific analysis, and the culminating process in this chapter is to present scientific findings in human terms. Sensitivities for using narrative affordances like plot, character, and time are developed in culture over time for specific purposes that become increasingly refined, varied, and available. Those implicit strategies of narrating in life must, thus, be the explicit focus of scientific analysis. Narrative analyses applied across individuals, even to large groups, need not run counter to qualities valued by humanistic scientists. Agency, consciousness, and particular experience are hallmarks of narrating, so those dynamics become beacons for outcomes of narrative inquiry. Likewise, narrative researchers can present results as case studies of individual narrators or as research reports about many narrators or situations.

Principles of dynamic narrative design and analysis also guide processes of identifying and reporting findings. Activity-meaning system designs set foundations for group and individual outcomes without losing details of individual consciousness, agency, and interaction that are rationales for narrative studies. As outlined in Chapter 2, activity-meaning system designs are consistent with narrating in life because these designs sample for meaning making in diverse relationships, with diverse tools, and for diverse uses. Activity-meaning systems are designs embedded in cultural practices, which ensures ecological resonance as well as systematic sampling. The natural uses of narrating in everyday life, applied to analysis, then lead to strategies including values analysis, plot analysis, script analysis, significance analysis, character mapping, and time analysis.

Although it may seem that dynamic analysis deconstructs narratives, what it does is understand narratives and narrating as relational performances, constructions, and reflections. It's as though values, plot, script, significance, character, and time yield pieces of a puzzle—rich, detailed descriptions—that a researcher can assemble to reveal the big picture.

The next section offers suggestions that researchers who have completed some narrative analyses can use to identify outcomes of their research.

OBSERVATIONS AND MEANING

Researchers enjoy the narrative analysis process, in part because examining discourse closely for its dynamic nature brings previously hidden meanings to the light. Nevertheless, even a rewarding data analysis process inevitably leads to questions like Now what? How do I think about what I and others have learned from these analyses? How do I turn these analyses into outcomes and findings that contribute to my area of inquiry and research questions? Dynamic narrative analyses allow for observations of meaning making in use, in relationships, and in settings of practice.

An **observation** in dynamic narrative inquiry is a description of results of analytic strategies. Each analytic strategy is a process for researchers' interactions with their studies, the materials gathered for analyses, and reflection about those analyses. Each design and analysis strategy in this book is represented with tables for guiding and compiling results. Those tables become material for making observations about narrative meaning, identifying patterns across analyses, and reflecting on observations to address research questions.

Over the course of a study, researchers review and decide on materials, analytic results, and notes that appear to have special relevance to answering (or revising) the research goals and questions. These materials include transcriptions of activities and interactions in the field, narratives, supporting documents, images, charts of analyses, memos, and readings guiding the research. Observations are what researchers notice from analyses of participants' uses of narrating in activities to do things that matter in daily life, in culturally relevant interventions, or in laboratories. When study designs and analyses include context, observations drawing on those methods neither deconstruct nor reproduce narratives. In this way, rather than the story itself, observations based on dynamic narrative analyses like those discussed herein connect story with purpose and context through theoretically relevant analytic processes. Observations are qualities of human consciousness and agency that constitute narrating in the first place—in the development of narrative abilities, in narrative use across the life span, in the uses of narrating across activity and institutional contexts, such as health, education, nation, and social service. In this way, context is embedded in analysis.

Table 7.1 on page 231 offers a framework for preparing to make observations from dynamic narrative analysis strategies. As the table shows, each type of analysis strategy has one or more purposes, such as identifying performed, contested, and transformed values by individuals and groups. In addition to the goals of each analytic strategy, the table indicates ways to organize results of narrative analyses, such as with lists of values, frequencies, and percentages. Underneath the Table 7.1 row listing those organizational strategies is a place for generating observations from the compilation of results. The bottom row of the table indicates an example of the relative contribution of each type of analysis. A researcher creating such a table would summarize the goals, potential observations, and contributions of each dynamic narrative analysis strategy.

The array of observations, findings, and possible contributions presented in Table 7.1 indicates how analyses potentially constitute a complex picture of narrative meaning making. As discussed in Chapter 4, for example, a plot analysis reveals the interactive focus of narrative meaning making with the environment, generated from and supported by plot structure elements (high points, resolutions). The interaction of plot with environment differs from and complements the psychosocially oriented nature of conformity with scripts. These observations and descriptions of contributions are illustrative for other researchers extending analyses to findings.

Table 7.2 includes the categories for organizing results and observations presented in Table 7.1, with blank spaces for you to complete your own analyses and observations. To complete Table 7.2, gather the tables, notes, and original narratives from the activities you have done in Chapters 3 through 6. Working from those materials, you can prepare to identify patterns by creating lists, frequencies, percentages, or indications of most and least common features, such as values, plot elements, scripts, significance markers, character maps, and/or time analyses. Based on the organized elements, make observations about, for example, the values that emerged across stakeholder expressions (Chapter 3), most and least common scripts (Chapter 4), and/or characteristic significance markers (Chapter 5). The phrasing of such observations, ideally, honors the nature of narrative quality to address research questions.

Making observations from narrative analyses is not an end in itself, but a means of describing patterns of narrative use to address questions about meaning. Access to observations also provides material researchers can consider with participants, who, although they may not be experienced researchers, can

Table 7.1 Preparing Observations of Narrative Analyses

	Values analysis	Plot analysis	Script analysis	Significance analysis	Character analysis	Time marker analysis
Goals	Intra- and intercultural agreements, contestations, transformations	Focal issues and orientations to resolve	Named common scripts built from common plot structures	Highly and/or specifically evaluated narrative sections, characters	Framing of meaning as character voices	Orientation to narrative problem and context expressed in time
Ways to organize and compile narrative analysis results	Lists, frequencies, percentages, X = majority of values performed, contested, centered by narrative group	Lists, frequencies, percentages, X = majority of named issues for compiled high points; list pragmatic function of resolution strategies by narrative group	Lists, frequencies, percentages, X = majority of each script type by narrative group	Lists, frequencies, percentages, ratios of all or each evaluative device(s) by narrative group	Patterns of character-evaluative action meaning; lists, frequencies, percentages, ratios, X = majority, across and within group, stakeholders	
Observations (use this space to state observations about meaning based on each analysis and important part or highlight of the analysis)						
Relative contribution to overall meaning	Indicates deep structure	Indicates focus	Indicates conformity	Indicates individuality and nuance	Indicates relational voicing	Expresses meaning

Note: "X = majority" refers to summary chart indicating results with most and least frequent resulting categories.

Table 7.2 Preparing Observations of Narrative Analyses in Your Research

Using this table: With Table 7.1 as a reference point, fill in results and observations of each type of dynamic narrative analysis strategy you have done in relation to your study or practice activities in this book. You can begin anywhere in this table, adapting any sections, such as "Goals," to your study, and including descriptions, examples, or computations for any relevant analyses.

	Values analysis	Plot analysis	Script analysis	Significance analysis	Character analysis	Time marker analysis
Goals						
Organizing results of analyses and highlights						
Observations about the result(s)						
Relative contribution to overall analysis of meaning						

reflect on their own narratives and results of narrative analyses in an extended research team. Collaborative reflection about observations of narrative analyses, like those in Table 7.1, can support, extend, or question researchers' previous interpretations. The section below defines results of analyses presented in Chapters 3 through 6 as observations.

Observations From Values Analysis

As noted in Table 7.1, a major goal of values analysis is to examine narratives and other kinds of documents by diverse stakeholders related to an issue of interest to identify patterns of performing, contesting, and centering or transforming values. Toward that end, values analysis yields data for making several types of observations: a list of values expressed across stakeholders and stakeholder expressions sampled in the study and a subsequent list of values the diverse stakeholders perform, contest, and/or transform. The researcher can compile these lists into frequencies or percentages of values by stakeholder and relational activity (performing, contesting, transforming), as illustrated in Chapter 3. Observations include summarizing lists to state the values with examples by individuals and various stakeholders, followed by describing the values that are performed, contested, and transformed by individual stakeholders and across stakeholders. Observations may also be converted into tables with frequencies or percentages across narratives by an individual and/or across stakeholders. These observations can be noted in Table 7.2. This process is, moreover, helpful for selecting illustrative quotes, such as examples of values and value negotiation processes that emerge as most prominent from the analysis.

Another method for making observations is to indicate with a symbol (like X) those values that a majority of stakeholders use to perform, contest, and/or transform, as illustrated in Chapter 3. Table 7.3 provides a template for charting the most and least common features in this summary way, for observations from values analysis and other analyses.

Examples of observations from values analyses in previous studies are "Analyses of teachers' personal stories and classroom discussions indicated that most of them (six of nine) performed the value that conflicts can always be resolved, while three teachers contested that value by not including conflict resolution strategies in their personal stories and by not emphasizing conflict resolution in class discussions about literature. These same three teachers tended instead to focus on the escalation of interpersonal conflicts." Such observations based on analytic results can then be illustrated with an excerpt for each descriptive point—an excerpt of a teacher's personal story including, for example, the presence or absence of conflict resolutions, an excerpt of a teacher guiding a class discussion of literature focusing on conflict resolution, and an example of a discussion focusing on escalation. Based on the compilation of values expressions across participants and narrative examples, the researcher can make a range of observations about common and diverse narrative features and uses by individual participants, across individuals, and across groups.

The bottom row of Table 7.1 states that values analysis can reveal the deep structure of meanings enacted and questioned across stakeholders. In other words, values analysis indicates the broad issues of difference and confluence in a society as indicated in statements by diverse stakeholders. There may be other possible contributions of values analyses in specific contexts, so

Table 7.3 Charting Major and Minor Incidences of Narrative Analyses Features

Using this table: After completing a table like 7.1 for your study and making observations from any/all the narrative analyses you have done, use this table to note observations about the most and least common dynamic features emerging from narratives by individuals and/or groups in your study. In this table you can state the value, high-point issue, or other narrative feature that emerges as a highlight and pattern worth considering as a finding to address research question(s).

Narrative analysis	Most common feature by individual	Least common feature by individual	Most common feature by group	Least common feature by group
Values analysis/ values performed by stakeholder(s)				
Values analysis/ contested by stakeholder(s)				
Plot analysis/high point				
Plot analysis/ resolution				
Script analysis				
Script 1				
Script 2				
Significance feature(s)				
Significance function				
Character map				
Time analysis				

researchers should consider those in relation to the contribution of values analysis in their own studies. Related to the observation above that most teachers performed the value that interpersonal conflicts can be resolved whereas a few teachers emphasized the value that interactions often escalate conflicts, the researchers considered the deep structure of this pattern—the underlying social reason. Observing the different values across stakeholders in the context of other details of the narratives, the researchers suggested that the narratives pointed to teachers' different experiences with conflicts and, thus, different communications about them to their students. When the researchers related the narrative patterns described briefly above to other teacher demographics, it turned out, as a matter of fact, that the three teachers who emphasized escalation identified with minority groups in the United States—African American and Latino—thereby making them sensitive to the fact that not all conflicts can be resolved, in part because of institutional racism. Therefore, researchers paying attention to how conflicts escalate can gain insights about narrative uses common among members of an ethnic or social group. Rather than determining ahead of time that all teachers identifying as African American or European American, for example, narrate in the same way, their narrating activities about lived experiences and analyses of those narratives, such as with values analysis, *reveal* shared experience. The details of that study are relevant to this discussion of research outcomes primarily to offer an example of how observations from values analysis can be stated and then considered with other analyses, like plot analysis.

Observations From Plot Analysis

The primary goal of plot analysis is to identify how narrative structure provides people with a means for interacting with issues in the environment. Plot analysis yields information for observations about narrative structure in terms of various plot elements, such as issues addressed with combinations of high points and resolution strategies. As presented in Chapter 4, the plot analysis process involves identifying plot elements in each narrative sampled for the research, for example, as in several prior studies, the elements of high point and resolution strategy. After the researcher identifies the high point of each narrative, gathering all the high points is next, followed by identifying the issues expressed in the high points of individual or groups of narratives. After identifying issues expressed with the high points, the researcher generates a list of those issues. As listed in Table 4.4, issues such as "social relations," "differences of opinion," and "physical altercations" generated from plot analyses can then be checked against the original narratives. Similarly, the researcher identifies resolution strategies.

The researcher then compiles the resolution strategies according to the pragmatic approaches they employ to resolve the conflict. Because resolution strategies are narrative attempts (sometimes multiple attempts in a single narrative) to resolve the plot, their discursive function is pragmatic—that is, in service of resolving the situation, drama, or dilemmas depicted in the plot conflict. While high points revolve around issues (conflicts typically built from initiating actions and complications), resolutions are solutions and, thus, function in relation to the plot. Steps in making observations of resolution strategies include identifying the resolution strategy or multiple strategies of each narrative; gathering all the resolution strategies is next, followed by identifying the pragmatic nature of resolution strategies in individual or groups of narratives. After listing the types of resolution strategies, the researcher generates a list of those issues. As listed in Table 4.4, resolution strategies often resolve plots (or attempt to resolve them) in ways that are "communicative" (such as characters engaging in or imagining conversations), in ways that are "psychological" (such as a character deciding to stop being stubborn or deciding to consider the adversary's point of view), in ways that involve "other intervention" (such as an uninvolved person helping to resolve an interpersonal problem) or with "collective action" (such as a group of people planning a protest). Of course, different resolution strategy types might emerge from the specific nature of the narrative database. After generating the types of resolution strategies, the researcher can check these against the original narratives.

In terms of the relative contribution of plot analysis to meaning in a narrative study, plots—especially initiating actions, high points, and resolutions—indicate the authors' interactions with their environments: the settings, issues, and means of resolving issues in environments depicted symbolically in narrative form. The next section briefly discusses the unique contribution of observations from script analysis.

Observations From Script Analysis

As discussed in Chapter 4, scripts are common plot organizations by groups of participants and individuals. As also explained in Chapter 4, script analysis builds on basic plot structures, smoothing over the structural elements, to indicate a bigger picture or story type. For example, the relatively large database of narratives by young people growing up during the 1990s wars across the former Yugoslavia (discussed in terms of design and different analyses in Chapters 2, 4, and 6) revealed three common scripts organizing youth narratives of conflicts among adults. After following the steps in script analysis (Chapter 4), the researcher grouped narratives according to apparently similar scripts, named the scripts, and checked the narrative script categories against each narrative again. Observations then focused on the most and least prevalent script types across the four country contexts of the study. A major contribution of script analysis to participant meanings is the conformity to collective ways of knowing. These scripts, however, may vary by author-narrative-audience relation, as conformity differs across contexts where people share their stories.

Observations From Significance Analysis

The goal of significance analysis is to offer insights about individual, particular, and even peculiar meanings in relation to collective ones, like those in values and script analysis. Possible observations based on significance analysis are numerous, in part because of the richness of evaluative devices and the prevalence of evaluation especially in narrative discourse but also in other genres. As presented in Chapter 5, significance is marked by overall use of evaluation, use of specific evaluative devices, combinations of evaluative devices, and functions of evaluative devices. Significance analysis, thus, offers information for observations about patterns of difference and nuance in scripts, insights about how authors are humanizing characters in narratives, expressing them with thoughts and feelings, or other meanings.

A researcher focusing on significance, in particular to highlight the individual unique communications of participants, might decide to identify all devices and then narrow to those most characteristic of the individual, situation, or group. For example, when evaluative devices in a narrative cluster around a plot high point, a researcher can observe not only the nature of the high point—such as that it revolves around a threat to mortality—but also that the point is emphasized. If such a pattern of high points about threats to mortality occurs in more than one narrative or narratives by more than one person, the researcher can describe either of those facts. If some narratives or authors emphasize the brush with mortality while another narrative or author emphasizes a resolution, those differences are also notable for description. This step toward description involves researchers in a process of interacting with the original narratives, the data that narrative analyses have offered, descriptions about the narratives, and back again to the impact of the actual narrative(s) with these new insights.

Sometimes a researcher has a hypothesis about a specific evaluative device, such as that affective states will be relatively extensive in personal experience (autobiographical) narratives compared to their less extensive use in narratives focused on others. In the absence of a specific hypothesis about how evaluative devices indicate meaning, a researcher would identify the range of evaluative devices, do descriptive assessments of whether and how these observations of significance differ across and within stakeholders by situation and time, and then focus on those devices that indicate unique meanings by an individual or group, relative to the research questions. Observations of significance patterns can be descriptions of the evaluation patterns and the meanings they add to explicit statements of plot or other aspects of the narrative. Character mapping is an especially interesting companion to significance analysis when researchers are extending from analysis to observation. Time analysis employs yet another narrative element for additional insights about meaning.

Observations From Character Mapping and Time Analysis

The goal of character mapping is to examine diverse expressive voices within narratives as symbolic enactments of experiences, issues, and ideas that the author lays out as connected in some way. Observations of character mapping include the mention, emphasis, and patterning of characters in and around the narrative, the roles of those characters, and their functions. Close examination of the patterns of evaluation also can support observations of functions like minimizing and others discussed in Chapter 6.

The goal of time analysis is to pay attention to another major narrative feature where additional or conflicting meanings may reside. In the narratives from Colombia, for example, community members used past time markings to perform solidarity against attacks on their communities, for lost loved ones, for their stolen way of life, and for attempts to persevere; present time markings to establish feeling and intentionality; and imagined time to express their will to survive and to move beyond givens.

After writing observations from tables of narrative analyses, the researcher shifts to a consideration of patterns. Patterns include observed similarities, differences, change, and other comparisons. Narrative analysis offers a systematic way to extend observations to findings through the process of identifying patterns of meaning.

IDENTIFYING PATTERNS OF MEANING

Researchers who value narrative because it is rich, experiential, particular, and communicative appreciate complexity and want to analyze for it. Dynamic narrative design and analyses provide strands of meaning to identify from patterns and, ultimately, to report as findings about complex experiences, knowledge, and intention shared in the narrative realm. Research questions typically imply the identification of certain patterns. For example, a research question highlighting process is "How do young immigrants understand their being called 'illegal'?" A research question highlighting a pattern of difference is "How do young immigrants who are refugees, such as from natural or human-made crises, understand their being called 'illegal' differently from immigrants whose parents came to the United States without visas?" Research questions can, thus, guide a researcher to identify patterns of results. Identifying patterns may also lead to unexpected findings or to the establishment of a refined set of research questions.

What is a pattern and why are patterns important to narrative inquiry? Patterns of relationships and difference (such as authors' connecting to different audiences from different perspectives and participants sampled from different experiential situations for different purposes) create the weft and warp of narrative meanings woven together. By examining and comparing strands of meaning, the researcher can gain a greater appreciation of the content and purpose of narrative in use.

Four kinds of patterns are characteristic of dynamic narrative inquiry. Narrative meanings pattern in relationship to the nature of experience the researcher expects from people in different positions, the types of narratives sampled, and the narrative analyses applied. In terms of an activity-meaning system design, the researcher would expect relationships of meanings across stakeholders in the system, such as a relationship of similarity, difference, or partial overlap. For example, a study eliciting narratives by immigrant high school students in the United States and their U.S.-born peers examined the two groups' patterns in relation to one another (Lucić, 2012). Immigrant and U.S.-born youth may not interact all that much, but the formulations of each group toward the other and toward the contexts where they live are expressed in their narratives. Certain meanings may be similar across groups, such as that immigrants have been singled out in public and local discourse in recent years, while other meanings may differ, such as the understanding among immigrant youth that their positive contributions to the society are greatly undervalued.

Similarity

Patterns of similarity may occur across narratives or other expressions by an individual, across analyses of narratives by two or more individuals, across materials by several stakeholders, or across another combination of research participants. Similarities occur not in exact words but in similar uses of narrating as indicated in analyses of plots, values, and other cultural tools. If you have completed Tables 7.2 and 7.3, identify patterns of similarity and write statements about those patterns.

Difference

Patterns of difference may occur across narratives by an individual, across analyses of narratives by two or more individuals, across materials by several stakeholders, and across other combinations of research participants. Patterns of difference could also open complexities within individuals or groups when the research design elicits or gathers narratives requiring different narrative stances in relation to an issue, audience, or purpose. Patterns of relation are available in contexts defined by narrating for multiple audiences, from multiple perspectives, in multiple activities, and in multiple genres.

A focus on patterns of differences of scripts in narratives of conflicts among adults (discussed in Chapter 4 and in the section on observations above) offered the finding that a majority of participants in each of the four countries narrated conflicts among adults in everyday life conforming to a similar script. Of the narratives by youth in BiH, 62% conformed to a "tensions abound" script, while 68% of narratives by youth in Serbia conformed to a "reflect on societal divisions" script, and 56% of narratives by youth in Croatia and 52% of narratives by refugee youth from the former Yugoslavia conformed to a "move beyond difficulties" script. The researcher with such findings could reasonably make an observation about different narrative scripts that emerged in each context—that is, conformity to different ways of organizing experience, at least around conflicts among adults.

Change

Change is an interest in social science research. Reasons for examining change include determining results of an intervention in health practice, community participation, education, or other institutional activity. Change is relevant to research designs and questions that sample over time, such as over the course of policy innovations, introduction of an environmental change, or some other situation the researcher expects to have an impact on participants and their narratives. Researchers who have designed studies over time, diverse situations, or other differences should have analyses available to observe for patterns of change. Research with the goal of identifying change typically seeks diverse results of analyses but must check as well for similarities.

Examining results of an intervention requires sampling across time appropriate to a task. Another kind of change emerging in contemporary theory about the social nature of human diversity, as in dynamic narrative inquiry, is change over situations. If human knowing, development, and behavior are sociocultural phenomena, then change would occur across situations (not only over time). Situations include narrating for different purposes and audiences, and from different stances. Cross-situational changes in narrative and other expressions would require the time to participate in those situations, but it is the nature of the situations that is most relevant to explore, rather than the period of time for an intervention to take. In fact, the change of narrating situation is an intervention, if one thinks about how people interact with narrating as a cultural tool that changes them as well as any message conveyed within it.

Narratives sampled before, during, and after an intervention may indicate changes in values, structure, or significance as a result of the intervention. For example, the classroom-based study of 7- through 10-year-old children's narratives of conflict over a year with a violence prevention program showed that children's autobiographical narratives conformed to the values of the violence prevention program increasingly over the year, while their fictional narratives conformed less to the values of the violence prevention program over the course of the year. The research design and inclusion of different narrative genres (autobiographical and fictional) indicated change over time and relation. Changes over time differed for autobiographical and fictional narratives, revealing patterns of relation, diversity, and change. The children's uses of narrating changed in relation to the curriculum, author-audience relation, and time. The curriculum introduced specific values of how people should and should not deal with conflicts and disagreements with peers; the autobiographical narrative genre exposed the author as a character enacting conflict, and the school year with the curriculum allowed ample time for such changes.

The study of how middle school youth in an after-school program used narrating about experiences at work before and after interacting with a computer game simulating a work situation in which the young people played the role of bank teller expected to conform to certain rules (discussed in Chapter 3) revealed a different pattern (Kreniske, 2012). The pattern of change in values in narratives of prior experiences embedded in a "letter to a boss" and a "letter to a friend" in that study differed for the younger (sixth-grade) and older (seventh- and eighth-grade) participants. That study occurred over a short period (within an hour) of playing the banking simulation game, and the differences in whether and how students of the different age groups used narratives to different audiences to enact a new set of values became prominent. With these examples, one can see how the sampling of narrators and narrative activities offers observations about relationship, diversity, and change in meaning making. These patterns may be, moreover, between groups (such as age groups), within groups (such as youth in different countries), or between and within groups given another design.

Coherence

Narrative inquiry often seeks a coherent representation of autobiographical accounts (Baerger & McAdams, 1999; Georgakopoulou, 2006; Hermans & Hermans-Jansen, 2001; Linde, 1993; McAdams, 2005). Narratives are organized in terms of coherent structures like plot, values, and focal issues. Coherence may occur in extended narratives by an individual or group within a time and place or over extended space-time dimensions. Research emphasizing coherence tends to be a priority in health fields, especially mental health, sociological and social psychological studies of group process, and certain studies of development. Dynamic narrative inquiry researchers are, however, also open to exploring how conflict and contradiction operate in narrative meaning making.

Conflict and Contradiction

From the perspective of a theory of use, narrating is a process of relating experiences, knowledge, and intention from diverse perspectives across diverse spheres of activity (personal, interpersonal, social, political). In addition to structures that foster coherence, like script, narrative elements trade on trouble—that is, breaches in the normal course of events (Bruner, 2002)—and thus conflict. While script is a concept acknowledging the smoothing over of complexities toward a collective coherent account, plot in most cultures requires some conflict, which may or may not be resolved. This and relations among characters as well as relations among author, narrator, narrative, and context also reveal tensions and conflicts across those spheres of activity.

Observations of patterns from various analyses can be examined for their interrelations. Observations can be described as diverse strands of meaning fitting together as complementing one another, in tension, in sequence, or in causal relation. Observing those different patterns of similarity, difference, and change contributes to an account of cultural meaning and nuance gleaned from narrating by people in diverse positions with diverse interests in a system. Observations in tension with one another allow contradictory meanings to become evident. Such tensions or contradictions signal relational dynamics like power relations, problem solving, or development and, thus, the life-like processes that often interest researchers. Observations presented as causal or impact relations refer to the narrating context in ways that reveal complex author/speaker stances. For example, as discussed in Chapter 6, narratives about the plights of others (third persons in narratives) often express more negative affect than those about one's own (first person expressions). As such, a sequence of narratives usefully opens diverse perspectives that occur for individuals as well as across them. We researchers working with narratives should welcome those tensions to observe life-like meaning.

In summary, like archaeologists, dynamic narrative inquirers scan the narrative landscape broadly and impressionistically, both before and after the detailed analysis work is completed. The central research work, however, which enhances researchers' sensitivity to the richness of narrating, is to dig, to find shards, perhaps gems, beyond the obvious to later re-create the broader scene and improve the picture with the benefit of having explored deeply. Narrative researchers identify living cultural products—plots, characters, values, time, and significance—considering how these work together and with those of historical relevance to convey complex ecologically valid meaning addressing research questions.

FROM OBSERVATIONS TO FINDINGS

Research questions also define the scope of relevant findings. After noting observations indicated by your analyses and focusing further to identify patterns of similarity, difference, change, and/or coherence, you can begin to state findings addressing the research questions established for your study. Findings expressed as statements to address your research questions are claims based on observations of results of analyses, patterns, and combined patterns. Insights that could be helpful when you are creating claims from observations begin with the consideration of different kinds of research questions and the outcomes implied. The phrasing of research questions directs expectations of research reports and should, ideally, remain in the researcher's creative/scientific process.

Questions of existence ask for how specific individuals or groups understand an issue, such as in the question "How do people involved in a certain situation understand/participate in/want to change the circumstances of their experience?" Questions of association seek connections across individuals and groups, either with one another or with some other phenomenon, such as a situation, as in the question "How do young people growing up in different circumstances understand/participate in/want to change their experience?" Questions of impact promise close examination of activities and effects, such as with an intervention, the passage of time, or some other specific alteration of what would be the normal course of events. This is suggested in the question "What changes occur after a focal participant or a group of people in a similar situation as that participant participate in an activity or intervention?"

Table 7.4 provides a worksheet you can use for moving from observations (noted in Tables 7.2 and 7.3 and/or in notes you made in the analysis process) to findings.

Table 7.4   Preparing to Summarize Outcomes of Narrative Inquiry

Write your research questions here:

1.

2.

3.

What are these research questions asking or implying about the nature of findings in your narrative inquiry?

Descriptions

Individuals:

Groups:

Other:

Analyses—patterns of

Relationship (what kind):

Difference (what kind):

Change (what kind):

Coherence

Conflict, Tension

Certain kinds of experiences:

Findings your questions imply

Existence:

Association:

Impact:

Other:

Based on this analysis, rewrite or edit your research questions to account better for what your method allows.

Findings

Some narrative research questions focus on identifying the experiences of underrepresented or marginalized persons. When asking, for example, "How do young people brought illegally to the United States feel about their legal and life situations?" a researcher might focus on describing each participant's explicit statements about citizenship, legality, and related matters. Studies addressing such questions might interview from 3 to 20 people in the given group, perhaps sampled over a range of factors that could interact with the effects of living undocumented in the United States, such as gender, age, and ethnicity. Some questions in such an interview would be phrased explicitly, while questions designed to elicit narratives might prompt for "a time when . . ." Because narrating is an illustrative—apparently documentary—medium, showing rather than explaining experience, researchers find few explicit statements to draw on for insights about the nature, depth, nuance, or complexity of respondents' feelings. That is one of the reasons for doing narrative analyses, but, as discussed above, detailed analyses must translate into observations and findings that reasonably describe one or more participants' (stakeholders') representations related to a question. Reports from such analyses might present illustrative extracts of explicit statements of risk and related circumstances. Such studies are consistent with the report rationale discussed in Chapter 1, and, as some have reported, lead to new ways of thinking about issues of interest and perspectives of those who have been previously excluded.

Researchers also want to make scientific contributions from narrative studies contributing findings that identify realities beyond descriptions.[1] Analysis involves working with the details of discourse—or another phenomenon—such as by reading/listening very closely to narratives in context. In addition to the importance of concrete detail in narrative analysis is the importance of being able to test analytic results, with multiple analyses and in different relationships. With observations about the explicit phase of narrating (what is said) and the evaluative phase (how it is said), multiple meanings emerge, and the researcher's theory is key to integrating information from the various analyses to address the research questions. Analytic findings address research questions that go a step further than describing experiences of individuals or groups to offering more general results and contributing to theory as well as new knowledge in a field.

Outcomes of narrative inquiry are, in summary, generated from analyses of values, plots, scripts, significance, character mapping, and time markers. Observations are, in turn, considered for patterns of similarity, difference, and change, thereby again maintaining particular and general, individual and social, diversity and connection. With guidelines for transforming analyses into observations and findings, active users of this book would have some summary

Table 7.5 Guiding Questions for Working from Analyses to Observations to Findings and Toward Presentations

Using this table: Writing responses to the following questions should be helpful as you summarize steps thus far in your narrative inquiry project. It is possible that some questions will not be relevant to your study or that you will have only partial responses at this time. Do what you can as a way of determining where you are in your project.

What are your research questions?

What is your research design?

What is the activity-meaning system context?

Who are the stakeholders (number and reasons why selected)?

Which narratives do you need for analysis?

    Created in what context?
    In what form?
    How many?

Which narrative analyses have you completed or tried?

What results do you have from those analyses? (Include charts, notes, or other analysis results.)

What observation is indicated by each analysis?

Drawing on that observation, what finding can you state to address the research question or a revised research question?

findings to use in drafting research presentations. Table 7.5 provides a framework for summarizing progress in a narrative inquiry project.

The following section defines three approaches to writing narrative inquiry reports, articles, or chapters.

PRESENTING DYNAMIC NARRATIVE RESEARCH

The previous chapters of this book have presented and, ideally, engaged readers in dynamic narrative inquiry—design and analyses of narrative discourse and narrative analyses of non-narrative discourse.

Having found that certain analyses offered findings, readers now must combine them into a research report, article, or book to address research questions.

> . . . narrative nonfiction books or articles are fundamentally collections of scenes that together make one big story. . . . [Nonfiction] narrative requires more research than traditional reportage, for writers cannot simply tell what they learn or know; rather, they must show it . . . strive for accuracy even when ideas and information are presented as scenes. (Gutkind, 2012)

Narrative inquiry focuses on eliciting and appreciating individuals' expressions of experience related to an issue or phenomenon of research interest. The dynamic narrative inquiry theory and method presented in this book, with activity-meaning system designs (including a fuller or more partial complement of stakeholders) and any or all of the analytic strategies, provides data for a range of approaches to writing research reports, articles, or books. Thus far, this chapter has offered a guide for generating observations—a collection of scenes, if you will—toward presenting a coherent research report. The pragmatic nature of any research report is an argument, a kind of story, that sets the scene with a rationale for a study, states a research question or two, an approach for how the question will be addressed, and an explanation of how the study led to a certain conclusion. Different formats of research reports resemble narratives more or less, as discussed briefly below. Nevertheless, a researcher can usefully think of the presentation of findings as telling a kind of story, as suggested by Gutkind in the quotation above.

The findings of narrative inquiry address research questions. Questions guiding narrative inquiry would ask "how" relevant persons experience a certain phenomenon or issue of interest, "how" that phenomenon occurs in diverse ways across groups positioned differently around the issues, and "how" individuals relate to the issues in different situations when sharing their experiences with different audiences and for different purposes.

The findings of narrative research combine into an argument the researcher contributes to the specific line of inquiry or theory. One can think of this argument as a nonfiction story. Findings of my analyses of narratives with young people growing up in the midst of wars combined to shift the story of the effects of war from a story that "life was fine, then one day war disrupted everything, children were the major victims thereby experiencing trauma . . ." to a very different kind of story that "life was fine, then over time tensions rose, children interacted intensely with the people and situations most salient where they lived, and those historical circumstances then became the frameworks of their ways of perceiving the world and themselves."

Having generated observations and findings from analysis, a researcher can address several questions to guide the process toward presenting a research report. Questions guiding the presentation of a dynamic narrative inquiry include the following:

- What questions motivated your study?
- What design have you used to elicit experiences and knowledge related to these questions?
- Reviewing the tables you created with guidelines in this chapter and others, what findings seem most interesting, solid, or important in some other way?
- How do you summarize the finding(s) of each analysis? What statement expresses the result?
- How do you summarize any combined findings from various analyses?
- How do these statements address your research questions?
- What do these responses to the research questions offer to theory and/or previous research?
- What continued research questions would follow from your study?

With notes addressing these questions, a researcher can consider the format of a research report. Ideally, that process begins with deciding on an appropriate publication context—an oral presentation, an article to submit to a specific scholarly journal, a chapter for a book, a book, or a journalistic or policy piece. Examining models of any considered publication source is a good way to identify the features.

With all that you have learned from your dynamic narrative inquiry design and analyses, you can consider findings as indicating meaning in context. With sensitivity to the relational and diverse use of the dynamic approach, you can consider narrative meaning as it unfolds in conversation (Mishler, 1991). With that respect of narrating in everyday life, you can proceed to presenting your research with a variety of options.

Case Study Approach

Staying true to the individual, as scholars say is a "hallmark" of narrative (Riessman, 2007), is important. One way to do that is to present case studies focusing on an individual's experience and meanings. There are also other ways, such as seeking common, diverse, and interacting meanings relevant to an issue within and/or across individuals and groups.

Case studies, also referred to as life story narratives, emphasize narrating as a process that constitutes development of self-concept or self-representations. The primarily descriptive approach defines the person in terms of narrative coherence, with some theories allowing for narrative affordances like chapters (McAdams, 2005) or time (Freeman, 2009). Theoretical concepts of interaction such as positioning of multiple voices in an individual's life story offer a researcher tools for understanding personal complexity and for interpreting the individual's story.

Dynamic descriptive cases consider representation and positioning, rather than the content of self-representations alone (Wortham, 2001). Different from presenting the story literally as an interviewee expressed it, a dynamic narrative case study interprets and presents the interview in terms of actual and virtual conversations enacted in the expressive activity. While some researchers present participant interviews exactly as expressed, those with a dynamic narrative orientation present diverse "selves" as indicated by different characters in diverse relations to one another. A dynamic narrative description is presented in terms of relational concepts (characters, voices, positions) over time (past, present, and future selves). Rather than a case study expressed as a coherent albeit changing self over time, a dynamic narrative case is presented as a character interacting in scenes. This difference between a literal case study description and a literary case study description has implications for the organization of a narrative inquiry report and, thus, the contribution of the narrative inquiry.

For example, the dynamic case study of Jane, presented by Wortham (2001), mentions the number of episodes defined by life events and Jane's direct interactions with the interviewer. Rather than organizing these scenes chronologically in the research presentation, Wortham presents major and minor characters in Jane's life story and different types of relations among those characters, among other theoretical analytic frames. Headings in the chapter focus on Jane's different ways of representing herself and the challenges in her life, including "passive voice," "active voice," and "assertive voice." The researcher presents the major life challenges Jane focused on, including "institutionalizations" in orphanages, "parenthood," and "abortions."

While coherence in one orientation might be self with self, coherence in the other is of speaker with context and each context of telling/writing. A dynamic approach foregrounds tensions because tensions are evidence of interaction—when we assume that people use narratives to do something, each use involves some acknowledgment and interaction with context. Use then becomes paramount to coherence, so tensions that emerge across uses highlight a personal dynamic in relation to the sociocultural context.

Sociobiography Approach

Sociobiographies offer comparative cases of individual and social meanings in terms of common and diverse narratives of experience and knowledge around an issue or phenomenon of interest. **Sociobiography** is a unit of analysis that integrates individual and society in terms of dynamic relations. Sociobiography is a concept defining individual perspectives in relation to the social and physical environments (Daiute, 2010). Sociobiographies bring relationships among diverse stakeholders to life. This view is consistent with theories explaining that all discourse is social because it embodies meaning in activity (Bakhtin, 1986; Bruner, 1986; Harré & van Langenhove, 1999).

Organizational structures of sociobiographical presentations of narrative inquiry can begin with scripts or values—different representations of shared narrative orientations by groups of individuals. Headings can name the scripts, followed by highlighting of the unique enactments of those scripts by individuals who conform to them. As shown in one study and discussed above, a majority of participants in Bosnia and Herzegovina wrote narratives of conflicts among adults with an organization characterized as "tensions abound," while within that group, individuals differed in various ways in how they did that (Daiute, 2010).

Case studies of how individual young people make national scripts their own inform us of the interactive nature of human development and social change. The study identified individual cases from contributions by participants within BiH and the other countries involved. The following criteria guided the selection of cases: Participants completed all activities in the workshop, one or more of the narratives conformed to the local script pattern, and the resulting four participants from each country include a male and a female in the younger cohort (ages 12 to 18) and a male and a female in the older cohort (ages 19 to 27).

After compiling the data for these individuals, the researcher compared the approach of each individual to the relevant national scripts. Analyses revealed several dimensions of variation for transforming scripts into personal stories: location of the narrator (direct or indirect), narrator connection to the conflict (emotional or rational), historical orientation (past, present, or future), tone (earnest or ironic), and any other notably unique discursive elements. Questions guiding the case analysis included "How is the national script enacted differently by this individual?" and "What variations, consistencies, and contradictions appear across the data for this participant?"

After beginning broadly to characterize the political-violence system and then the national responses, the researcher considered individuals interacting with those environments via the details of everyday life. An analysis accounting for differences in significance, character mapping, and time use by participants conforming to a national (or other) script yields the "biography" within the "sociobiography" format. In this way, specific narratives become evident as useful for differentiating among individuals' perspectives within a broader social frame. Sociobiography is, thus, a way to consider narrating as a mediational process.

Individual variations revealed that although children growing up in political violence develop understandings in direct relation to their environments, as evidenced in their uses of common country-specific scripts, individuality also flourishes. Differences identified herein relate systematically around scripts, such as claiming more or less responsibility to address societal divisions among participants in Serbia, more or less individualistic orientations to moving beyond difficulties in Croatia, more or less practical and emotional orientations to tense circumstances in BiH, and more or less otherworldly solace to deal with exclusion among participants in the United States. These options relate to scripts, so they are not completely open, but choice emerges as an option, especially when issues are open for examination.

Traditional Research Approach

Because dynamic narrative inquiry methods offer systematic analyses amenable to reliability checks and presented with comparative computations, some researchers seeking publication in certain kinds of research journals can use a format typical of scientific academic discourse. The format for such journals is to begin with a theoretical and research rationale for the study, a research question, descriptions of methods (including design plan for sampling participants), data, and detailed data analysis plan. A section on results follows, with data tables, reports of reliability, statistical texts, implications, and conclusion.

In summary, a case approach is characteristic of much narrative inquiry. The sociobiography approach is one developed for case studies sensitive to social, political, and other environmental factors. An approach to traditional scientific research is also possible from dynamic narrative inquiry designs and analyses. Both approaches appreciate narrating, albeit in different ways. A descriptive approach tends to equate results with specific narratives and authors. A socio-biographical approach draws especially on the activity-meaning system research design to consider similar and different experience and knowledge across groups and individual stakeholders in relation to a question of interest. A traditional research approach organizes findings in terms of scientific inquiry to yield generalized results.

CONCLUSION AND MAINTAINING A DYNAMIC APPROACH

This book began with a discussion about different ways of appreciating narrative in an interactive research process. The ideal of interaction has been a beacon of much qualitative inquiry and narrative studies in particular, with numerous thoughtful approaches. These approaches have sought to define research in terms of interaction with people whose experiences have not been in the mainstream foundations of knowledge, to craft a research process that honors participants' voices, sometimes by blurring distinctions between researcher and subject, sometimes by presenting research in narrative form, and sometimes by blurring distinctions between narrative and narrating. Interactive narrative inquiry also includes relationships between society and individuals and groups whose goals and ways of knowing are defined in very different ways.

Chapters in this book have explained and illustrated an inquiry approach consistent with the appreciation of narrating as a powerful human tool for doing important activities in everyday life. By learning about these processes for research, you are recognizing what speakers of a language—in this case English—do every day. Table 7.6 presents a list of just some of these amazing everyday narrative skills, summarizing the major inquiry skills presented in this book. If some of these narrative processes help a researcher listen or read more carefully, the journey of narrative inquiry has begun.

The explanation of how researchers have built their studies on different functions of narrating began with a theory of dynamic narrating, with four principles applied to narrative inquiry in research in the human sciences. As readers have seen, this theory of narrative use also applies practices of spontaneous narrating to specific methods of design and analysis. Dynamic narrative inquiry builds on a notion of interaction extending the field in a different way—a way that connects researcher and subject, particular and broader stories, solidarity

| **Table 7.6** | Activities of Dynamic Narrative Inquiry |

Using this table: Mark the activities you have (1) applied, (2) tried, (3) need to practice further, (4) still have to get to, or (5) don't understand. Also, write notes about possible contributions of each narrative inquiry activity to your study.

_____ Developing research question(s)

_____ Activity-meaning system research design

    _____ Identifying time and space locations of narrative interactions relevant to the issues and questions of research interest

    _____ Identifying stakeholders who interact with and in narratives, explicitly and implicitly

    _____ Identifying relevant stakeholder expressions:

_____ Values analysis

    _____ Identifying values in sampled narratives and documents across stakeholders

        _____ List of topics addressed

        _____ Values implied by those topics

        _____ Beginning with more explicit narratives, documents, moving to implicit

    _____ Identifying values performed, contested, transformed across stakeholders

    _____ Summary of most frequently performed values across stakeholders

    _____ Summary of most frequently contested values across stakeholders and by stakeholders

    _____ Summary of transformed values across stakeholders, by stakeholders

    _____ Possible contributions of values analysis:

_____ Plot analysis

    _____ Identifying plot elements

        _____ Setting

        _____ Initiating action

        _____ Complicating actions

        _____ High point/turning point/climax

(Continued)

Table 7.6 (Continued)

_____ Resolution strategy(ies)

_____ Coda/moral stated

_____ Possible contributions of values analysis:

_____ Script analysis

_____ Identifying draft scripts

_____ Identifying basic plot (initiating action, high point, resolution strategy[ies])

_____ Identifying logical connections holding plot together

_____ Identifying groups of narratives conforming to each draft script

_____ Making any necessary revisions of script to yield general ones

_____ Naming each script for the apparent conforming social/collective narrative message

_____ Significance analysis

_____ Identifying evaluative devices

_____ Psychological state expressions

_____ Affective states

_____ Cognitive states

_____ Reported speech

_____ Intensifiers

_____ Negatives

_____ Qualifiers

_____ Causal connectors

Familiarity with functions of significance markers

_____ Humanizing

_____ Minimizing

_____ Qualifying

_____ Connecting logically

_____ Connecting socially

_____ Character mapping

    _____ Identifying characters

        _____ First-person singular characters

        _____ First-person plural characters

        _____ Third-person singular characters

        _____ Third-person plural characters

        _____ Other characters

    _____ Identifying focal characters and peripheral characters

        _____ Character frequencies

        _____ Character placement in the plot

    _____ Identifying character roles

    _____ Identifying significance functions for the focal and other characters

    _____ Summarizing symbolic uses of different characters in the narrative

    _____ Possible contributions of character mapping:

_____ Time analysis

    _____ Identifying time markings

    _____ Categorizing time markings

        _____ Past

        _____ Present

        _____ Imagined times

    _____ Summarizing uses of different time markings in the narrative, across narratives

    _____ Making observations from analyses

    _____ Identifying findings (from observations) to address research questions

    _____ Possible contributions of time analysis

and conflict in terms of language and activity as intelligent tools for relationship and diversity for the collective development of humanity.

How "development" is defined in different circumstances across the globe is contentious during this 21st century, when inequality and injustice are increasing. Narrative inquiry is one activity for addressing questions about experience, goals, and context, because much of the bad and good is done with narrative means. To maintain inquiry that acknowledges such global and local dynamics, researchers can continue to apply and stretch principles of narrative use—relationship, diversity, materiality—to people using narratives and other cultural tools to do things that are mostly good but certainly are defined in terms of their ongoing dreams and challenges to those dreams. With a theory and method of narrative use based in those principles, researchers can learn from their inquiries, address research questions, and contribute new knowledge to their fields. We cannot provide absolute answers, but we can offer reasoned observations and findings from narrative analyses. We can, moreover, maintain the dynamic nature of inquiry that inevitably extends interesting findings with new questions to pursue.

Note

1. An advance in narrative inquiry is to do analyses that can be checked for reliability, ensuring stability of each category of analysis. Reliability checks of analytic concepts and procedures are important for researchers wanting to maintain consistency in their analyses over time, for readers of the works wanting to check their agreement on any examples presented, and for future applications of the method.

Appendix

Process Checklists

The checklists below summarize the major activities involved in the research design, analysis, and interpretation strategies in this book. Each chapter discusses the concept, prior use in research, and process in detail.

THE DYNAMIC NARRATIVE DESIGN PROCESS CHECKLIST

Narrative research design can be dynamic and critical with a sampling and analysis of expressions by diverse actors (stakeholders) who interact explicitly or implicitly around a set of experiences and/or issues of interest. This process is activity-meaning system design.

1. Identify a research focus and read previous related research to learn about what is already known and what is still unclear.

2. In addition to reading previous related research, familiarize yourself with the relevant participants, settings, narratives, and related expressions. Ways of doing this include, but are not limited to, the following:

   2a. Make notes from your own experiences and observations.

   2b. Identify narratives available on the Internet as you consider appropriate narratives and narrating activities for your study.

   2c. Visit settings and do informal observation.

   2d. From those settings, create or gather narratives, interactions with narratives.

   2e. Identify a few sample narratives, conversations, or other materials that seem similar to what you would hope to have as data for your research.

3. Draft some research questions.

4. Draft an activity-meaning system design for narrative inquiry.

4a. Consider elements of activity-meaning system designs:

4a1. Identify time-space dimensions of narrative interactions.

4a2. Identify stakeholders in these narrative interactions.

4a3. Identify stakeholder expressions.

4a4. Make notes about possible outcomes of the study.

4a5. Make notes about any hypotheses you have about what you might find.

5. Review the activity-meaning system design draft, and consider how narrative interactions across them might play out.

VALUES ANALYSIS PROCESS CHECKLIST

Values analysis is a process for selecting and analyzing norms and principles that organize narrative expressions across stakeholders (participants) in an interacting social system. On the view that each narrative is a response to others across relevant time and space, values are performed, contested, or transformed, depending on narrator stance, audience, and other circumstances.

1. After reviewing your research question, identify stakeholders: societal (global, national, local), institutional (within relevant practices), group (with common histories, goals, and so on), individuals, individuals' different situations (possible intra-personal diversities).

2. Select narratives and other expressions to enact key stakeholders/actors for the values analysis relevant to your research question.

3. Identify values across stakeholder expressions, remembering that values are norms, principles to live by, and common assumptions, stated explicitly or, more often in narratives, implicitly. Identify values by sentence; later in the process, this will help you identify predominant values by narrative (see item 5, below).

3a. Identify explicitly stated values, underlining sentences (or "t-units"— thought units of independent clauses and the dependent clauses and/ or phrases that go with them grammatically) expressing them; for example, there may be a phrase or word that states or implies judgment, like "good," "bad," or "beautiful."

3b. Identify implicitly stated values; see item 3a, above.

3c. Continue to identify values by using methods such as beginning with societal stakeholders (going from the bottom up as well as from the top down) and beginning with policy statements.

4. Write down the values of each stakeholder, indicating which stakeholder expressions state each value.

5. Identify predominant (most common) and somewhat expressed values for each narrative.

6. Examine the values negotiation process—performing (uptake of societal and institutional values), contesting (ignoring or denying or expressing values counter to the institutional values), centering (creating some new form of values)—across your selected stakeholder expressions.

7. Summarize the values (groups of values and the overall values) within and across stakeholder spheres, groups, and individuals that are mutually taken up (performed), are not taken up (contested), and are transformed in some way (centered as unique in some way).

8. Compile results of the values analyses.

9. Consider the contribution of the values analysis to addressing your research questions and/or to suggesting other research questions.

PLOT ANALYSIS PROCESS CHECKLIST

Plot analysis identifies the basic structure of a narrative and as such can apply to a single narrative, many narratives, groups of narratives, interviews, letters, or other time-marked discourses. Plot analysis identifies the structure of a plot—most simply beginning, middle, and end—comprising initiating action, complicating actions, plot conflict or turning point, resolution strategies, and ending.

1. Read each narrative, then read it again. When you think you are familiar with the narrative, take a first step at identifying what seem to be its major movements by identifying what you perceive as the beginning, middle, and end sections, and more specifically the plot elements.

2. Identify the plot elements, including the following:
   2a. Setting
   2b. Characters

Primary character(s)

Secondary character(s)

Character(s) of apparently minor importance

2c. Initiating action

2d. Complicating action(s)

2e. High point (turning point, climax)

2f. Resolution strategy(ies)

2g. Final resolution or ending

2h. Coda

2i. Narrator stance

3. Make an outline of the major plot elements: initiating action, complicating actions, high point, resolution strategies. Notice, in particular, the major—plot-central/plot-turning—issue or conflict enacted in the high point.

4. Compile the conflict issues across the relevant set of narratives (and/or single narratives) in this plot analysis.

5. Compile the resolution strategies, final resolution/ending.

6. Observe similarities and differences of high points and resolutions across narratives.

SCRIPT ANALYSIS PROCESS CHECKLIST

Script analysis identifies shared general plot structures.

1. Begin with a plot analysis of narratives in your data set.

2. After identifying the plot elements of each narrative, try three strategies for identifying the script:

2a. Smoothing the plot

2b. Making logical connections

2c. Applying master narratives (expected or novel)

3. Identify common and diverse scripts across groups of narratives in your study, by groups of participants or by individuals in different narrating activities, such as over time, narrative task/genre, and so on.

4. Map these common and diverse scripts for each narrative you are analyzing; identify common structures across a group of individual narratives.

5. Discuss the collective nature of scripting in terms of power relations, persuasion, and individuals' management of pressures to narrate certain knowledge and interpretations and not others.

SIGNIFICANCE ANALYSIS PROCESS CHECKLIST

The process of significance analysis involves identifying evaluative devices in one or more narratives or narrative excerpts by an individual or groups.

1. Read each narrative; then read it again. Appreciate the narrative; note your reactions.

2. Underline evaluative devices, going through this step several times.

3. Identify evaluative devices, for each device or going through sentence by sentence. Repeat this step several times.

4. Identify frequencies of evaluative devices and different types of evaluative devices.

5. Identify patterns of evaluative device expressions by individual, group, or some other factor relevant to your study, based on frequencies, densities (number of evaluative devices per overall number of words in the narrative), and placement of evaluative devices of different kinds. Observe similarity, difference, and change over context, time, or other qualities relevant to your research questions and design.

6. Consider the effects of the significance patterns you identify, first by paying attention to the effects of evaluation on you as a reader and then by considering some of the common functions along with different kinds of evaluative devices. That is, does the narrator do a lot of humanizing via uses of psychological state expressions? Which kinds dominate? Or does there appear to be a minimizing, for example with the use of negatives and hedges? Or is there intensifying overall, around specific plot elements or characters?

7. Summarize your findings.

8. Consider how these patterns illuminate narrative meaning, in particular to address your research questions or to suggest other questions.

CHARACTER MAPPING PROCESS CHECKLIST

Character mapping is a process of identifying characters, character mentions, character roles, and character psychological states and, thereby, considering the functions of characters in narrative meaning.

1. Read the narrative several times to become familiar with it.

2. Identify characters in the narrative.

3. Note character mentions and focal characters (based on frequency in the narrative). Consider the effect of different character mentions on the meaning of the narrative.

4. Identify the actions and psychological states of each character. Identify patterns of character-action-psychological state patterns you notice.

5. Consider whether characters play specific roles in the web of meanings offered in the narrative.

6. Consider the role the narrator plays.

TIME ANALYSIS PROCESS CHECKLIST

Time analysis involves noticing tense and time words in a narrative and considering the contribution of the different patterns of time marking across characters and overall in the narrative.

1. Identify time markings in a narrative or excerpt where you expect that marking time will offer additional insights to narrative meaning.

2. List the past, present, and imagined (future, conditional, subjunctive) times in the appropriate columns of Table 6.7, following the instructions in the table. After this process, what do you notice about differences, if any, in the uses of each time for narrative meaning?

3. Do patterns of past, present, and imagined time shape narrative meaning? If so, how? These patterns might be of emphasis (frequency) and/or of function (apparent purpose for the author).

4. Having examined and made observations based on the frequencies of different time orientations, consider the possible functions of different time orientations to narrative meaning.

CHECKLIST FOR SUMMARIZING OBSERVATIONS, PATTERNS, AND FINDINGS

A major step toward writing research reports from narrative inquiry is to summarize findings.

1. Note your research questions or revise them as appropriate. Identify the patterns these research questions state or imply, such as (but not limited to) the following:

   1a. Patterns of similarity

   1b. Patterns of difference

   1c. Patterns of change

   1d. Patterns of coherence

   1e. Patterns of conflict and/or contradiction

   1f. Other patterns

2. Summarize observations you have made based on narrative analyses. Summarize observations from narrative analyses you conducted:

   2a. Values analysis

   2b. Plot analysis

   2c. Script analysis

   2d. Significance analysis

   2e. Character mapping

   2f. Time analysis

3. Identify patterns of meaning in terms of the research questions.

4. Write notes with your findings in terms of each research question.

5. Decide on a format for your report after considering possible presentation or publication sources.

References

Amsterdam, A., & Bruner, J. (Eds.). (2000). *Minding the law: How courts rely on storytelling and how their stories change the way we understand the law and ourselves.* Cambridge, MA: Harvard University Press.

Austin, J. L. (1962). *How to do things with words.* Cambridge, MA: Harvard University Press.

Baerger, D. R., & McAdams, D. P. (1999). Life story coherence and its relation to psychological well-being. *Narrative Inquiry, 9*(1), 69–96.

Baker, P. (2012, September 5). At the Democratic Convention, an emphasis on social issues. *New York Times,* The Caucus blog. Retrieved from http://thecaucus.blogs.nytimes.com /2012/09/05/at-the-democratic-convention-an-emphasis-on-social-issues

Bakhtin, M. M. (1981). Discourse in the novel. In M. Holquist (Ed.), *The dialogic imagination* (pp. 259–422). Austin: University of Texas Press. (Original work published 1935)

Bakhtin, M. M. (1986). The problem of speech genres. In C. Emerson & M. Holquist (Eds.), *Speech genres and other late essays* (pp. 60–102). Austin: University of Texas Press.

Bamberg, M. (2004a). Considering counter-narratives. In M. Bamberg & M. Andrews (Eds.), *Considering counter-narratives: Narrating, resisting, making sense* (pp. 351–371). Amsterdam: John Benjamins.

Bamberg, M. (2004b). Positioning with Davey Hogan: Stories, tellings, and identities. In C. Daiute & C. Lightfoot (Eds.), *Narrative analysis: Studying the development of individuals in society* (pp. 135–158). Thousand Oaks, CA: Sage.

Bamberg, M. (2008). Selves and identities in the making: The study of microgenetic processes in interactive practices. In U. Müller, J. I. M. Carpendale, N. Budwig, & B. W. Sokol (Eds.), *Social life and social knowledge: Toward a process account of development* (pp. 205–224). New York: Taylor & Francis/Lawrence Erlbaum.

Bamberg, M., & Georgakopoulou, A. (2008). Small stories as a new perspective in narrative and identity analysis. *Text & Talk, 28*(3), 377–396.

Berman, R. A., & Slobin, D. I. (1994). *Relating events in narrative: A crosslinguistic developmental study.* Hillsdale, NJ: Lawrence Erlbaum.

Billig, M. (1995). *Banal nationalism.* Thousand Oaks, CA: Sage.

Botero, P.G. y Palmero, A.I. (2013). La utopia no esta adelante: Generaciones, resistencias, e instituciones emergentes. E-book—(Grupos de trabajo de CLASCO: Asociacion Argentina de Sociologia: CINDE y Universidad de Manizales.

Brown, P., & Levinson, S. C. (1987). *Politeness: Some universals in language usage.* New York: Cambridge University Press.

Bruner, J. S. (1986). *Actual minds, possible worlds.* Cambridge, MA: Harvard University Press.

Bruner, J. S. (2002). *Making stories: Law, literature, life.* Cambridge, MA: Harvard University Press.

Cazden, C. B. (2001). *Classroom discourse: The language of teaching and learning.* Portsmouth, NH: Heinemann.

Charmaz, K. (2006). *Constructing grounded theory: A practical guide through qualitative analysis.* Thousand Oaks, CA: Sage.

Chase, S. E., & Rogers, M. F. (Eds.). (2001). *Mothers and children: Feminist analyses and personal narratives*. New Brunswick, NJ: Rutgers University Press.

Clandinin, D. J., & Connelly, F. M. (2000). *Narrative inquiry: Experience and story in qualitative research*. San Francisco: Jossey-Bass.

Corbin, J., & Strauss, A. (2007). *Basics of qualitative research: Techniques and procedures for developing grounded theory*. Thousand Oaks, CA: Sage.

Cresswell, J. W. (2013). *Qualitative inquiry and research design: Choosing among five approaches*. Thousand Oaks, CA: Sage.

Cundall, J. (1851). Goldilocks and the three bears. In J. Cundall (Ed.), *Treasury of pleasure books for young children*. London: Grant and Griffith.

Daiute, C. (2004). Creative uses of cultural genres. In C. Daiute & C. Lightfoot (Eds.), *Narrative analysis: Studying the development of individuals in society* (pp. 111–134). Thousand Oaks, CA: Sage.

Daiute, C. (2006). Stories of conflict and development in U.S. public schools. In C. Daiute, Z. Beykont, C. Higson-Smith, & L. Nucci (Eds.), *International perspectives on youth conflict and development*. New York: Oxford University Press.

Daiute, C. (2007). *Dynamic storytelling by youth* [Research workshop activity guide]. New York: Graduate Center, City University of New York.

Daiute, C. (2008). The rights of children, the rights of nations: Developmental theory and the politics of children's rights. *Journal of Social Issues, 64*, 701–723.

Daiute, C. (2010). *Human development and political violence*. New York: Cambridge University Press.

Daiute, C. (2011). "Trouble" in, around, and between narratives. *Narrative Inquiry, 21*(2), 329–336.

Daiute, C., & Botero, P. (2012, July 11). *Narrating displacement through Colombian community development dealing with violence*. Paper presented at the meeting of the International Society for the Study of Behavioral Development, Edmonton, Alberta.

Daiute, C., Buteau, E., & Rawlins, C. (2001). Social-relational wisdom: Developmental diversity in children's written narratives about social conflict. *Narrative Inquiry, 11*(2), 1–30.

Daiute, C., & Caicedo, D. (2012). *The community college as agent of change in the 21st century immigration crisis*. New York: Graduate Center, City University of New York.

Daiute, C., Campbell, C., Cooper, C., Griffin, T., Reddy, M., & Tivnan, T. (1993). Young authors' interactions with peers and a teacher: Toward a developmentally sensitive sociocultural literacy theory. In C. Daiute (Ed.), *The development of literacy through social interaction* (pp. 41–66). San Francisco: Jossey-Bass.

Daiute, C., Eisenberg, Z., & Vasconcellos, V. (2012). Parece que e' uma coise ate' meio normal, ne'? Analise de narratives sobre "risco" em creches de favelas [It seems like it's normal, even: Narrative analyses of "risk" in early child care in favelas]. *Revista Educação em Foco–UFJF*, 209–228.

Daiute, C., & Griffin, T. M. (1993). The social construction of written narrative. In C. Daiute (Ed.), *The development of literacy through social interaction* (pp. 97–120). San Francisco: Jossey-Bass.

Daiute, C., & Morse, F. (1993). Access to knowledge and expression: Multimedia writing tools for children with diverse needs and strengths. *Journal of Special Education Technology, 12*(3), 1–35.

Daiute, C., & Nelson, K. A. (1997). Making sense of the sense-making function of narrative evaluation. *Journal of Narrative and Life History, 7*(1–4), 207–215.

Daiute, C., Stern, R., & Lelutiu-Weinberger, C. (2003). Negotiating violence prevention. *Journal of Social Issues, 59*, 83–101.

Denzin, N. K., & Lincoln, Y. S. (Eds.). (2011). *The SAGE handbook of qualitative research* (4th ed.). Thousand Oaks, CA: Sage.

Donald, M. (1993). *Origins of the modern mind: Three stages in the evolution of culture and cognition.* Cambridge, MA: Harvard University Press.

Educators for Social Responsibility. (n.d.). Resolving Conflict Creatively Program (RCCP). Cambridge, MA: Educators for Social Responsibility. Retrieved from http://esrnational.org/professional-services/elementary-school/prevention/resolving-conflict-creatively-program-rccp

Elliott, D. S., Hamburg, B. A., & Williams, K. R. (Eds.). (1998). *Violence in American schools.* New York: Cambridge University Press.

Engeström, Y. (2009). The future of activity theory: A rough draft. In A. Sannino, H. Daniels, & K. D. Gutiérrez (Eds.), *Learning and expanding with activity theory* (pp. 303–328). New York: Cambridge University Press.

Engeström, Y., Miettinen, R., & Punamäki, R.-L. (Eds.). (1999). *Perspectives on activity theory.* New York: Cambridge University Press.

Erikson, E. H. (1994). *Identity and the life cycle.* New York: W. W. Norton.

Etengoff, C. (2013). *Family and individual development around issues of sexual and religious identity.* New York: Graduate Center, City University of New York.

Fairclough, N. (2010). *Critical discourse analysis: The critical study of language* (2nd ed.). New York: Pearson.

Foucault, M. (2001). *The order of things: Archaeology of the human sciences.* New York: Routledge.

Freeman, M. (2009). *Hindsight: The promise and peril of looking backward.* New York: Oxford University Press.

Georgakopoulou, A. (2006). Thinking big with small stories in narrative and identity analysis. *Narrative Inquiry, 16*(1), 122–130.

Gilligan, C. (1993). *In a different voice: Psychological theory and women's development.* Cambridge, MA: Harvard University Press.

Graves, D. H. (1983). *Writing: Teachers and children at work.* Portsmouth, NH: Heinemann.

Gutkind, L. (2012, December 17). Three R's of narrative nonfiction. *New York Times,* Opinionator blog. Retrieved from http://opinionator.blogs.nytimes.com/2012/12/17/three-rs-of-narrative-nonfiction

Harding, S. (Ed.). (1988). *Feminism and methodology: Social science issues.* Bloomington: Indiana University Press.

Harré, R., & van Langenhove, L. (Eds.). (1999). *Positioning theory: Moral contexts of intentional action.* Malden, MA: Blackwell.

Heath, S. B. (1983). *Ways with words: Language, life, and work in communities and classrooms.* New York: Cambridge University Press.

Hermans, H. J. M., & Hermans-Jansen, E. (2001). *Self-narratives: The construction of meaning in psychotherapy.* New York: Guilford Press.

Howell, J. C. (1997). *Youth gangs* [OJJDP Fact Sheet 72]. Washington, DC: U.S. Department of Justice, Office of Justice Programs, Office of Juvenile Justice and Delinquency Prevention.

Immigration Policy Center. (2012, June 22). "Economic Benefits of Granting Deferred Action to Unauthorized Immigrants Brought to U.S. as Youth." Retrieved from http://www.immigrationpolicy.org/just-facts/economic-benefits-granting-deferred-action-unauthorized-immigrants-brought-us-youth

Jović, S. (2012, May). *Cognitive management of self-presentation in the self-presentation technology era.* Symposium presented at the annual conference of the Jean Piaget Society, Toronto.

Killen, M. (2007). Children's social and moral reasoning about exclusion. *Current Directions in Psychological Science, 16,* 32–36.

Korobov, N. (2009). Expanding hegemonic masculinity: The use of irony in young men's stories about romantic experiences. *American Journal of Men's Health, 3,* 286–299.

Kreniske, P. (2012, October). *Middle-school students negotiate a workplace simulation with threats to authority and supportive friends.* Poster presented at the meeting "Transitions from Adolescence to

Adulthood," Society for Research on Child Development, Tampa, FL.

Labov, W. (1973). *Language in the inner city: Studies in the Black English Vernacular.* Philadelphia: University of Pennsylvania Press.

Labov, W., & Waletzky, J. (1997). Narrative analysis: Oral versions of personal experience. *Journal of Narrative and Life History, 7*(1–4), 3–38. (Original work published 1967)

Lieblich, A., Tuval-Mashiach, R., & Zilber, T. (1998). *Narrative research: Reading, analysis, and interpretation.* Thousand Oaks, CA: Sage.

Linde, C. (1993). *Life stories: The creation of coherence.* New York: Oxford University Press.

Lucić, L. (2012). *How do youth make sense of interpersonal interactions and resolve conflicts with diverse groups?* (Doctoral dissertation). New York: Graduate Center, City University of New York.

MacWhinney, B. (2000). *The CHILDES project: Tools for analyzing talk* (3rd ed.). Mahwah, NJ: Lawrence Erlbaum.

McAdams, D. P. (2005). *The redemptive self: Stories Americans live by.* New York: Oxford University Press.

McCabe, A., & Peterson, C. (Eds.). (1991). *Developing narrative structure.* Hillsdale, NJ: Lawrence Erlbaum.

McLean, K. C., & Pratt, M. W. (2006). Life's little (and big) lessons: Identity statuses and meaning-making in the turning-point narratives of emerging adults. *Developmental Psychology, 42,* 714–722.

Messina, V. (2013). *Soldiers to students: Experiences of transitions of Iraq and Afghanistan war veterans.* Unpublished manuscript, Graduate Center, City University of New York.

Miller, P. J., Hoogstra, L., Mintz, J., Fung, H., & Williams, K. (1993). Troubles in the garden and how they get resolved: A young child's transformation of his favorite story. In C. A. Nelson (Ed.), *Memory and affect in development* (pp. 87–114). Hillsdale, NJ: Lawrence Erlbaum.

Mishler, E. G. (1991). *Research interviewing: Context and narrative.* Cambridge, MA: Harvard University Press.

Nelson, K. (1998). *Language in cognitive development: The emergence of the mediated mind.* New York: Cambridge University Press.

Nelson, K. (2007). *Young minds in social worlds: Experience, meaning, and memory.* Cambridge, MA: Harvard University Press.

Ninkovic, M. (2012). *Changing the subject: Human resource management in post-socialist workplaces.* (Doctoral dissertation). New York: Graduate Center, City University of New York.

Ochs, E., & Capps, L. (2002). *Living narrative: Creating lives in everyday storytelling.* Cambridge, MA: Harvard University Press.

Oliveira, M. (1999). The function of self-aggrandizement in storytelling. *Narrative Inquiry, 9*(1), 25–47.

Opie, I., & Opie, P. (1980). Hansel & Gretel. In I. Opie & P. Opie (Eds.), *The classic fairy tales.* Oxford: Oxford University Press.

O'Reilly, K. (2012). *Ethnographic methods.* New York: Routledge.

Parker, I. (2005). Narrative. In *Qualitative Psychology: Introducing Radical Research.* (pp. 71–87). Maidenhead, England: Open University Press.

Peterson, C., & McCabe, A. (1983). *Developmental psycholinguistics: Three ways of looking at a child's narrative.* New York: Plenum.

Polivanova, K. N. (2006). On the problem of the leading activity in adolescence. *Journal of Russian and Eastern European Psychology, 44*(5), 78–84.

Polkinghorne, D. (1991). Narrative and self-concept. *Journal of Narrative and Life History, 1*(2–3), 135–153.

Ranciere, J. (2010). *Dissensus on politics and aesthetics.* New York: Continuum International.

Reyes, A. (2005). Appropriation of African American slang by Asian American youth. *Journal of Sociolinguistics, 9,* 509–532.

Reyes, A. (2011). "Racist!": Metapragmatic regimentation of racist discourse by Asian

American youth. *Discourse & Society, 22,* 458–473.

Ricoeur, P. (1990). *Time and narrative* (Vol. 3). Chicago: University of Chicago Press.

Riessman, C. K. (1993). *Narrative analysis.* Thousand Oaks, CA: Sage.

Riessman, C. K. (2007). *Narrative methods for the human sciences.* Thousand Oaks, CA: Sage.

Ruck, M. D., Park, H., Killen, M., & Crystal, D. D. (2011). Intergroup contact and evaluations of race-based exclusion in urban minority children and adolescents. *Journal of Youth and Adolescence, 40,* 633–643.

Ryan, D. W., & Bernard, H. R. (2003). Techniques to identify themes. *Field Methods, 15,* 85–109.

Sassen, S. (2008). Unsettling master categories: Notes on studying the global in C. W. Mills' footsteps. *International Journal of Politics, Culture, and Society, 20,* 69–83.

Schieffelin, B. B., & Ochs, E. (Eds.). (1987). *Language socialization across cultures.* New York: Cambridge University Press.

Schiffrin, D. (1994). *Approaches to discourse.* New York: Wiley-Blackwell.

Scott, J. C. (1992). *Domination and the arts of resistance: Hidden transcripts.* New Haven, CT: Yale University Press.

Sladkova, J. (2010). *Journeys of undocumented Honduran migrants to the United States.* El Paso, TX: LFB Scholarly Publishing.

Smorti, A., Del Buffa, O., & Matteini, C. (2007). Narrazione autobiografica di eventi dolorosi: Analisi degli aspetti formali e contenutistici del testo [Autobiographical narrative of the painful events: Analysis of the formal aspects and content of the text]. *Rassegna di Psicologia, 24*(3), 11–33.

Smorti, A., Pananti, B., & Rizzo, A. (2010). Autobiography as tool to improve lifestyle, well being, and self-narrative in patients with mental disorders. *Journal of Nervous and Mental Disease, 198,* 564–571.

Solis, J. (2004). Narrating and counternarrating illegality as an identity. In C. Daiute & C. Lightfoot (Eds.), *Narrative analysis:*

Studying the development of individuals in society (pp. 181–199). Thousand Oaks, CA: Sage.

Spence, D. P. (1984). *Narrative truth and historical truth: Meaning and interpretation in psychoanalysis.* New York: W. W. Norton.

Stein, N. L. (1982). What's in a story: Interpreting the interpretations of story grammars. *Discourse Processes, 5,* 319–336.

Strunk, W., & White, E. B. (1999). *The elements of style* (4th ed.). New York: Longman.

Surat, M. M. (1990). *Angel child, dragon child.* New York: Scholastic.

Tolman, D. L. (2005). *Dilemmas of desire: Teenage girls talk about sexuality.* Cambridge, MA: Harvard University Press.

Tomasello, M. (2005). *Constructing a language: A usage-based theory of language acquisition.* Cambridge, MA: Harvard University Press.

Turkle, S. (1997). *Life on the screen: Identity in the age of the Internet.* New York: Simon & Schuster.

Vasconcellos, V. (2011). *Agente auxiliar de creche: Educador da infância carioca.* [Teacher's aids: *Carioca* infant–early childhood care educator]. Rio de Janeiro: Faperj Scholarship Report.

Vygotsky, L. S. (1978). *Mind in society: The development of higher psychological processes.* Cambridge, MA: Harvard University Press.

Walker, P. (1996). *Voices of love and freedom.* Iowa City: Perfection Learning.

Watts, R. J. (2003). *Politeness.* New York: Cambridge University Press.

Wertsch, J. V. (2002). *Voices of collective remembering.* New York: Cambridge University Press.

Wertsch, J. V., & Tulviste, P. (1992). L. S. Vygotsky and contemporary developmental psychology. *Developmental Psychology, 28,* 548–557.

Wittgenstein, L. (1953). *Philosophical investigations.* Oxford: Basil Blackwell.

Wortham, S. (2001). *Narratives in action: A strategy for research and analysis.* New York: Teachers College Press.

Glossary of Concepts for Dynamic Narrative Inquiry

Concept/Term (chapter defining and focusing on the concept): Definition.

Activity-meaning system (2): A concept guiding research design, based on the theory that people use narratives and other cultural tools to interact in the world; a system of explicit and/or implicit relationships and interactions in which each narrative occurs.

Activity-meaning system design (2): Design that makes visible and audible the network of relationships and interactions in which each narrative occurs.

Actors/stakeholders (2): *See* **Stakeholders/actors.**

Addressivity (1, 2): A quality of each meaningful utterance, word, brief narrative, or novel, responding to others in the present, prior, or future moments of history; addressees for narrating, whether in the room or in the imagination, are others who have created some motivation for an utterance—a definition, explanation, justification—and a basis for response or resistance by the speaker/author of the narrative.

Analysis (3): A systematic approach to reading beyond the literal expression, from a specific theoretical perspective, to understand meaning or some other phenomenon.

Audience (2): Actual and imagined others influencing, interacting with, or potentially interacting with narratives; actual audiences are physically or virtually present, while imagined audiences are historical (such as in echoes of or other kinds of responses to past narratives) or potential audiences, those to whom a narration may be directed.

Author (2): The person speaking or writing a narrative, as (sometimes) distinguished from the narrator and characters in a narrative, including the "I" character referring to the author.

Centering (3): *See* **Values negotiation.**

Character (6): An element of narrative, symbol of a person or other animate or animated actor, often represented with consciousness.

Character mapping (6): The examination of characters in a narrative and their roles, based on the frequency, paths of their mention, and animation with psychological states and evaluative devices.

Coda (4): A final reflection on the entire narrative, once completed, typically from the narrator or author/speaker perspective, outside the events, unless otherwise stated; could also be a moral of the story.

Complicating action (4): A narrative plot element involving actions building from initiating actions toward a high point/turning point/climax.

Construction (rationale for narrative inquiry) (1): A focus on narrating as a developmental process—whereby persons become themselves through the stories they tell.

Contesting (3): *See* **Values negotiation.**

Cultural-historical activity theory (2): Explanation that human development occurs in meaningful activities and relationships, via culturally-created means. With some variation, a theory also referred to as "activity theory," "sociocultural theory," and "sociohistorical theory".

Cultural products (3): Narrative and other commonly used symbol systems that result from and are used in social life and human social activity.

Cultural tool (1): A symbolic process developed in human relations for interacting purposefully in the world; language, the quintessential cultural tool, which people use to interact with one other, their environments, and the myriad symbolic realities created in cultural histories.

Culture (1): The product of social life and human social activity and the enactment of cultural products to do a variety of important engagements in life.

Development (1): Biological, historical, situational changes of individuals and societies; achieved with cultural activities like narrating, as mechanisms of these intersecting developmental processes. "Development" is an interactive process of biological, social, cultural, and situational factors in daily life; the term "change" is also often used to suggest these complex interactions.

Diversity principle (1): A principle referring to within-person and within-group differences, as well as differences across individuals and groups, in narratives and narrating.

Dynamic narrating (1): The theory that narrating is a social process people use to make sense of social and physical environments and interactions with those environments, and how they fit; the extension of this explanation of narrating to research as applied in this book; defined by four principles (use, relation, diversity, materiality) and consistent practices of research design, analysis (values analysis, plot analysis, significance analysis, character mapping, time analysis), and presentation of findings.

Dynamic narrative inquiry (1): Inquiry that involves designing and analyzing narrative expressions for what they do as much as what they say; applying principles of dynamic narrating to other relevant expressions as well as those that are strictly narratives, focusing on narrative expressions and relevant expressions as they interact with situation and purpose toward the ultimate end of identifying context-sensitive meaning.

Evaluative devices (5): Linguistic devices indicating the evaluative phase of meaning, typically adjectives, adverbs, psychological state expressions, and other verbal categories, as well as graphic markers of speech qualities like "!" indicating emphasis. Evaluative devices constitute categories of author/speaker significance—that is, the reason why the narrative is being shared; these categories include intensifiers, psychological state expressions, negations/hedges, and qualifiers.

Evaluative language/evaluative phase of meaning (5): The implicit meaning—also referred to as style or personal inflection; phase of meaning expressing the significance of the narrative to the author; meaning expressed in the small words such as "really," "sort of," "then uh," markers like "!" in the sentence, and other inflections. *See also* **Referential phase of meaning**.

High point (4): Pivotal conflict of the plot (character motivations in conflict with another aspect of the story)/turning point or climax where complicating actions reach an apex and then begin to recede to resolution strategies.

Imagined time (6): Time used creatively in narrating, such as with past events presented in present tense. Events presented in future, conditional, or hypothetical tenses or expressions are imagined time, when past and present times are used as recorded (agreed upon).

Indexicals (1): Linguistic devices (words, phrases, and so on) that point outside the narrative text. Examples include pronouns such as *she* or *it*, referring to people or objects outside a narrative and adverbs indicating location, such as *there* and *here*.

Initiating action (4): Action that launches and motivates the plot, with trouble or breach in what the author/speaker has established as normal or expected.

Joint attention (4): Attention that results when an adult directs a baby's gaze by pointing and making sounds, affirmations, and other signals toward where to look.

Landscape(s) of action (1): Events represented in narrative.

Landscape(s) of consciousness (1): Psychological states in narrative and psychological functions of narrative that render the events meaningful.

Materiality principle (1): The principle that narrative is composed of qualities (such as lifelike depictions of events and consciousness and common structures [within cultural bounds]; evaluative language), elements (such as characters, high points, resolutions), and interactive connections to contexts (such as indexical pronouns and other pointers to the environment) that express meaning augmenting the literal meaning of words.

Meaning (1): Expression, intention, and interaction, stated and implied, in verbal and nonverbal discursive activity.

Mediate (1): The use of narratives and the narrating process to interact with life and self, to figure out what is going on in the environment, how one fits, and sometimes even to change situations. Also referred to as sense making or meaning making.

Narrating (1): A uniquely human means of symbolic intelligence, expressed in verbal and nonverbal media, interacting with contexts in ways that render relationships among the qualities and features of narrative aspects of meaning.

Narrative(s) (1): Most strictly, oral and written expression of time-ordered event representations; more liberally, lifelike accounts of experience or knowledge, conversations developing into narrative-like accounts, and referring to ways of knowing (as in *script, worldview,* and *master narrative*).

Narrative analysis (2): The systematic examination of narratives and analyses of other verbal and nonverbal expressions according to narrative qualities, elements, and dynamics of narrative use.

Narrative inquiry (1): A research process involving design of data collection and analysis of narratives and/or the application of principles and features of narrative to the analysis of other discourses to address research questions or aims.

Narrative interactivity (2): The interaction of narratives and their specific features with contexts—prior narratives, actual and potential audiences, cultural traditions, environmental circumstances, and other narrative via specific linguistic features (*see* **Indexicals, Evaluative devices**) and the functions of narratives and narrating (*see* **Use principle**).

Narrative meaning (1): The interplay of expressions and the meanings they enact among people whose perspectives merge and diverge in social and political processes in life and in research.

Narrative systems (2): Actual and/or virtual interaction among people, environments, and ideas with narrative as one among expressive interactions. Classic narratives, small stories, and ways of knowing expressed as narrative or non-narrative discourse as relevant to a study.

Narrator perspective (also Narrator stance) (4): The point of view crafted in the narrative by the author/speaker; with a combination of plot elements, such as high point, resolution strategies, and coda, as well as narrative qualities of significance, character, and time.

Observation (7): A description of a result of narrative analysis strategies; connects story with purpose and context through relevant analytic processes.

Outcome (7): Results of research analyses, as described herein, with processes of narrative inquiry design, analyses, observations, findings, and patterns of findings.

Participant (2): A research subject, often in narrative inquiry implying some active rather than passive involvement in the research.

Performing (3): *See* **Values negotiation**.

Perspective (2): Personal understanding, interest, goal, experience, and knowledge that play out and matter in activities.

Plot (4): The skeleton of a story, typically imperceptible under the story's flesh and dressing; a cultural device for relating to others and the broader world, drawing on lifelike elements including a setting, initiating action, and subsequent rising and falling actions in events. *See also* **Plot elements**.

Plot analysis (4): Analysis that involves identifying the basic structure of narratives, allowing for comparison and consideration of how narrators are using plot.

Plot elements (4): Certain lifelike and symbolic elements, including characters, setting, complicating actions (usually with some in the past), a high point (turning point or climax), resolution, ending, and sometimes coda or moral of the story.

Positioning (3): Diverse author/speaker/narrator stances in relation to the topic/issue purpose, and actual/potential audiences.

Power relation (2): Explicit or implicit interaction and/or effect of a person, group's, or institution's influence, resources, in particular as such are enacted in in narrative sense-making and expression processes; such influence can be mutual among participants and fluid rather than only rigid, and narrating is one way such dynamics occur.

Practical theoretical concepts (2): Theoretical narrative concepts that can be operationalized in research design and analysis tools.

Referential phase of meaning (5): The explicit statement of meaning, also referred to as content or theme. The referential phase of meaning is typically conveyed with words that can be looked up in the dictionary. *See also* **Evaluative phase of meaning**.

Relation principle (1): The principle that highlights that narrating is a social-relational activity and that narrators interact with present and implied others, objects, and ideas in environments.

Report (rationale for narrative inquiry) (1): A focus on narrative as the actual, remembered experience, knowledge, and truths of the individual. This rationale involves no or little emphasis on the interactive nature of narrating.

Research (1): Systematic activity conducted with the aim of gaining new knowledge.

Research design (2): The organization of activities in existing situations, situations created in lab settings, or archived/media situations to gather narrative and related materials in ways that address research questions and goals.

Research questions (2): Questions phrased in terms of the knowledge researchers are seeking with their projects, designs, and analyses.

Resolution/ending (4): The culmination of resolution strategies or simply an end to the narrative.

Resolution strategies (4): Attempts to resolve the main plot issue. A plot need not contain more than one resolution strategy, and the strategy need not result in an ultimate resolution.

Script analysis (4): Analysis that involves identifying the combined plot logic organizing a group of narratives: conflicts, resolutions, and causal connections among those major plot elements.

Scripts (1, 4): Commonly used plot structures, including similar elements and connections between the elements; shared ways of knowing, interpreting, acting in the world. Scripts are ritual narrations created in social interaction and organizing perception and action; they are also referred to as social scripts, dominant ideologies, ways of knowing, cultural scripts, master narratives, and collective memories.

Sense making (1): *See* Mediate, Narrative meaning, **Use principles**.

Significance (5): The personal inflection of narrative to the author/speaker, as indicated by the use of certain linguistic devices (evaluative devices).

Significance analysis (5): Analysis of the individual perspective (inflection) of the author in narrative meaning for a specific telling; a means of studying narratives for indications of an implicit strand of meaning with the author's evaluation of the narrative—why he or she is sharing a particular story at the time. Significance analysis involves identifying evaluative devices, including psychological state expressions (affective, cognitive, communicative), intensifiers, qualifiers, causal connectors, negations and hedges, the placement of evaluative expressions, and functions.

Small stories (2): Conversations in everyday discourse that develop into narrative-like accounts among the conversational group, for others (such as for a researcher in a focus group), and for the conversants themselves.

Sociobiography (7): The relational and unique perspective of an individual; research report that focuses on the individual perspective in social relation to relevant others, society, and culture.

Stakeholders/actor(s) (3): Individuals, institutions, and groups who have participated in narrative exchanges, directly (such as face-to-face, via correspondence, or through media) or indirectly (such as in ways that might be influential, from more to less influential), and resource-rich forces (families/ancestors, governments, teachers, news media, popular culture, special interest groups to individuals, marginalized and less influential groups) and mutually influencing persons (peers, subsequent generations with innovations). Stakeholders/actors have shared and diverse interests, orientations, and activities across a sociocultural system—as expressed in cultural products like documents, mission statements, news reports, curricula, and personal narratives.

Strategies (of narrative analysis) (1, 3–6): Specific analytic approaches, including those highlighted in this book: values analysis, plot analysis, script analysis, significance analysis, character mapping, and time analysis.

System (of narratives) (2): Narratives by different stakeholders around an issue and a sequence of narratives by people.

Time (6): A cultural concept referring to perceived natural cycles (day/night, seasons, bodily changes); devices like calendars and clocks; the organization of events into past, present, and future; and historical or ideological periods with certain features, like the Renaissance or the modern era. Time in narrative draws on and extends these and other concepts to create meaning.

Time marking (6): The use of cultural tools to identify meaning in time, like verb tenses, time words, and historical terms.

Use principle (1): The principle that highlights the fact that discourse is an activity and that narrating functions as a tool to mediate individual and societal interactions.

Values (3): The principles and beliefs that people live by; may include enduring moral codes and situational norms, and may be flexible and changing over time, situation, or some other factor. Values are culturally specific goals, ways of knowing, experiencing, and acting in response to environmental, cultural, economic, political, and social circumstances.

Values analysis (3): Analysis that involves examining the values organizing relevant stakeholders' narratives or pertinent expressions to identify shared and divergent meanings related to a research interest.

Values negotiation (3): The process whereby individuals do or do not take up values of others, in conversations and narratives created in the same setting or implicitly in interacting expressions across stakeholders. Values negotiation involves **performing** values (taking up, echoing the values of others), **contesting** values (not performing them when that might be the expectation, or directly resisting performing them), and **centering** values (transforming or changing existing values in some way). This extends to what some scholars refer to as positioning.

Ventriloquy (6): The expression of an individual's thoughts and affects through others, such as authors do with third-person characters and/or narrators in narrative discourse, to divert controversial meanings away from the author/ speaker to other characters.

Index

Page references followed by (table) indicate a table; followed by (figure) indicate an illustrated figure.